In the Shadow of Enlightenment

In the Shadow
of Enlightenment

A Girl's Journey through the Osho Rajneesh Cult

Sarito Carroll

Published by Heroine Publishing LLC, 2024

ISBN: 979-8-9916866-1-7

INTRODUCTION

*"Our lives begin to end the day we become silent
about things that matter." —MLK*

IN THE winter of 1985, Rajneeshpuram—the so-called utopian commune
built around Bhagwan Shree Rajneesh, later known as Osho—collapsed
under a storm of criminal charges, conspiracy, and scandal. For seven years
of my childhood, I had lived inside that movement, both in India and at
Rajneeshpuram. At sixteen, when the commune crumbled, I was thrown
into the real world, utterly disoriented and completely unprepared.

The commune had been my home, but as I navigated life beyond its
gates, I was forced to confront the trauma I had experienced within. Yet,
acknowledging that trauma went against everything the Osho community
espoused—catchphrases like "just get over it," "be positive," and "let go of
the past" dismissed any pain as a personal shortcoming. When I couldn't
simply "let go," I blamed myself. The tenet "you create your own reality"
haunted me. If I was unable to heal, wasn't it my fault? At the same time, I
burned with rage at being dismissed by these shallow platitudes.

Even after I distanced myself from the movement, its mindset clung to
me. My own voice felt constantly at war with the commune's, which had
lodged itself deep in my psyche. It took years to unravel the tangled web of
trauma before I could believe in myself and find my own voice. Finding the
courage to use that voice took even longer.

I had wanted to tell my story for decades. The urge first struck during a
college English class thirty-five years ago. We were reading *The Handmaid's
Tale* by Margaret Atwood. Though my life was far from that dystopian
nightmare, the themes of coercion and control struck a deep chord. The
power of words moved me, and I thought, *I need to tell my story.* But each
time I tried, I hit a wall of fear and doubt. Was I afraid of letting the community down? Despite my efforts to break free, a part of me still longed to

belong. I stayed silent, hoping I could just "get over it," but the resentment inside me only grew.

Over the years, I became more disillusioned with the Osho movement. I knew I couldn't stay silent forever. Osho's vision for a "New Man"—one liberated from conditioning, living in freedom and awareness—had a dark side, a side that excused harm and masked abuses in the name of spiritual growth. This book is about that hidden side, the unspoken things that happened in the shadows. But these are precisely the truths that the Osho community refuses to acknowledge, dismissing any criticism as "negativity." In the past, each time I tried to speak, fear pulled me back—the old longing to belong never fully let go.

Now, nearly forty years after the fall of Rajneeshpuram, I've found the self-respect and courage to take the leap. This is my way of releasing the shame, rage, and fear that have gripped me for so long. Remaining silent felt like abandoning myself. Writing this book has been a way to gather the fractured pieces of my past and see them for what they truly were. The more I wrote, the more I believed myself—some of it felt so insane, even to me. I wasn't making it up. Some of it *was* truly bat-shit crazy.

In many ways, this book is a tribute to my younger self. Speaking out now is my way of affirming that she mattered. It's about standing up to a bully and saying: *This was not okay.* It's a way to reclaim the truth, shed the shame, and tell those who hurt me: *Take back your poison.* It's about honoring my principles and standing up for myself in a way I couldn't back then.

This memoir is my story, told as accurately as I can remember. Though memories may blur with time, this is the truth as I lived and felt it. The names of many individuals have been changed to pseudonyms, and in a few cases, other identifying details have also been altered, to respect their privacy. While the dialogue is reconstructed from memory and not a verbatim account, it is consistent with the character or nature of the person speaking. Every block quote is presented exactly as it appears in its original source.

PART ONE

Wandering Hippies

CHAPTER ONE

TUMBLEWEEDS

I WAS BORN during the counterculture revolution of the late '60s, fueled by the rebellion of the beatniks and the free-spirited hippies. My parents met in Tompkins Square Park, the pulsating heart of New York City's alternative scene. My mother, Judy, had arrived in 1963 to attend Barnard College. Tom, my father, was a native New Yorker steeped in the Beatnik ethos. He moved through the East Village art scene with a vibrant, free-spirited charm, capturing the city's soul through his camera lens.

Judy was an artist at heart too. She had even wanted to study art in college, but her strict intellectual Jewish parents said they would disown her if she did, so she majored in mathematics. However, unbeknownst to her parents, she took art classes at the New School, and she quickly immersed herself into the East Village scene. She found her tribe of other free-thinking rebels who banded together in rejecting the repressive values of the '50s in favor of feminism, civil rights, anti-war activism, and non-materialism.

Tom and Judy's chance meeting quickly evolved into a relationship. They shared similar anti-establishment ideals and bonded over art. He was everything Judy's parents disapproved of. He was living the hand-to-mouth artist's life. Plus, he wasn't Jewish, didn't have a college education, and was ten years Judy's elder. Being with Tom was a way for her to metaphorically spit in her parents' faces, defiantly asserting her individuality.

Tom supported himself through sporadic photography gigs at clubs like the Fillmore East, where the likes of The Who and other up-and-coming musicians played. He was just scraping by. Soon Judy learned that Tom had a history with drug use. At that time, he insisted that he was clean. She also learned that he had a son and daughter who had recently landed in foster care because his ex-wife was consumed by a heroin addiction. Tom didn't try to get custody of his kids, claiming he didn't have the means. As she learned more about his shady history and minor run-ins with the law, she didn't think much of it—it was "sticking it to the man." I guess they were in love.

When Judy graduated from Barnard in 1967, she and Tom got married and moved into an apartment over a fish shop where the rent was cheap. Judy landed a job putting Wall Street data onto mainframe computers, which must have rubbed up against her anti-establishment stance. However, she needed to make a living, especially since Tom couldn't. He had started taking drugs again, sometimes disappearing for days on end, only to return in a cloud of volatility.

This is when Judy learned she was pregnant with me. In the brief moments that Tom wasn't high, he was excited about the pregnancy. Judy savored those moments, clinging to any shred of hope that their relationship could survive.

* * *

Judy went into labor on December 13, 1968, the day the New York hospital staff was having their holiday party and were thus shorthanded. My father was off on one of his benders, high as a kite. She was on her own.

Judy's labor was not progressing. After twenty-four hours of intense labor pain, a doctor examined her and determined that I was posterior—sunny side up. I would have to be turned before I could be delivered. Several hours later, a midwife with magician's hands positioned me correctly. Shortly thereafter, I arrived, a hardy nine pounds.

I don't know if my mother felt joy for my being born. I imagine that she was not just utterly exhausted, but also distraught that her husband was not there for her. I don't know if she held me. She must've been overwhelmed, possibly thinking to herself: What have I done? What have I gotten myself into? I can't handle this. I often wonder if we bonded, because as young as I can remember, there was a rift between us. I felt responsible for putting her into the predicament of motherhood.

After my birth, Tom fell deeper into his addiction. He would take whatever he could get his hands on, but heroin was his drug of choice. Now, instead of capturing the dingy, unglamorous underbelly of the city with his photographs, he fell into the grime himself and shot up in the shadows. When methadone clinics opened, he enrolled, promising to follow the program. Instead, he sold his methadone on the street and then used that money to buy more heroin.

Now, with a baby, and Tom growing more secretive and even violent, Judy started saving money to a secret bank account. When I was three months old, she left him. If I put myself in her shoes, I would have felt intense grief and heartbreak. Being young and naive, I am sure she thought Tom would change, and his changing would prove his love and her worth. That wasn't reality. My mom took me and left New York. For the next three years, we moved around the country—from California to Washington to Boston, and everywhere in between. I don't remember any of it.

After three years on the road, we returned to New York City where Judy felt most at home and could study art again. Upon our return, Tom once again said he was clean. Judy allowed him to visit me on occasion.

My earliest memory is of my parents looming above me, yelling at each other. I was standing beneath the towering New York City skyscrapers. The buildings, like giants, cast shadows on my small frame. I stood there staring at the pavement, my legs like lead.

Days later, my mom had packed all our stuff into her blue VW Beetle, and we left New York again. This time for good.

* * *

For the next two years, we kept moving. We blew in and out of towns like tumbleweeds, as if we were guided by fate. I don't know if Judy was looking for something in particular. Maybe she was just running. One thing was certain, she wanted to be independent and free.

What I remember most is the ground moving under the tires as I stared out the car window. The landscape morphed from wide-open expanses, to specks of green trees joining into forests, to fields and fields of corn. We passed through many places. Sometimes we stayed a few weeks, sometimes a few months. We never stayed anywhere long enough to put down roots. I have memories, like vivid etchings, of places we stopped, but with no place to ascribe them. I recall picking cherries in a lush orchard, which must have been in the Northwest. I also remember eating canned corn at a homeless shelter in a dusty town somewhere. One place I do remember well is Utah, where a group of people were building a commune around

Dr. Christopher, a formidable herbalist well known in the '70s. While there, I walked along the sandy arroyos where I played alone in my own imaginary kingdom. Up on a mesa, I found arrowheads that I wrapped in cloth and stored like treasure in my little suitcase. Since we moved so much, I didn't often play with other kids. I existed mostly in solitude.

Before long we left Dr. Christopher's place and were back on the road. I never liked the goodbyes. Every time we left wherever we were, tension coursed through my body, perhaps because I wasn't sure where we would land next. Plus, I could feel my mother's unease and worry, and I was keenly aware that we had little to no money. I always wanted to hide when my mom asked people for favors, like for a place to crash for a couple of nights. I just wanted to be normal.

As we zigzagged across the country, we met many who were hitchhiking or floating as freely as we were. We often stopped to talk to people Judy could tell were part of her free-spirited clan by their long hair and flowery flowing clothes. She trusted people who weren't "straight," as she put it. She thought straight people were closed-minded and unliberated.

Many of the people we met seemed to live close to the earth, their faces coated in dust, their hair ruffling in the wind. They all stood for love, peace, and organic farming. They were usually inclusive, loving, and often kind of dreamy. They would dance, play music, hug, and just hang out for hours. Looking back, I realize their spacey aura was probably because many of them were stoned. Nonetheless, most of them were nice. Plus, they seemed to like me, saying things like, "You look like Shirley Temple," or "Look at those beautiful blue eyes." Sometimes people would even give me little gifts like a polished piece of tiger's eye that I'd put in my pocket and rub for good luck.

However, being on the road was also scary at times. Since we met so many people, some of whom were a little unhinged, I felt like I was always on guard until I could sense if they were safe or not. My mom, on the other hand, seemed to trust all hippies and misfits. One time we were driving somewhere on a wide-open road, when my mom saw a hitchhiker up ahead.

"Shall we pick him up?" she asked me.

"No," I said. I was wary of new people. I didn't know why, but I didn't trust people; I always expected them to do something bad. She stopped the car anyway, not considering my response.

"Who knows if we might need the same favor someday. It's good karma," she said. The man opened the back door, tossed in his backpack, and got in. I sat in the front seat stiffly. Something about him gave me the creeps. As the car started moving, he bolted forward, stuck his head between the two front seats and said, "Want some speed?" There was a moment of silence. What was speed? I wondered.

"No, I don't," Judy said. He leaned back in his seat, put his legs between the two front seats, and planted his feet on the dashboard. Judy asked him to remove them. He pulled his legs back, then bolted forward screaming and flailing right in our faces. "You women are all the same, you think you're so independent. You're full of shit." I was scared. I looked at my mom wide-eyed hoping to find reassurance, but all I saw in her eyes was fear.

"Please sit back," my mother said. Eventually, he calmed down. My mother and I stole silent glances. I didn't make a sound. I feared the crazy man would erupt into a fit again. I stared ahead hoping a town would appear on the horizon, and finally one did. We stopped at a gas station. By this time, the guy was sprawled out on the back seat muttering to himself. My mom and I got out of the car as quietly as we could. She walked to the payphone and called the police. Then we went into the gas station to wait. Once the police arrived and told the guy to get out of the car, we got back on the road.

As the weeks and months passed, rage towards my mother brewed inside of me. I didn't know why exactly, I only knew what my body told me, and it was tense and buzzing. I had a profound sense that I was mute, though nothing was wrong with my voice. I didn't know how to get my mother's attention. She seemed focused elsewhere, somewhere far away and unreachable. I threw full-out screaming, fist-clenching temper tantrums, but even such great exertions of energy barely seemed to get her attention. She retreated and collapsed, as if she was powerless in the face of attacks by a four-year-old. I sensed that all her bad feelings were my fault. I thought I was a burden, unworthy of demanding anything. I was most certainly not a source of joy.

Yet, somehow, I knew she loved me, but instead of reassuring me that I was safe, she withdrew further into her own cocoon where I couldn't reach her. My rage and frustration grew. I couldn't even call her mom. I never did. The word was tainted for me. In another act of defiance, I even rejected my own name, Jennifer. First, I insisted my name was Gittel, my Hebrew name, then Joy, then Clementine, after my love of the song "Oh My Darling Clementine." Sometimes we would sing as we drove: "You are lost and gone forever, dreadful sorry, Clementine!" The song expressed a sadness I could not find a way to express myself.

CHAPTER TWO

THE HUERFANO (ORPHAN) VALLEY

THE BLUR that was the first few years of my life comes into focus at age five. There was stillness, no engine running, and ground beneath my feet. I remember a house with linoleum floors and a kitchen with white Formica countertops. Outside I was surrounded by amber hued mesas dotted with sage brush and twisted pine trees. It was Dixon, New Mexico. We stayed for a whole year, and I attended preschool. One of the few photos I have of my early childhood was taken during that time, a school portrait, I believe. I wore a stained maroon shirt, my short hair tied away from my face with a piece of red yarn, and smudges of food on my cheeks and around my mouth.

My mother's new boyfriend, Clay, lived with us. He was tall with dark hair and menacing dark eyes. My instinct was to keep my distance, and I avoided him the best I could while living in the same house with him. At least my mother seemed less downtrodden and sad since she was with him, and I felt less like the single source of her unhappiness.

It turned out that Dixon was not the new way of life for which my mother was searching. So, when Clay spoke of a conglomeration of communes, just three hours away in the Huerfano valley in southern Colorado, my mother was all ears. "There's a whole bunch of amazing people there, living off the land, taking care of each other's children, and cooking together," he told her. He had friends in one of the settlements named Archulettaville, and one of the dwellings was available. It sounded just like what my mom was looking for.

I was still an angry child, perhaps even more vociferously than I was previously, since I was now old enough to speak. Judy thought and hoped that living communally, giving me freedom, and sharing her parental duties with others, would be the best way to help me calm down. We packed up what little we had and headed to Colorado.

An amber haze enveloped the Huerfano valley as the light hit the dust in the air. On one side of the road giant mountains stretched up high in the sky; on the other side, I saw an expansive tapestry of green farm patches.

When we arrived at Archulettaville, all I could see was a row of nine or ten cavernous animal stalls made of dirt and stone that were etched into the mountainside along the road. I could tell people lived there because the stalls had been fitted with doors and windows. Native American tapestries were being used for curtains. Several people, grungy like us, sat at a table on the dirt terrace in front of the stalls. A couple of children ran around naked, their skin crusted in dust.

Across the road sat a white ranch style house with red trim. It was the home of Dan Archuleta, the man after whom Archulettaville was named. He was a Chicano whose family had farmed the land for generations. He owned the fields surrounding his house. When some hippies approached him asking if they could crash in his abandoned goat shelters across the road, he agreed. The settlement evolved from there. Dan, never married, must have been lonely and liked the company.

When we arrived, Dan hobbled out of his house to meet us, rocking from leg to leg like a penguin. Maybe he was bowlegged from riding horses all his life. He wore a white cowboy hat stained with hand grease and the dust of the valley. His face looked worn like old leather, with deep lines etched around his eyes and mouth.

When my mom introduced us, he smiled brightly, tipped his hat with one hand, and reached out his other to shake mine. "Nice to meet you, Jennifree. You're a real pretty girl," he said.

"Thank you," I said. "Do you have horses?"

"Oh yes, Jennifree, I do. I even have a pony you can ride," he said. I was so excited.

*   *   *

Archulettaville was just one of the small communities that popped up along county road 580 in the mid '70s. The valley's most infamous was Libre, a community started by artists who wanted to live off the grid, focus on their art, and break free of conventional societal constraints. Some people lived in shacks, others built houses or geodesic domes, and still others lived in group settlements like us. The hippies and Beatniks who traversed the country from coast to coast, often in colorfully painted VW busses, stopped to visit the communities in the valley. Even the likes of Alan Ginsberg paid a visit. Everyone seemed to know everyone else, and there were often gatherings where everyone converged.

The once animal stall, which was now our home, was a single room about ten feet by ten feet. The walls and floor were dirt. A small loft up above was accessible by a makeshift rope ladder. One of the stalls in the middle of the row was used as a communal room with a small kitchen, a couch, and a table.

Judy and Clay set up their bed downstairs. I didn't have a bed per se, just a sleeping bag, so I slept wherever, often in the loft.

Dan took an immediate liking to me. Too much of a liking. I was apparently the apple of his eye. He gave me a pony—more a figure of speech than actually giving it to me for real. He would saddle it up for me and take me riding. I loved it but ended up having an asthma attack. I was allergic to horses, and pretty much all furry friends, much to my dismay. But Dan found other ways to interact with me. He would invite me into his house and give me candy. Once, he even took me to Walsenburg, the nearest town, about an hour away. I sat in his pickup truck trying to stay as close to the passenger door as I could. I didn't know how I knew, but I sensed not to get too close. In town he bought me gifts, including a pair of black patent leather shoes. I'd never had anything so pretty or shiny before. As beautiful as they were, I felt uncomfortable receiving them, as if I was then obliged to Dan. I felt a little like his pet.

At the same time, my repulsion towards Clay only grew stronger. I have no memory of him doing anything to me, I just felt uncomfortable and scared in his presence, even imagining him to be the devil. When he entered the room, I wanted to be as small as possible, or even better, not be there at all.

My anger towards my mother persisted too. Now I shunned her touch. When she tried to show me affection, I would instinctually retreat like a clam in its shell. I often felt like I would vomit, as if expressions of love were toxic and disingenuous. I wanted to get away from her—I hated her. And I loved her and needed her. I stomped, screamed, tried to pound on her with my little fists. I felt like I would explode. She'd throw her arms in the air seemingly defeated, unsure how to deal with me. I was instinctually looking for her to set boundaries of protection, but she wanted to live without boundaries. She didn't understand me, and took my tantrums personally, seeing herself as a victim. If anyone asked why I was so upset, she said I was an angry girl and that she didn't know what to do. She told them I had rejected her. The more I acted out and cried for help, the more distance and freedom I was given. When I wasn't throwing fits at her, my anger drilled inward. I felt like I was defective and unworthy of needing anything.

Convinced my mother didn't want me, I sought refuge wherever I could. Soon I befriended Mary Jo, one of the women in the community who took a liking to me. She was a sturdy and steady earth mamma, with dark brown hair and tanned skin from working outdoors. Her presence was reassuring. When people showed me they were trustworthy, like Mary Jo did, I would slowly open up a window to myself that was by default firmly shut. A goofy, quirky, spontaneous part of me emerged, and I got a glimpse of what it felt like to belong. Before long I was spending most nights with Mary Jo and her boyfriend John, not my mother.

Yet, as much as I shunned my mother, I would fall into a panic when she ventured too far away. I was terrified she would forget me. One of my most memorable fits of defiance was when she went to Denver for a few days. As soon as she left, I marched my way to the communal room, found a pair of scissors, and furiously chopped off all my hair. I think I was hoping to get a reaction out of her, to get her attention, to express my feelings. At six years old, I didn't have the vocabulary. When she returned and saw my hair, she was unfazed. In her eyes, she was just letting me be free.

When Mary Jo was busy, I'd walk in the fields around Dan's house. I'd lay on the ground and stare at the sky, daydreaming and imagining castles and unicorns in the clouds as they transmuted into different shapes and dissolved into blue. I felt stuck in my body, unable to rest—like an unrelenting sense of being on guard. At least the ground and the sky offered some comfort.

Then, Mary Jo told me she and John were going to hitchhike to Boston and be gone for a while. I begged her to take me with her. I asked my mom if I could go. She agreed, and even reminded me that my grandparents lived there. A plan formed in which Mary Jo and John would drop me off with them while they were in Boston and then pick me up a week or so later.

I didn't actually know my grandparents. The only time I met them was when I was too young to remember. My mom rarely even talked about them, and when she did, it was with distain. From the little my mom said, it was clear that they disapproved of her lifestyle and everything she did. Nonetheless, I imagined that if I visited, they would shower me with love, affection, and gifts, as I thought grandparents were supposed to. I couldn't wait to meet them.

Soon Mary Jo, John, and I were standing on the side of the road with our thumbs out. We slowly inched our way across the country. Some nights we stayed in motels, but after a while we started sleeping under highway overpasses. I lay there frozen in fear, imagining the warm welcome I would soon get from my grandparents, but I also worried we wouldn't make it. I overheard Mary Jo and John saying they had only a few dollars left and that we would have to spend it wisely so we could all eat. I wanted to curl into a ball like a roly-poly and disappear. I didn't want them to spend their money on me.

A couple days later, we showed up on my grandparents' doorstep unannounced. I stood there in my moccasins and worn-out clothes, covered in grime from our travels. When they came to the door, they glared at me flatly, as if their faces were frozen and they couldn't smile. Mary Jo introduced me, "This here is your granddaughter, Jennifer. She wanted to come see you." I'm not sure who responded, but what I remember hearing was "we didn't know about this, and we weren't expecting her." They looked me over in a way that made me feel like a dirty animal. I sensed they'd prefer I didn't enter their house. I gripped Mary Jo's hand trying to plead not to leave me there with these unpleasant people.

Hesitantly, they took me in and Mary Jo and John left. First, they put me in the bath. I was mesmerized by the running water, and even more so by the spiral that formed when the water drained. I hadn't seen anything like that before. They must have washed my clothes or gotten some new ones. Then they sat me down in front of the television, yet another thing I hadn't seen before. I watched *Mr. Rogers Neighborhood* and *Sesame Street*. I loved Mr. Rogers. I wished I could walk into the television set and stay in his neighborhood, instead of with my grandparents. When Mary Jo and John returned a week later, I was relieved. Soon we were back in the Huerfano valley, the closest thing to home.

★ ★ ★

After a while, Clay left the Huerfano and moved to Hawaii. I thought he and my mom broke up, but then a few weeks later, my mom announced she was going to Hawaii too. She said she just wanted to see what it was like and would come back for me soon. She must have grown restless again, or maybe she wanted to be with Clay, or get away from me. Mary Jo agreed to take care of me while she was gone.

Then late one afternoon, when I was sitting outside gazing at the golden light cast across the valley, Mary Jo came and sat with me. She was more serious than usual. She looked me in the eye. "Your mom isn't coming back to get you. She has arranged for you to travel to Hawaii with a woman named Susan and her two children." My body froze.

"Why isn't she coming back?" I asked.

"I don't know. But she wants you to join her in Hawaii."

"No, I don't want to go," I said.

"It's going to be okay. Your mom is waiting for you. She'll be happy to see you." I stared at the ground, tears rising up. I didn't want to move again. I didn't want to leave Mary Jo.

"Susan will come pick you up tomorrow," she said.

"No!" I said. Who was Susan? Even Mary Jo didn't know who she was. Mary Jo explained that was somebody my mom knew. That night, we packed my suitcase.

The next morning, Susan pulled up in front of the homestead in a brown station wagon. Her two boys sat in the car staring at me. Susan and Mary Jo spoke for a few minutes, and then Mary Jo walked back to me and explained that Susan and her boys were driving to California, and then from there we would all fly to Hawaii. She explained that Susan agreed to take me along, and that my mom would be waiting for me when I arrived in Hawaii. I clung to Mary Jo's leg, my suitcase sitting on the ground next to me. She bent down, hugged me, then put her hands on my cheeks. "You have to go now, sweetheart. Soon you will see your mother."

"No, I don't want to go. I want to stay with you," I said. The fear of leaving cemented my feet to the ground. I clung to Mary Jo even harder. I hoped my most pure wish and prayer would be heard. If I just wished hard enough, I thought, I could stay and not get into the car with this unknown woman.

Susan yelled from the car, "Ready to go?" I could sense that her two sons were impatient.

"Yeah, we're coming," Mary Jo responded. I stared at Mary Jo, tears in my eyes, desperately sad. She was no longer going to be my person. In fact, I would only see her one more time, many years later when I met her for lunch as I drove through the Southwest.

I got into the back seat of the car, placing my suitcase next to me like a security blanket. Then we drove off. I stared into that vast Colorado sky to say goodbye.

I sat in the back seat, clinging to my sides. Susan's two boys were rowdy and unfriendly. They teased me saying things like "something's wrong with her, she's scared, she can't even speak."

I don't know how long the journey took, but it felt endless. It didn't take long for me to realize that Susan found me to be a burden. Perhaps she wasn't getting paid enough, or even anything, for the hardship of transporting me to Hawaii. Or maybe she just didn't like me. Something about her wasn't right. She was always mad. I sensed that she could do something crazy at any minute. She said that she had cancer and showed me a grape-sized black bump on her foot. She said she was going to Hawaii to heal herself. I stared at the bump, horrified. I had heard the word cancer before and knew it was bad, but not what it actually meant.

At one of the rest stops, we were both in the women's bathroom. I was washing my hands when Susan screamed from inside the stall, "I just shat out part of my intestine." I was scared. I didn't quite know what she was saying. My thoughts raced. I stood by the sink, frozen. She came out, hysterical, with a white ropy thing in her hand. "Look," she said. "This is my intestine."

"What does it mean?" I said.

"I don't know what it fucking means. It probably means I'm going to die soon, or it means my cancer is spreading," she yelled. I just looked at her, knowing I had to be careful what I said, or else she would yell at me more. "Ok, let's go, no use staying around here. You just remember I am doing you a big favor, so make no bother for me, I have enough on my plate," she said.

"Ok," I said and followed her out to the car. I got in my seat and felt I didn't even deserve to breathe. I wanted Mary Jo, or even my mother.

CHAPTER THREE

HAWAII

I WAS FINALLY reunited with my mother on the Big Island. Shortly after I arrived, I turned seven. First, we stayed with Clay in a tepee he had pitched deep in the jungle up a dirt road, but we weren't there long. Soon they broke up for real. With no other tether to anyone on the island, we drifted with random hippies we met at the local food co-op or the beach. We stayed in an assortment of treehouses and jungle huts. There were always people coming and going, talking about such and such a place, or what certain people were doing. Someone we crossed paths with had just returned from Molokai, and told Judy about Halawa Valley, a sparsely inhabited part of the island with waterfalls and lush unadulterated land. She was intrigued, and since we weren't really living anywhere, she decided we should go see it for ourselves.

Molokai was, and still is, the least populated of the Hawaiian Islands. We arrived in 1976, when, according to census data from around that time, the population was less than six thousand. The only way to get to Halawa Valley was via a single lane road that ran along the perimeter of the island.

At the top rim of the valley, Hawala looked like an oasis with distant waterfalls in one direction and the vast blue ocean and sky in the other. The steep road into the valley was rugged, probably deterring many from making the journey.

On our very first day there, we met Julie and Jamie, and their young son, Jamuna. They had a house that Jamie had built himself. Not a real house, but a hippie house, meaning there were walls, a roof, and a floor, but no plumbing or electricity. To me it was palatial. It was more of a house than our stall in the Huerfano or Clay's teepee. I wanted to live in a house too, but we barely had enough money for anything. So, like many other "back to the earth" types, Judy set out to find a place where we could squat for free.

Not far from Julie and Jamie's, Judy found a clearing that was level. She got permission from the landowner to squat there, and then got straight to work. First, we cleared the land and made a path from the beach with a machete. Next, she carefully located four trees that would become the corners of our hut. When all the prep work was done, she and Jamie built an eight foot by eight foot plywood platform that they hoisted into the air and secured to the four trees, about six feet above the ground. Above the platform, they secured a couple of cross beams to the trees, over which they laid a thatch roof made of palm fronds that we picked in the jungle. As a finishing touch, Judy attached rolled up tatami mats to the sides that we could roll down at night or when it rained.

We moved in. We slept upstairs in the loft; we kept the remainder of our meager belongings and our camp stove downstairs. Mostly we lived outside. The valley was once abundant with taro fields, and the terracing from the past farming was still intact, albeit overgrown. It was fertile ground for growing pretty much anything. Judy got to work digging and planting a garden. She had a green thumb. Soon we had an abundance of vegetables, flowers, and herbs.

The beach was just a short walk away. There was rarely anyone there. I spent hours splashing in the water. I mostly bathed in the ocean, or sometimes in one of the pools by a waterfall. To water our garden, Judy siphoned water from a creek up the valley. Sometimes, if you were really quick, you could use the warm water that was baking in the hose to take a quick hot shower before the cold water caught up. We didn't have a toilet or an outhouse. We went to the bathroom anywhere we wished within the jungle. We would simply dig a hole or move a rock and do our business there. Instead of toilet paper, we wiped ourselves with the leaves of a soft fuzzy plant we called the toilet paper plant.

When it poured, there was not much we could do except lay in our loft listening to the rain pounding on our roof. The construction of our hut was far from perfect, and it wasn't unusual for the roof to leak. We would put pots or cups under the leaks and attempt to fix them when the sun returned.

Judy signed up for food stamps and enrolled me in Molokai's public school. I woke up each morning at dawn to get ready, which involved very little. My mom would braid my wild mane of hair, I'd put on my little sundress and flip-flops, then walk to the road to be picked up by a Mahu who drove me to school. Mahu were native transgender people who were once the priests and healers of the Hawaiian culture and were still revered. He was a plump, teddy bear kind of person. He looked a little intimidating at first due to his size, but he was a gentle soul, and I soon felt at ease with him. I am sure I was just as odd to him at first, as I was one of only two white students in the entire Molokai public school system.

As we drove up the steep slope out of the valley, and all the way to Kaunakakai, the main town, he hummed or sang Hawaiian tunes that made me happy. Sometimes he talked to me in either broken English or Pidgin. After school he came and drove me home again. During the two hours a day we spent in the car, I learned Pidgin too.

Being at school was no fun. I stuck out like a sore thumb. I was tall and gawky with blond hair and blue eyes. I didn't look like the rest of the kids who were mostly native Hawaiians. On the playground during recess, the other kids taunted me, yelling, "Stupid haole girl." Haole is the Hawaiian word for white, not native like them. The nicer ones just called me "Jennifer giraffe," which I didn't really mind since I liked giraffes. To the best of my ability, I tried to keep to myself and be invisible. I didn't want any trouble. However, I did wonder if I was actually stupid. I didn't seem to know what most of them knew, like the Pledge of Allegiance. Why couldn't I just be normal, I wondered.

After school I sometimes visited Julie and Jamie and played with Jamuna. They were a real family. They had things I could only dream of having, like luscious skin cream that smelled like flowers, which Julie would rub on my sunburned arms and shoulders. I liked hanging out at their house, but never wanted to overstay my welcome.

Mostly I spent hours and hours alone wandering on the beach or in the jungle. I picked strawberry guavas and lilikois, eating as I went. I never wore shoes, except when I went to school. My soles had grown a thick layer of protective skin, so rocks and thorns didn't hurt me. I liked feeling the muddy squishiness of the mossy jungle floor between my toes. I felt protected in the jungle, like it was my shelter. It was where my imagination wandered into magical fantasies. Though I was accustomed to solitude, being alone only with my imagination could be lonely. Yet, it was safer than getting attached to people and then having to say goodbye.

The highlight of the week was going across the island on Sundays to the free vegetarian feast at the Hari Krishna ashram. I loved how welcoming they were. The women and girls wore orange saris, some with interwoven strands of silver and gold. They seemed so happy, and their clothes were so beautiful. Their walls were covered in intricate textiles that looked fit for kings and queens. There were also lavish paintings of a man with blue skin with a flute held to his lips. He stood against an idyllic landscape with cows smiling at him. They told me he was Krishna, their master, who embodied pure love. They said when he played his flute, animals would follow him. I was enchanted.

Not long after that I was visiting one of the other hippies who lived in Halawa Valley. Her house always smelled like incense. The smoke rose from an altar she set up with statues and a large photo of a man with an afro and a halo. It was not Krishna. She told me his name was Sai Baba, her guru. He was also from India, and she told me he performed miracles. India was starting to sound magical with so many holy people who loved everyone. Even more than that, I liked the idea of miracles. I asked the woman lots of questions about Sai Baba. That's when she gave me some magic powder, wrapped in a little paper pouch, called vibhuti. She said Sai Baba manifested it out of thin air. I was so excited. When I got back to our hut, I opened the little packet, poured a little in my hands, clenched my fists, and prayed. I prayed for a real house with lots of rooms, and for friends. I sat with complete commitment, repeating, "Please, please, please."

⋆   ⋆   ⋆

After I finished the school year on Molokai, my wish came partially true. We moved to Kauai to a house in a guava orchard. It was made mostly of plywood, had walls, a real roof, floors, and a front porch where we could hang a stalk of bananas to ripen. There was still no running water or electricity, but it was an actual house. And my mom scored and bought a big white car for fifty dollars, which I named Gardenia. Our new neighbors, Akala and Roland, and their two sons, Tai and Jora, lived just up the river. They and my mother paid their rent by picking the guavas for their landlord, Jack. They dressed like us and lived off the land like us. We all became instant friends.

At our house, my mom let me have the one bedroom, while she slept in the loft in the living room. We didn't have money for furnishings, so we headed to the dump, where my mom always found treasures. She didn't understand why people threw away such good stuff. That day at the dump, we scored. I found a whole bag of clothes that looked new and were my size. Maybe I wouldn't look so different. Then my mom called from several yards away. "Look, look, I found you a dresser." She stood there proudly, as if her find proved her theory that we didn't need to buy things from stores. The dresser was perfect: It was white with little green vines and violet flowers painted on the drawers. It even had a mirror that attached to its back.

Back in my room, I put my belongings in the dresser drawers, and my Flower Fairy books, that I loved so much, atop the dresser next to my kerosine lamp. I even had a bed off the floor with a real mattress, on which I arranged my stuffed animals. In time we made several other trips to the dump and gathered things from other people. Soon we had a futon couch, dishes, and a battery powered boombox. I listened to Hawaiian music, Bob Dylan, and other singer-songwriters for hours as I stared into space.

My mother enrolled me in Island School, a private alternative school that had just opened. I would be in third grade. She arranged to teach folk dancing in exchange for my tuition. To this day this puzzles me, as I have never known my mother to be a dancer, and I certainly never learned folk dancing at school, or ever. Nonetheless, I liked school, and although I was still different, I wasn't as different as I was at the school on Molokai. Now, instead of saying the Pledge of Allegiance each morning, all us kids gathered in a circle and did yoga. I was so nimble that I could do Raja Bhujangasana, king cobra pose, like a pro, bending backwards and placing my toes on my forehead. It was my special talent, and other kids congratulated me. I wasn't used to other kids being nice to me.

We had English class, science class, and theater class. My favorite was science class, taught by Tom, my favorite teacher. I secretly hoped he would marry my mother. He wasn't slimy like Clay or the other guys who tried to be her boyfriend. He was kind and fun and found creative ways to teach us math and science. Sometimes he took us on excursions into the jungle where we looked at tadpoles and plants. He encouraged me and praised me when I did good work. He even told my mom I was good at math.

I was starting to feel like I fit in. I even made two friends at school, a rich Jewish girl named Torah, who invited me to her birthday party, and Raven, my first crush. Raven and I often sat together at recess and made up songs and stories. But having friends was also uncomfortable. I was shy and ashamed. I worried they would find out how poor and odd I really was. Plus, now that I had seen Torah's house, I realized that I still didn't live in a real house. I didn't want my new friends to know that we didn't have a bathroom or running water.

One of my favorite pastimes was to lie on my bed and browse the Sears and JCPenney catalogues. I would fantasize about having a house with running water, flushing toilets, and a sprawling lawn. First, I would pick out all the beautiful clothes I would buy. New clothes. Then I would browse the section with home goods like lawn mowers. I imagined that I was grown up, married, and that I lived in a big house with a shiny driving mower sitting out front.

Before long I spent most of my free time at Akala and Roland's house. Whenever I could, I took care of Jora, their young son. He was a fixture on my hip. I loved him and never wanted to leave him. I would carry him to the river, play in the water with him, and feed him. Akala seemed to like the help. She often let me eat meals with them too.

I was with them so much that I think my mother's feelings were hurt. She still told people that I rejected her. When I was with her, I felt her sadness as if I could feel her heart. I still felt like it was because of me. I don't think I was as angry or incessantly throwing tantrums, but I still didn't feel at ease with her. I thought she'd be happier if I stayed out of her hair. Plus, I was embarrassed by her.

She showed up to school wearing loose flowing dresses, often with stains, and no bra. The lunches she made for me were vegetables and whole wheat tortillas filled with tahini. I imagined that the other kids gawked at my food as they at their peanut butter and jelly sandwiches on white bread. That was bad enough, but then she started wearing orange—and only orange. Not long before that a man who also wore orange seemed to be around a lot. He had recently returned from India and gave my mother several books written by his guru, Bhagwan Shree Rajneesh. Whatever she read must have made her wear orange too, but I didn't understand why.

A few weeks later she told me she had become a disciple of Bhagwan, and that she had a new name, Ma Prem Shreya. Ma denoted she was a female, Prem was a prefix that meant love, and Shreya was what I was to call her from now on. Not long after that, when we picked up our mail from our PO Box, she excitedly opened a parcel that had arrived. It was a wood beaded necklace with a locket containing a picture of her new master. She said it was called a mala and that she was supposed to wear it at all times. I asked her why. She said it was to show she was a disciple. I didn't really know what that meant. To me it was just another thing that made her stand out and seem weird. I didn't see anyone else wearing a necklace with some Indian man's picture in the locket.

★ ★ ★

Two weeks before I finished third grade, my mom said she wanted to speak to me about my upcoming summer vacation. That evening we sat on the floor of our makeshift living room. I braced myself.

"Since you have three months off for the summer, I would like to travel to India," she said.

"Why?" I asked. I didn't want to go anywhere. I was finally settling in and felt like I was beginning to belong somewhere.

"I want to visit the Rajneesh ashram and meet my new guru," she said. "We'll be back in time for you to go back to school."

"I don't know." I could sense that she had already made up her mind, and that whatever I said wouldn't matter.

"I promise we'll be back in just a couple of months," she said.

"Can we visit Sai Baba?" I was still enthralled with his halo and his magic powder.

"Sure, after we go to the Rajneesh ashram, we can see him too," she said. I was still reticent. However, if we would be back soon, and if I could meet the man who made miracles happen, I figured it would be okay. I remembered our visits to the Hare Krishna ashram on Molokai, which conjured up images of Krishna with his luminous blue skin. I gleaned that India must be the most exotic place on earth, where saints walked the streets and blessed the people and the animals. Maybe they would bless me too.

When the school year ended, we packed a suitcase each. For some reason we also packed up everything else we owned. I didn't understand why since my mom promised we would be back soon. And somebody else was moving into our house. Where would we live when we got back?

A couple days before our departure, we loaded the boxes with all our important stuff into the car. Shreya explained that somebody she met agreed to let us store the boxes under their house for safekeeping. But, when I saw that the house stood on stilts near the ocean, it didn't look safe to me. Nonetheless, we unloaded our boxes, which included all our photographs from my childhood, as well as the arrowheads I collected in

Utah, and the paintings I did in school. We tried to put the boxes in the most protected place we could find, but I feared a heavy rain would still get them wet, or maybe the mongooses would get into them. As we drove away, I took a good look at the ocean. I felt sad that I had to leave the things that had become familiar to me. I wasn't certain we would actually return.

PART TWO
Pune

CHAPTER FOUR

ARRIVAL

THE BOMBAY airport was chaotic. Everyone moved quickly and with no sense of order. If I didn't stick close to my mom, I could have easily been caught up in it all and swept away. As soon as we got our luggage, pushy people were trying to carry our bags or sell us taxi rides and accommodations. Just outside the airport, elegant Indian women draped in vibrant silk saris and adorned with colorful glass bangles stood in stark contrast to the emaciated beggars who reached toward us, pleading, "Baksheesh, baksheesh." Some of the beggars didn't even have shirts. Some of them looked like they were starving. I could see their every rib. Meanwhile, rickshaws honked and wove to and from the curb in every which way. Worst of all was the stench of sewage and fumes, and the trash all over the street. My senses were overloaded.

Somehow, we eventually found our way to the train station where Judy, I mean Shreya, bought our tickets to Pune. On the platform, vendors sold snacks, and the aroma of spicy, greasy food hung in the air. A man stood by his tea cart, yelling, "Chai, chai," as he poured hot tea from one pot to another with great flair, steam rising in the air. He then poured the tea into small terra cotta cups. Travelers bought the cups of tea, drank it, and threw the cups on the tracks before boarding their trains.

When our train pulled up, everyone pushed and shoved to get on. We made it aboard. We were in third class along with all the locals and even chickens. My mom was all about roughing it anyway, though I think in this case it was that we had very little money, so she bought the cheapest tickets. The seats were all occupied, so there I stood, uncomfortable with the forced closeness. Those around me looked at me with pleading eyes. It seemed they wanted me to do something to ease their suffering. I was helpless to do anything. India was nothing like the images I saw at the Hari

Krishna ashram on Molokai. It was no paradise at all, and there was no sight of the likes of Krishna blessing the people and the animals.

Dazed with jet lag and so many new sights, sounds, and smells, we arrived in Pune and got a room in a rundown hotel close to the train station. I felt like I would fall asleep while standing, but first I looked out our window. Down on the street, things were lively and loud. It felt like a strange dream. I was used to the noises of the jungle, with its comforting hum of insects and birdsong. I longed for my own bed, even if it was nothing fancy.

Too tired to take a shower, I lay down on the bed fully clothed. A couple of hours later, I awoke, my skin crawling. I jumped up. "Shreya, wake up, something's biting me!" My body was covered in bedbug bites. So far, I hated India.

★   ★   ★

The next morning, we caught a rickshaw to 17 Koregaon Park, the address for the Shree Rajneesh Ashram. The rickshaw dashed around people, cows, and other vehicles in the street as horns honked from every direction. There was no logic or organization to the flow of traffic—it was more like a circus. Amazingly, somehow, we didn't crash.

When we entered the Koregaon Park neighborhood, there was a hint of serenity. Large mansions sat behind wrought iron gates, and massive banyan trees sprawled wide with tentacles hanging to the ground. Soon there was a spattering of Westerners, dressed in orange, ambling down the street.

The rickshaw stopped in front of the ashram's large, ornately carved, brass-embellished wood gate. Above the gate, "Shree Rajneesh Ashram" was etched into the marble facade. We passed through the gate as if entering a different world. It was an immaculately clean oasis—a complete contrast to the dirty, chaotic world just outside. Lush greenery flanked a central walkway. A sea of orange-clad, smiling people strolled the path wearing loose, flowing clothes. Many of the men wore only a lunghi or shorts, their chest hairs glistening in the sun. Everyone wore a wooden beaded mala with a central locket with a photo of Bhagwan, just like my mom's. My mom fit in perfectly. I stood out in my blue skirt and flip-flops.

The people at the front gate welcomed us warmly, gave my mom a schedule of the daily activities, and pointed to the front office where she could meet with one of the people in charge to schedule a meeting, called darshan, with Bhagwan. As we walked further into the ashram, everyone smiled at us. People had a softness and vulnerability in their eyes, their pupils dilated with joy. Unlike in the real world, where people didn't often gaze into my eyes, here they did, as if they wanted to see deep inside of me. It felt welcoming, but also a little strange, like there was no privacy.

Many congregated along the two-foot-tall stone wall, called the Zen wall, that snaked on either side of the central path. Some conversed, others stood or sat and hugged each other for ages. Not far from the front gate was Krishna House, the main office. The central chamber had floor-to-ceiling windows and marble floors. Behind the windows sat three high-backed chairs that looked like thrones. The center chair was on a pedestal, clearly denoting a hierarchy. It was where Bhagwan's personal secretary, Ma Yoga Laxmi, sat. To her right was Arup, a sturdy Dutch woman who scheduled people for therapy groups and darshan with Bhagwan. To Laxmi's left was Ma Anand Sheela, Laxmi's assistant.

We were told that Bhagwan didn't interact with the public except in the mornings when he gave a lecture or in the evenings when he met with a smaller group of disciples for darshan. His house and gardens were behind a fence. The gate to his compound was guarded by sannyasin men trained in martial arts, called samurais.

As we wandered through the ashram, we found Vrindavan, the canteen where you could buy amazing food, the therapy chambers where people did groups, and a boutique where you could buy red clothes. Soon, I heard music coming from Buddha Hall, a huge auditorium with shiny stone floors, a canvas roof, and a white marble chip road surrounding it like a moat. It was where Bhagwan met with his followers each morning for lecture, also called discourse. During the day, the hall was used for all sorts of meditations. Lush, perfectly maintained gardens with bamboo and flowers filled the spaces between the buildings. The back of the ashram was where the permanent residents lived and was off-limits to me as a new arrival.

★   ★   ★

The next morning, we joined the throngs of devotees standing in line waiting to enter Buddha Hall for discourse. When we were close to the entrance, the line became single file, and two sniffers, standing on either side of us, bent forward and smelled our heads to make sure they didn't detect perfume or other scents. We were told Bhagwan had asthma and ailing health, and absolutely no scents were allowed. If a sniffer detected a smell, you would be turned away and could listen to discourse at a section of the Zen wall where a speaker was installed.

We sat down on the floor with the hundreds of others already seated in silence. They sat cross-legged, their backs erect, many with silk shawls wrapped around their shoulders. Their eyes were closed, waiting for Bhagwan to arrive. It was the first time I witnessed meditation, though I didn't know what it was, other than closing your eyes without going to sleep. There was a deep sense of peace in the hall, like bathing in the warm sun. I figured that nice feeling was created by the meditation.

Then I heard the sound of car wheels on the white marble chip path. Bhagwan's limousine pulled up behind the podium at the front of the hall. Everybody raised their hands into prayer position either in front of their hearts or lips. Bhagwan came into view, wearing a crisply ironed white robe that hung to his ankles. His bald head glistened, and his long wispy beard hung down to his chest. With his hands held in prayer position, or namaste, he walked slowly and deliberately to the podium and sat down on the throne. After a long silence, he began to speak. His voice was deeply resonant, slow, and with elongated S sounds. He took long gaps between sentences, as if nothing was urgent. His voice was almost hypnotic, lulling a collective calm in the auditorium. He spoke of other religions and all sorts of things I knew nothing about nor understood. I sat there silently taking it all in, trying to be present and listen like the adults did. Ninety minutes later, he said, "Enough for today," stood up, and slowly walked back to his Rolls-Royce to be driven back to Lao Tzu House a mere five hundred yards away. After he left the auditorium, people sat silently for a while longer, blissfully basking in their master's energy, before getting on with the day.

CHAPTER FIVE

INITIATION

S OON AFTER our arrival, my mom met Bhagwan for evening darshan. These more intimate meetings took place in a smaller auditorium called Chuang Tzu, which was attached to Bhagwan's house. In these meetings, Bhagwan would give initiation, called sannyas, or speak to sannyasins, like my mom, who took initiation through the mail. He would answer their questions and usually prescribe several therapy groups that he thought would best help them break through their hang-ups and uncover their true selves. I didn't attend, but afterward, my mom said Bhagwan told her to do two groups, one called Enlightenment Intensive and one called Prema. I wondered what the groups would be like and what she would have to do.

I was still Jennifer and wore regular clothes. I was keenly aware and uncomfortable that I didn't fit in. I wasn't sure what any of it was about. I just knew that everyone was there because of Bhagwan. He was said to be awakened, and everyone was there to learn from him. I wasn't sure what being awakened meant. What I liked was how welcomed I felt. The people were always smiling and hugging, and they were nice to me. I wanted to be part of the loving family and wear orange too. So, before my mom started doing groups, which she said would take up all her time, I asked her to get me some orange clothes. That afternoon, we caught a rickshaw to MG Road, the bustling shopping hub in the heart of Pune, and purchased an orange kurta with a lace bib around the neck and matching pants.

The next day, when I returned to the ashram wearing my orange outfit, people beamed wide smiles at me. Some stopped and asked me when I would take sannyas. I hadn't really thought about that. What was sannyas? From what I could understand, taking sannyas would mean I would belong. And to belong, I would be given a new name as a symbol of shedding the old me and emerging into a new me. I was far less interested in being a disciple than I was in belonging. But if taking sannyas meant I would belong,

I would do it. Before long, when someone asked me when I would take sannyas, I responded, "Soon." They liked that answer.

On August 5, 1978, I stood outside Lao Tzu gate waiting to enter Chuang Tzu Hall. I insisted on going without my mother. I didn't want to be associated with her; I thought I was so mature at the age of nine that I didn't need a chaperone. I had seen many other kids in the ashram without adults, so why would this be any different?

I was sniffed and ushered into Chuang Tzu Hall alongside thirty or so others. We all sat on the cool floor in a semicircle facing Bhagwan's empty chair. Behind us was a dense wall of trees and gardens. Birds sang and squawked, and in the distance, I could hear car horns and the hum of civilization. I felt awkward and unsure of what I was supposed to do. I felt apprehensive about meeting Bhagwan, being in front of so many people, and the ceremony to come. I even worried that I was doing something that couldn't be undone. As we waited, I hugged my knees to my chest, as if my legs were a shield to hide behind.

Then the door from Bhagwan's house into the hall opened. Everyone sat up straight and placed their hands in namaste. There again stood Bhagwan in his crisp white robe with his sandaled feet peeking out. He stood at the door for several moments, his hands in namaste too. He slowly scanned the room, as if greeting each one of us. He then sat down in his chair. His bodyguard, Shiva, sat on the floor to his right, and his secretary Laxmi sat on the floor to his left. People were called up one by one.

When my name was called, I got up and bashfully moved to the front, aware that all eyes were on me. "Have a seat," Bhagwan said. I sat down. "Close your eyes, and listen to the sounds," he continued. I had never meditated before, but I closed my eyes and concentrated on the sounds, exactly as he told me to. He was very important—I didn't want to disappoint him. I heard birds chirping, then car horns in the distance, then my breath. After a couple of minutes, he spoke again. "Very good, you can open your eyes." The guard signaled me to move closer. I knelt right in front of Bhagwan, leaning forward while he placed a mala over my head. He then placed his thumb on my forehead, between my eyebrows, smiled, and looked deep into my eyes. After a few seconds, he said, "You can sit down." He reached to his side and handed me a piece of stationery where he had written my new name. "Your new name is Ma Prem Sarito," he said. "The prefix Prem means love, and Sarito means river. River of love." I don't remember what else he said or whether he was done talking to me, but I promptly rose to my feet and returned to my seat.

A few months later, a new darshan diary, a book that recorded people's meetings with Bhagwan, came out. I was amazed when I saw my photo and the comment: "She scuffled back to her mum." Nope, she was not there. I remember sitting there feeling sad I was on my own, like I wanted someone to congratulate me or tell me I had done a good thing.

CHAPTER SIX

ASHRAM KIDS

WHILE MY mother did groups, I hung out on the Zen wall watching people go by. I was shy, but not so shy that I wouldn't talk to someone if they approached me. Many adults stopped to say hello, sometimes telling me I was adorable or inquiring where I was from. It wasn't long until I recognized people.

My mom was in silence. She and all the people doing groups wore "in silence" badges so they could be fully immersed in their group. In contrast to the general aura of joy, the people in groups seemed serious, often looking down. I guess they were trying to avoid eye contact so they wouldn't be tempted to speak. Sometimes I'd even see somebody with their arm in a sling or with a black eye. Nobody else seemed alarmed by it. To me, it was confusing.

I soon learned that people sometimes got injured in the therapy groups, where they would go berserk and let out all their anger. I did sometimes hear screaming coming from the therapy chambers as I passed by on my way to Vrindavan, the cafe next door. I was told they were breaking through their conditioning to uncover their true selves. It sounded scary, and I was relieved to learn my mother wasn't doing one of the violent groups. She was currently doing Enlightenment Intensive, where participants sat across from each other all day asking or answering the question, "Who am I?" I didn't really understand that either, but at least nobody got hurt.

Everyone knew there were lighter groups and more scary groups. The groups that sounded scary to me were Tantra, Primal, and Encounter. They were the ones where people beat each other up or had sex with each other. It seemed like making it through one of those groups was like a rite of passage, a test of devotion. I even overheard people talking along the Zen wall saying, "Ha! You were assigned Primal group, brace yourself!"

Despite my naiveté, certain things were crystal clear from the get-go.

First and foremost, Bhagwan, as an enlightened being, was the leader and was revered. His words and instructions were taken as doctrine. If he told somebody to do a group, it was for that person's own growth. What was most important was to surrender, which I understood to mean doing whatever you were told. There was a lot of talk about letting go of your ego. When I asked someone what ego meant, I was told it meant our identities, our sense of self. There was even a sticker that many people plastered on their notebooks that said "Let Go." The letters E, G, and O were in a different color, so it read "let go ego."

Everyone felt it was a gift to be near Bhagwan—the closer, the better. He apparently emitted a field of energy that everyone called the Buddha-field. This energy was contagious and could lead you to awaken, just like Bhagwan did. At the very least, being near Bhagwan was a fast track to enlightenment, not only because of the energy he emitted but also because of his wisdom. Many thought they were lucky that their paths led them to Bhagwan, as if it was something cosmic. Bhagwan reinforced that belief, referring to all of us followers as the chosen ones.

★ ★ ★

I didn't see my mom during the day, but I felt comfort knowing she was somewhere within the ashram. I tried to act self-sufficient, even though I was far from it. But there were always friendly people asking me if I had eaten or trying to get to know me better. I felt safe, like people looked out for me. The woman who rented us a room in her apartment often checked on me too, and sometimes we even walked home together. I passed the days by drifting to different parts of the ashram, exploring alone, then talking to someone for a while, then wandering again until something else engaged me.

I was not the only kid wandering around. Many of the other kids I saw weren't with their parents either. They all wore orange clothes and malas, like I did now too. Some ran around together in the gardens or gathered in circles on the ground. Some were barefoot and some had wild, unbrushed hair. I also saw kids much younger than me, maybe four years old, alone. I worried they were lost as I watched them weaving between the adults. Sometimes someone would pat them on the head or stop and say a couple of words and then continue walking.

I was too timid to join the other kids. They seemed like a tribe, and I was scared they wouldn't like me. I just watched them from a distance. Then one afternoon, a towheaded girl with a kind of tough demeanor walked right up to me and introduced herself.

"I'm Maya."

"I'm Sarito." It felt strange to say my new name. It didn't feel like my name yet. Maya told me she was Australian, so I asked her about koala bears. Then we ran off to Vrindavan to see if someone would think we were cute and buy us a treat. Unlike me, she was bold and unabashedly approached people, saying exactly what she thought. When I was with her, I felt free to be precocious too, and I felt that if we were together, we didn't need any adult to take care of us. That was, of course, far from true, as I did go home with my mother each evening, and she always made sure I had money for food. Maya didn't seem to have a place to go home to. From what I could tell, she and her mother had trouble. She took care of herself. I don't even know if her mother was there; I never met her. She started staying with me and my mom most nights.

For a time, we were practically inseparable. We hung around the ashram, even visiting the back of the ashram where the permanent residents lived, and we weren't allowed. We'd walk in the gardens, then go visit Vipassana Go Down, the place where people packed up books to send to disciples around the world. The adults liked our visits, often admiring how free-spirited we were. When we were done in one place, we'd skip away to the next. We had nowhere we had to be. Nobody was tracking our movement, so we just followed our whimsy.

Maya already knew some of the other kids, which made me feel more at ease. Sometimes we played with them. Most of them lived together in a large hut at another property not far from the ashram's back gate. The parents worked in the ashram and lived elsewhere. The kids' hut was circular and very large. Beds were set up like a dormitory. The parents took turns putting them to bed at night and getting them up in the morning. But some of the bigger kids, who were around my age, said that sometimes whoever was supposed to be looking after them didn't show up. I think they relied on each other a lot for affection and other basic needs, like getting to their hut, eating meals, and getting dressed. Some of the kids were as young as four, so I'm sure the bigger kids looked out for them the best they could.

During the day, some of the children attended the ashram school nearby. I went along a few times, unsure of what to do. I sat on a swing and observed. Some kids played in the schoolyard, while others gathered inside an open-air hut. A woman teacher held a child on her lap while others vied for her attention. Nearby, a male teacher, shirtless with a beard and long hair resembling Jesus, played guitar as the children laughed and sang along. Later, he read to them, one of the girls sitting on his lap while the others huddled in close.It didn't seem like a normal school like Island School, where there was roll call or anything like that. I couldn't see any kind of structure. I wasn't really sure who the school was for or if I was even allowed to attend. It seemed some kids attended while others didn't. Or maybe kids just went to school sometimes. However it worked, nobody seemed to notice if I was or wasn't there. After a couple of visits, I never returned.

It seemed Bhagwan and my mother both thought children should have freedom. It didn't take long for me to learn that Bhagwan said all us kids didn't belong to our parents but rather to the commune. He even said that if parents weren't happy being parents, then to give it up. Many did that at least part of the time. And nobody was allowed to have babies. Bhagwan said that children were a hindrance to the spiritual path. I learned what sterilization and vasectomy meant. For women, it meant they had their "tubes tied," as many called it. For the men, it meant they didn't have sperm. I didn't really understand the technicalities, only that it meant women couldn't get pregnant. Bhagwan encouraged this so that people could have lots of sex and not worry.

I figured that since nobody was to have children, those of us kids who were allowed to be part of the commune were special. We were the ones who slipped through the cracks and were welcomed anyway. Even more than that, I thought we were lucky to be Bhagwan's disciples at such a young age since we hadn't yet been ruined by outside society. I knew this because I asked if I needed to do groups. I was told I didn't because I hadn't yet been ruined by societal conditioning.

CHAPTER SEVEN

MEETING VIDYA

As I GREW more accustomed to life in and around the ashram, I saw my mother less and less, except at night to sleep. She had finished her groups, but I wasn't sure what she was up to. I found myself intentionally avoiding her, a silent push away stemming from feeling unwanted or forgotten. When I was around her, I felt a confusing mix of disgust, attachment, love, and guilt. She had a heaviness about her, as if she was worried or unhappy. She didn't seem free and joyful like the other sannyasins. I wasn't sure if staying away and being angry made her sad or if staying away was what she hoped for so she could feel free. She never asserted herself and just let me do what I wanted. I felt so ashamed that she didn't seem to want me, but I tried to hide it and act like I didn't need her anyway. I was trying to go with the flow, like sannyasins liked to do.

Late one afternoon, I was lingering near the front gate, where a group of people were standing together laughing. I approached them to see what was going on. They were talking about a party. A well dressed non-sannyasin Indian man, wearing a white shirt, looked at me, smiled, and said, "You should come!" I looked at him confused. Did he realize I was a kid? One of the other adults must have seen my facial expression and reassured me.

"It's just down the road, and all us sannyasins will look out for you," he said. I had nowhere else to be, and I was trying to fit in better by being less shy and timid, so I agreed.

A couple of hours later, I was standing in the foyer of a swanky Koregoan Park mansion with marble floors and ceilings to the sky. The living room was crammed with boisterous, partying sannyasins. I don't know whose house it was, but I suspected it was the Indian man I met earlier. Maybe he liked all the fun and positive energy the sannyasins brought to his house.

I stayed close to the door, almost frozen, as I scanned the room to see if there were any kids or anyone I knew. I didn't recognize a single face. I felt ashamed being there alone, thinking it meant nobody liked me. Me and my shame were about to walk out when my eyes met those of a sturdy-looking blonde woman across the room. Was she really looking at me? I had never seen her before. She was still looking at me, now her eyes brightened, and a huge smile spread across her face as she gestured for me to come in her direction. As we moved towards each other, I watched as she smiled and boisterously said hello to people as she passed them. She seemed to know everyone, and some even looked at her with reverence. Who was she?

When we met in the middle of the room, she looked me right in the eyes. "Hello! I just had to come and meet you. Who are you? You are just adorable," she said with a South African accent.

"I'm Sarito," I said.

"I'm Vidya," she said. "When did you arrive?"

"I just moved here. I just took sannyas," I said. She looked me over as if greeting a loved one she hadn't seen in a long time. I basked in her kindness. I felt warmth in my chest. There was something about her that made me feel safe. I wanted to hug her and lean into her for protection, even though we just met.

"You must come see me in the office, come anytime," she said.

"You work in the main office?" I asked.

"Yes, if you ask for me, Vidya, at the front desk, they will know where to find me," she said.

"Okay," I said.

*   *   *

The next day, I walked around the ashram as usual, passing and almost entering the office several times. Each time I walked towards the marble steps and tall glass doors, I lost my courage and turned around. I thought the office was for important people, not a nobody like me—a girl wanting to belong somewhere. Finally, I pushed through my fear, stood up tall, pretending I had confidence, and walked straight into the fancy, air-conditioned chambers. At the reception desk, a young Indian woman asked if she could help me.

"Can I please see Vidya?" I asked.

"Do you have an appointment?" she asked. Vidya must have been some-one important if I was supposed to have an appointment.

"No," I said, feeling uneasy and unsure that the occurrence of the night before was even real. The receptionist saw the tentativeness on my face and smiled, trying to ease my tension.

"Is your mother supposed to be here too?" she asked softly.

"No, she is not. I am here alone," I said. She looked confused.

"I'll check for you," she said as she got up from her chair. I waited impatiently, fidgeting the time away. I could hear Vidya's unmistakable and rather loud voice from a room behind the reception area. It was a pivotal moment of waiting that I would never forget. Looking back, I realize that if things didn't play out as they were about to, my whole life would have been different. When the receptionist returned and said Vidya would see me, I was relieved.

I entered the room just behind the reception area with trepidation. The large room contained thirty or so desks in clusters. Vidya's desk sat against the wall facing the rest of the room. It appeared that the office was arranged around her. She was clearly the queen bee.

As I walked through the room and sat down in one of the chairs in front of Vidya's desk, eyes peered upon me from around the room, some with kindness, others with curiosity. I am sure they wondered what a nine-year-old girl was doing alone in the front office asking for a meeting with one of the women in charge of running the ashram.

I sat waiting for her to finish whatever she was doing. Then she raised her eyes and looked at me blankly for a second. Did she not recognize me from the night before? And then as if she came out of a trance, her eyes brightened, and a big smile spread across her face. "Oh darling, I am so happy to see you again, I'm so glad you came to see me," she said. "Please tell me your situation." I felt so bashful, and now that I found out she was an important person, I felt like a little mouse.

"I just arrived. My mom is Shreya and was doing groups, but she's done with that now. I have asthma," I blurted. I didn't expect to blurt out that I had asthma, but I had been wheezing a lot, and my mom thought it was from all the fumes outside the ashram. That got me to thinking how great it would be if I could live in the ashram. It would not only help my breathing because everything was so clean, since Bhagwan had asthma too, but it would also be a blessing that would mean I really belonged. It was a long shot, since the few kids that lived in the ashram itself were the children of the very special devotees.

Vidya asked me several questions about where I was living, what our plans were, and my health. I told her we had no plans, but that I hoped we would stay. She seemed to like that idea. She smiled so warmly and was so focused just on me. I felt uncomfortable—I wasn't used to feeling so seen.

"Do you want to live with the other kids?"

"Yes," I said, and then corrected myself in a moment of boldness. "Well, I want to live in the ashram to help my asthma. I don't want to live with my mother." She fell silent as she pondered. I felt like I may have said too much. At least she didn't just tell me my wish was absurd and come right out and say no.

"You know, your situation is quite unusual. I'm concerned about your health. But understand, the people who live in the ashram are people who work hard to keep this place running. Their work is their devotion to Bhagwan. You're a kid, and your mother and you just arrived. I will need to meet your mother," she said.

"Okay, I'll tell her to come see you," I said.

"Once I have talked to her, come back to see me. I need to think about this," she said.

"Okay," I said and rushed out, feeling a little shaky.

That evening I told my mother that I had gone to the office to see Vidya. She seemed surprised but not displeased. I insisted that she go see Vidya the next day before Vidya forgot about me. And so she did. I don't know what they talked about. I anxiously hoped the commune would find a place for my mom. I wanted to make sure she was safe and had a job so we could stay, and so my mom didn't have to worry about money. I knew we had very little.

The next afternoon I went back and met with Vidya. This time I just walked past the receptionist and entered the big room with all the desks. When she saw me, she motioned for me to come sit in front of her. I could barely wait to hear what she would say. "Darling, I will try to figure something out for you to live with the kids or in the ashram. It will take a few days until I know more."

"Thank you," I said, beaming. "What about my mother?"

"We'll give her a job and a place to live," she said. I was so relieved. "In the meantime, you can stay with Nira in Eckhart House." She pointed to a woman who sat at a desk in the corner to her left.

"Okay," I said hesitantly. I didn't want to burden this woman who was tasked to let me sleep in her room. And even though I was happy, I worried that my mom would be hurt that I was leaving her alone to go stay with someone else. "And you can come work with me. You can be my message runner," she added, pointing to the side desk to her left. "That will be your desk." I wasn't expecting that. I felt so lucky.

"Wow, really?" I said.

"Yes, I would love to have you around. I feel like you could be my own daughter," she said.

That night I packed up my suitcase of stuffed animals and my few pieces of clothing and ventured past the guards and into the private part of the ashram. I arrived at Nira's room, if you can call it that. It was, in fact, a hut, not much bigger than her large bed, on the roof of a white stucco horseshoe-shaped building. Hers was just one of several huts that covered most of the roof. When I arrived, Nira was inside her mosquito-netted room waiting for me. I didn't even know her, but she welcomed me so warmly. We sat on the soft bed and talked and laughed. I felt so safe and cared for. At the same time, I felt guilty that I was happy without my mom. I could feel her loneliness from afar. That night and several more after that, I slept there with Nira in her bed as if it was normal as anything.

CHAPTER EIGHT

MOVING IN

I STARTED WORKING in the office with Vidya. Shortly after that, my wish came true, and I moved into a room in the back of the ashram. The newly constructed Veggie Villas was a row of ten rooms that faced a large vegetable garden. It backed to the fence that surrounded Lao Tzu House. I felt so lucky I was going to live so close to Bhagwan. I would most certainly be in his energy field. Each room was furnished with three single beds, most on the floor, and a small shelf for each person. Since nobody had much more than a few orange clothes and a few personal items, the storage space was ample. I claimed the bed right by the window. Maya moved in too. Soon after that, a third girl named Taliya moved in. She barely gave us the time of day. She clearly thought we were below her. Her mother was a beloved member of the ashram's spiritual elite. We did a good job of ignoring each other.

After dinner, almost everyone gathered in Buddha Hall for music group. It was by far the highlight of the day. It was led by a charismatic German swami named Anubhava. He stood in the center of the hall in his orange robe, his long brown hair and beard swaying in the breeze as he played his guitar and sang. Behind him was a full band. He had a gift for inspiring devotion, as if his words flowed straight from his heart. We sang original compositions like "Drinking from Your Wine, Bhagwan, Drinking from Your Wine," and "Yes, Bhagwan, Yes." We never did anything halfway. We belted it out with full gusto, professing our love and surrender to Bhagwan as we danced with zest. It was a joyous celebration. Maya and I always went. We danced together, alone, or with other adults or kids. You could dance any way you wanted. It was about genuine expression.

One evening, I returned to our room to see that Maya's belongings were gone. My heart sank. Where was she? I didn't know what happened, only that she was called to the office and got into trouble for something. After that, I rarely saw her, and she seemed mad at me when I did see her. I clearly did something to upset her, but I didn't know what. I felt like I lost a sister. I filled my days in the office, where I doodled and ventured out to deliver messages. I hardly ever played with the other kids anymore. I spent most of my time with adults. They seemed to like me.

A few weeks later, Gita, a girl my age with straight dirty blonde hair and a crisp English accent, moved in and took Maya's bed. She was given a job in the office too. We became fast friends and sat up at night talking. Soon after that, Devi, a German girl our age, moved in a couple of doors down. She shared a room with two adult men, neither of whom were her father. I was in awe of her fancy stationery, angora sweaters, and leather shoes. She clearly didn't get her things from a dump. She and her busty and beautiful mother had recently arrived from Germany. Her mother had quickly caught Bhagwan's eye and was moved into Lao Tzu House with the other beautiful women who looked after his every need. Moving up the ranks that fast was unusual, and I imagine other women were envious.

Gita, Devi, and I hung out in our rooms and played. Devi and I even created our own language that only she and I knew how to speak. I don't know how we created it; it was a sound thing that just fell into place. I guess it was our own variation of pig Latin, which we all spoke sometimes. Our language used a lot of L's. For example, the word "dinner" was "dilavinalaver."

Soon a fourth girl our age joined our friend group. Kaya and I met in the main office, where Sheela introduced her to me as her new assistant. Kaya was Indian, with shiny black hair and striking green eyes. Sheela asked me to show her around the office and to teach her English. Sheela was always bubbly and full of energy, but also intimidating. I knew not to challenge her or ever refuse her request. I didn't want to say no anyway. I showed Kaya around, and each day taught her more English. She sat near Sheela in the big office with Laxmi and Arup. Sheela adored Kaya as much as Vidya adored me.

Soon Gita, Kaya, and I were dubbed "the office girls." Most people around the ashram came to see us as such. In time, we three office girls and Devi were like sisters. I still missed Maya, but my new friends helped fill the hole in my heart. Kaya moved into Veggie Villas with Gita and me, taking Taliya's bed. I was so glad Taliya moved out.

I don't know if the women in charge, whom everyone called "the Moms," had specific plans for us girls, like training us to take over someday, or if they just thought we were cute and liked having us around. Whatever the reason, we were our own little clan.

When the four of us weren't working, or in Devi's case, going to school, we did everything together or in pairs. I was happy to have friends with whom I could play and act my age, but when I returned to the office, I was like a little grown-up—at least more grown-up than my actual age. I thought that's how I was supposed to be, and many praised me for my maturity. My friends could be mature and responsible too. I think we all adapted to the culture.

After several months, I had taught both Kaya and Devi English, and with an American-ish accent to boot. For the first time in my life, I had real friends my age, and I didn't feel like I had to hide where I lived, what I ate, or what I thought.

Having a job, friends, and living in the ashram left very little time or need to see my mother. She now lived in the ashram too and worked in the publications department. On occasion, I would see her at the Zen wall after discourse. We would say hello, have a short conversation, and then go about our separate lives. Whenever she asked me how I was, I always told her I was happy being with Vidya and living in the ashram. I think she wanted to make sure I was fine, but she never said anything about what she felt, and never inserted herself into my life. I wasn't sure if she was relieved or sad that I was Vidya's sidekick and one of the special office girls. I hoped that not having to take care of me would help her feel freer. Yet, she still didn't seem that happy, and it felt like it was up to me to fix it. I felt torn inside. On the one hand, I felt like she didn't want me, and on the other hand, I could feel that she was hurt that I had attached to Vidya. It weighed heavily on me, and I felt less trapped if I didn't see her much.

CHAPTER NINE

LIFE IN THE ASHRAM

Each morning, I would go to discourse in Buddha Hall. I would sit there without moving, appearing to be the perfect little disciple. One of the most revered group leaders even stopped me one day after lecture and told me I was amazingly mature and spiritually advanced for my age. He was impressed that I could sit so still in meditation for the entire discourse. While I lapped up his praise like a puppy, I didn't believe him. I was just doing what I thought was expected of me, and I must have been good at it.

As I sat there with everyone else each morning, I tried to understand what Bhagwan was teaching, but my brain would get tied into knots. He talked about why other religions were toxic and were only brainwashing people, leading them further from their true selves. He talked about freedom and surrender. He talked about how ordinariness was extraordinary. He often contradicted himself, which made it even more confusing. Mostly he talked about awakening or enlightenment. I still didn't understand what that meant. What I did know was it was what most of the disciples were trying to attain. Bhagwan used so many different words to describe this vague thing he was guiding people towards. He called it nirvana, the ultimate truth, satori, bliss, and no-mind.

Why would anyone want to be nothing, I wondered. I didn't want to be nothing. If anything, I wanted to be something.

Many mornings I spaced out, and I was only jarred back to alertness when everyone in the hall broke into thunderous laughter at one of Bhagwan's jokes. He loved to tell jokes, especially dirty ones. Sometimes the crudity of the jokes made me uncomfortable. I didn't know much about sex except for what I saw in the ashram. I thought sex was supposed to be something sacred, like Bhagwan sometimes said, but hearing the graphic descriptions—referring to sex as "fucking" one day and "making love" the next—was confusing. When he used bad words or made it sound dirty, it felt slimy and a little nauseating. One thing I wasn't confused about was that he encouraged his disciples to be free sexually, to not repress themselves. He said, "Follow your energy." People did follow their energy all the time. Sex was very much out in the open. I saw a lot of people walking home arm in arm with a rotation of different partners on many occasions. I also saw a lot of kissing and hugging.

Though I didn't understand much of what Bhagwan taught, I figured maybe some of what he was saying seeped in anyway. Maybe just sitting in his presence anointed me with his enlightened energy, bypassing his words. I did notice that as I sat in discourse, I sometimes forgot about my discomfort and felt a deep stillness and peace inside. There was a certain silence and exhilaration that arose when we all sat together, like a union of energy aglow.

★ ★ ★

After discourse, I'd skip to Miriam Canteen, where I'd slather butter onto freshly baked fluffy bread. I would dip it into sweet chai. It was so delicious. Then I would meander my way to the office. I often took my time since I usually stopped to say hello to people I knew. I would act silly and make people laugh, and then skip off again.

In the office, I sat at my little desk next to Vidya. There wasn't a lot to do, except to be available if somebody needed me to run an errand. While I sat there, I would draw roses, and if one of my creations was especially good, Vidya would put it under the glass slab on her desk. She told me she was proud of me and that I was clever. Her praise quenched a thirst in me to be seen and appreciated. At times I believed her compliments, which infused me with pride.

As I doodled, I listened as a flow of people came to see Vidya about work assignments. She oversaw the ashram's personnel and was number three in command under Laxmi and Sheela. She was always nice to me, and to many others, but if you irked her or did something that was not aligned with the ashram's philosophy or work ethic, she was a bulldog. When she was upset with someone, her bubbly demeanor changed, and she would turn into a cold, sharp-tongued disciplinarian. Her face became stoic and flushed red with fury, and her voice grew stern and loud. She looked people straight in their faces and told them what they did wrong. Usually, people would be called out for being negative, not being surrendered enough, or not working hard enough. Everyone knew that negativity was unwelcome and that working hard was a measure of your surrender to Bhagwan. Nonetheless, sometimes people didn't do a good enough job. Nobody talked back or even tried to explain themselves; it was understood that her word was final. I think some found her scary, so they just stood before her, looking deflated. I felt bad for them.

I was starting to notice that all the women who ran the ashram could be harsh. I also noticed that there were very few men in charge. Women had the power, though Bhagwan had more power since they all worked in service to him. Maybe they felt comfortable being so harsh because they were carrying out Bhagwan's vision. At least in Vidya's case, she didn't seem shaken after she yelled at somebody. Instead, she always seemed sturdy and confident. She could be scolding one minute and loving the next. I guess it was just how things were done in the ashram.

The people being scolded thought it was part of their spiritual growth to be raked over the coals. I heard people talking about it, calling these encounters a "Zen stick." I was told that monks meditating in monasteries were hit on their shoulders if they weren't fully aware. In our commune, the term implied that the main purpose of harsh scoldings was an opportunity to surrender, drop your ego, and maybe even become enlightened. In that sense, surrendering to the Moms' will was part of the spiritual path— even a blessing.

The best way not to get in trouble was to not question the way things were done and be positive. Being negative wouldn't be good for the Buddhafield energy. We were constantly reminded how lucky we were to be there with Bhagwan, and as such, we were to embrace it fully and joyfully.

It became clear quite soon after I moved into the ashram that the Moms didn't like or approve of my mother. I don't know exactly what she did wrong, but she was always one to question authority. Since I rarely saw her, and certainly didn't know what she was thinking or feeling, I don't know what she questioned. However, I do remember her being called out a couple of times in front of a group of people as an example of how not to behave. I worried about her and wanted her to conform and fit in. I also wanted the women in charge to like her. At the same time, I was embarrassed to be associated with her. I heard that people who questioned anything or challenged authority would be told to leave. I worried that she would be kicked out if she didn't surrender. If she had to leave, I would have to leave too. I didn't want that. Fortunately, that never happened, and even though she was blacklisted, she was always given very responsible jobs, probably because she was smart and had skills that were useful.

*   *   *

I could tell that certain people or groups of people were special by the way other people treated them and by where they lived. Others saw them as further along the spiritual path. Once I saw the hierarchies, they were hard to miss. There were, of course, the women in charge, who seemed more focused on running the ashram like a business than on spirituality. Then there were the group leaders, the old sannyasins, the women who lived in Lao Tzu House, and the samurais.

The people who led the groups were especially revered because they were so far on the spiritual path that Bhagwan trusted them to guide others. Just like being near Bhagwan was an honor, so too was being in the presence of a group leader. While they were trying to help people drop their egos with their demands to "let go" or "be total," some of them didn't seem like they had dropped their own egos at all. They floated around the ashram with an air of superiority. And the male group leaders had their pick of women because of their status. I heard and saw a lot as I delivered messages or goofed off in the ashram. People openly spoke of how certain group leaders slept with lots of women, even women in the groups they were leading. I guess their positions of power made them desirable. Maybe the women thought having sex with them would be a spiritual experience. I also heard that group leaders would tell people to go home together at night and "make love," even if those paired together were repulsed by who they were partnered with. People just did as they were told because they were that devoted to Bhagwan.

Of all the special people, the disciples that had been with Bhagwan the longest did seem to embody a special quality. On the whole, they seemed humble and generous, almost quiet. They had meditated a lot. Some of them lived in Lao Tzu House, I assumed so they could meditate in peace and be close to Bhagwan. And it was also considered a great honor for Bhagwan to choose you to be so close to him. These special people were referred to as the "old sannyasins," even though some of them weren't very old.

That brings us to the women who lived in Lao Tzu. I thought they were all maidens. I was fascinated by their beauty and their serene, almost angelic grace. When I saw them, they seemed to float. They didn't circulate in the ashram as readily as everyone else. During the days, they took care of Bhagwan's every need, from cleaning and cooking to sewing his clothes and taking care of his large library. In the evenings, they usually went to darshan in Chuang Tzu. Since they were so close to Bhagwan, they were deeply immersed in his energy, so I thought they must be very special. Most special of all was Vivek, Bhagwan's closest confidant, who was always at his side. She was English with straight brown hair and bangs. Her skin was so pale and her lips so pink. Her beauty was delicate, almost ethereal. She was mysterious. I admired her from afar and dreamt I would meet her someday.

I did wonder if Bhagwan chose the women who surrounded him because they were so beautiful or because they were so devoted. I even thought maybe they were so beautiful because Bhagwan's energy made them radiate too. One strange thing I heard was that they saved all of Bhagwan's nail clippings and stray hairs. Anything that came from Bhagwan was holy. The hair and nails were put in little hand-carved wood boxes that the people in the mala shop made in addition to the beads and lockets we all wore. Bhagwan would give these special boxes to disciples as gifts. People cherished them and put them on altars, meditated with them, or held them to connect to Bhagwan.

I'm not sure that the samurais were as special as the other special people, but they were entrusted to guard Bhagwan's house and the ashram in general. It seemed that only strong men or handsome men were selected for the job. Shiva, Bhagwan's bodyguard and the head samurai, led all the men in regular karate classes so they were fit and ready to protect Bhagwan if needed. They even wore maroon uniforms inspired by Japanese samurai clothes. Many women drooled over them. They had their pick of women to sleep with. Their attractiveness was on par with the Lao Tzu women. And not surprisingly, the samurais often dated or slept with them, which appeared to be a badge of honor since those women were very selective.

★   ★   ★

I got to know most of the women who worked in the front office. Throughout the day, I would make my rounds, chitchat a bit, and move on. I became especially close to Ira, an American woman with freckles like me, who sat in the far right corner of the workspace. I didn't know what her job was. I didn't actually know what anybody's job was, only that they all worked for Vidya.

Ira seemed different from most sannyasins. She didn't have the same shiny bliss look; she was more practical. Her head was not in the clouds. Or as Vidya would say, "She had her head screwed on." Unlike most of us who wore Indian-style clothes, she wore nice orange and red clothes from the West. Also, unlike many of the sannyasins who didn't have money of their own or who had given all their money to the ashram, Ira still had some. At least enough to go back and forth to America sometimes and to buy treats from Vrindavan.

She looked out for me from the day we met. Most days, she would call me over to her desk, "Sweeto, come here." I loved it when she called me Sweeto. I would saunter over to her, and she would ask me if I wanted a treat. Of course, I did! She would hand me some money, saying, "Here, go get yourself something at Vrindavan, and while you're there, get me a croissant." I would crumple the money up in my hand and skip out of the office and down the marble steps. At Vrindavan, I would stare at all the fancy pastries trying to choose one. There were eclairs dipped in chocolate, cake with perfect icing, and cookies dusted in sugar. They all looked almost too pretty to eat. But I came to expect no less. Everything in the ashram was done with the utmost perfection. Every department was run like a tight ship.

When I returned to the office, Ira and I would sit at her desk and eat our treats together. Often when we were done, she would ask me to read to her or do some basic math. Since I loved her, I didn't protest. But I felt dumb as I struggled to mouth out the words. I couldn't really read or write, and I only knew a little math.

Other than Ira, nobody seemed to think I needed an education. I never stepped foot in the school again or even thought of school. I thought I was lucky that I didn't have to go. Bhagwan said education was brainwashing. That sounded bad. I most certainly didn't want to be brainwashed. It never crossed my mind that reading, writing, and arithmetic were basic skills that I would ever need. But when Vidya called me over one afternoon, excitedly proclaiming, "My sweet girl, I think it would be brilliant if you wrote a passage for the book flap for one of Bhagwan's books!" I was horrified. I didn't want anyone to know that I could barely read or write.

"What book?" I asked.

"*The Further Shore*. It's Bhagwan's new book that will come out soon," she said.

"Okay," I said flatly. How was I going to get out of this, I thought to myself. My mind was blank, and I didn't want to do it. But the other women who overheard the conversation were excited.

"What a privilege," one of them said.

"What am I supposed to write? What is the further shore?" I asked Vidya.

"Just write something about reaching the further shore—reaching enlightenment. Write about how lucky we are to be with Bhagwan," she explained. I pondered for a while and then sat with Ira, asking for her help. She encouraged me to just write something and not worry too much. So, I did. Trying to capture the concept that was explained to me, I wrote some gobbledygook in my chicken scratch. I rushed over to Vidya to show it to her, thinking she would help me make it better. But when she looked it over, she buoyantly exclaimed, "Oh, this is fabulous. Well done."

"Thank you," I said. I didn't quite believe her. I knew it was hideous, but I guess that didn't matter.

"I think we should print it in your handwriting. It captures the wisdom of a child," she said. I felt both honored and embarrassed. I barely did anything and didn't even know what I was saying, and I was being commended. All that mattered was that it was written by a kid. Surely everyone would read it, see how I could barely write, and think I was dumb.

The book came out, and there was my writing on the front book flap. Looking at it today, I still feel embarrassed. I'm pretty certain I didn't sound like the ten-year-old that I was.

The Further Shore

The old darshans didn't have as much energy that went all over the ashram. They had a lot of energy but that was not music and you would not hum and sway

the light would not go out

Bhagwan did touch people but they would just sway a little bit and still feel Bhagwan's energy for a while.

Now you don't know when it's finished

He talked more to people then Bhagwan does now.

Bhagwan is moving us to the further shore. The further shore is not so far anymore.

Remember that you're very lucky to be here with Bhagwan.

And also forget about the past and the future and be in the present.

CHAPTER TEN

BELONGING

I DIDN'T THINK of Hawaii or of meeting Sai Baba any longer. I had adapted to my new life in the ashram. I couldn't imagine being anywhere else. I didn't think of the future beyond whether somebody returning from a visit to the West would bring me chocolate or bubble gum. I had everything I needed. As the apple of Vidya's eye, I had certain privileges, lots of freedom, and lots of caring attention. I could do what I wanted. I could go to the Blue Diamond, the nearby five-star hotel, to swim, or spend hours goofing off with other kids on the streets out the back gate. And there was always the office where I could return and find somebody who was happy to see me.

At times I felt a connection with the community and with existence. I would run in the warm monsoon rain and get fully drenched as I heard music from one of the meditations blaring from Buddha Hall. The music became so familiar that it told me what time it was. I felt life pulsing through my body, my heart beating with delight, and a sense of surrender to life. I believed I was home and that I belonged. At times I didn't feel broken or unworthy.

At other times, I felt like a puddle. I hid a swell of emotion behind my shyness and introspection. I didn't feel sure of myself and did my best to be happy, or at least try to look happy when I was sad. Despite my attempts to hold it all in, a kind smile or a simple question would sometimes open a floodgate of sorrow. I cried and cried. I cried so much that the women in the office joked that my name meant "river of tears" not "river of love." I didn't fully understand the rawness of the grief I experienced. It just showed up as a gripping knot in my solar plexus that erupted. I couldn't will it away. I had a sense it had something to do with my mother. Looking back, I believed people's kindness touched the delicate, embryo-like part of me that felt abandoned. Eventually, the tears would stop, and I would revert back to my shy yet sassy demeanor.

As I became more comfortable and accustomed to my life in the ashram, I started venturing further away from the office. When I wandered around the ashram, people would often warmly invite me in to talk or listen to music. Sometimes people who had just returned from the West would show me the nice things they brought back.

One afternoon, during my explorations, I found a covered well behind the lush overgrowth that surrounded Buddha Hall. On hot afternoons, I would go there to swim under the platform. I liked having a secret place that I thought only I knew about. But a young swami, maybe twenty years old, found me there one day. He said hello, took off his clothes, and joined me in the water. He swam up next to me and pushed his body against mine, acting like he was playing with me. I didn't like it. It didn't feel right. I moved away from him, got out of the water, and put my clothes on. I didn't look at him, but I could feel his eyes looking at my body with pleasure. It felt gross. I was only ten and a half years old, but maybe I looked older because I was already starting to develop breasts.

When I returned a couple of days later, I looked around to make sure nobody, especially him, was around. I got into the water, splashing under the platform. Then suddenly the man was there again. He must have heard me. My body tensed all by itself. I acted as casual as I could, promptly got out, got dressed, and walked on as if there was somewhere I had to be. I learned how to play it cool and look calm even though I was uncomfortable on the inside. I had encountered other creepy men before. I didn't want to feel their slimy energy on me, so I did my best to ignore them and run off back to the office.

★   ★   ★

Some of the girls were good at getting money from sannyasins to buy themselves things. Devi was especially coy and sassy. Sometimes she sat on men's laps on the Zen wall, giggling and being adorable. Invariably, if she asked for some money to buy something, they would give it to her. I didn't have the courage to directly ask anyone for money. I felt too ashamed. But more than that, I didn't want to sit on the laps of swamis who wore nothing but a lunghi or seemed creepy like the guy at the well. I just wanted the means to buy things.

Instead of begging, I started going to MG Road to shop for supplies like biscuits and condensed milk for some of the wealthier sannyasins who lived in the ashram. They always gave me a list and a little money to buy something for myself. I would jump into a rickshaw outside the front gate and tell the driver, "MG Road, jaldee jao," meaning *go fast*. They would drop me off in the middle of the noise and chaos that smelled like cow dung, fumes, and rose water. I would weave through all the people—the women dressed in colorful saris with shimmering strands of silver and gold to the beggars dressed in rags. I learned to keep moving as men yelled at me to buy whatever they were selling. Soon one or two children, no older than six years old, would trail me, poke and prod me, pull on my clothes, and chant, "Chiclet, chiclet." They offered little packs of white or green Chiclets for fifty paisa. They would glare at me, batting their eyes. I learned to recognize their antics, and once I was firm and ignored them long enough, they would finally leave me alone.

The worst part was seeing the cripples with elephantiasis or without legs. With suffering in their eyes, they held out their hands, pleading, "Bakshees, bakshees." It made me so sad just to look at them. I felt like a coward as I averted my eyes and ignored them. But as much as I felt for them, they could become aggressive, acting like I owed them something. Yes, I was a foreigner and had my youth, but I had nothing to give them. If I had spoken Hindi, I would have told them that I barely had any money either.

I found my way and soon had a number of favorite shops. I especially liked the shop that sold black market candy and the shops where you could buy all kinds of silk or sparkling bracelets. The reams of cloth were piled up to the ceiling. The shop owners pulled different reams from the piles, telling me how high quality it was as they bobbled their heads from side to side. I daydreamed about the clothes I wanted a tailor to make me once I saved enough rupees.

After I goofed off for a while and stopped at one of the cafes for fresh mango pulp, a creamy blend of Alphonso mangoes and cream, dolloped with more cream, I would shop for the things I was sent to get. Then I was back on a rickshaw speeding back to the ashram.

One afternoon, I lingered in a swami's room after delivering the things I'd bought for him. He and his girlfriend often invited me to stay and chitchat. I liked to look at all his nice stuff, including his fancy bottles of liqueur. Sometimes he would let me have a sip of Amaretto or Bailey's Irish Cream. It was much more about the pretty bottles and the sweetness than the alcohol content. In fact, I didn't think I liked alcohol. Just recently, Kaya and I were in Sheela's room for some reason, probably just to hang out. We convinced her to let us try the green liquor, called Crème de Menthe, that we saw sitting there. She poured us each a little glass. When we tasted it, we both made sour faces at the same time. We thought it tasted like toothpaste.

On this afternoon, the swami offered me something different. He said he was cleaning things out. He handed me what looked like a briefcase. "I'm getting rid of these cassette tapes. Do you want them?" I wasn't sure what kind of cassettes, but I liked any kind of gift. I took the briefcase.

"Thank you," I said.

"They are now yours," he said. "They have brought me much joy, but I don't need them anymore." I suddenly felt small and undeserving of something so valuable to him. But I would try to take care of them.

When I got back to my room, I opened the case to find about fifteen cassettes that would become my close companions. The case contained Fleetwood Mac's *Rumors*, John Lennon's *Imagine*, Cat Stevens' *Tea for the Tillerman*, The Beatles' *Sgt. Pepper's Lonely Hearts Club Band*, Bob Dylan's *Blood on the Tracks*, Joni Mitchell's *Blue*, as well as albums by Van Morrison, Elton John, and Neil Young. I knew of some of the artists and couldn't understand why somebody would give up such a treasure in a place where such things were like nuggets of gold. It was the best gift I could have asked for. The only trouble was that I didn't have a tape player.

It was not often that I used my "cute card" to get something, but I admit, on this occasion, I did. I brought my case of cassettes to the office and showed Vidya. I was so excited. I coyly hinted that I didn't have a way to play them. It was unlikely that she had a tape deck sitting around since anything from the West was coveted, but it was worth a try. If anyone could get one, it was her. Within a couple of days, she surprised me with a little boom box that fit perfectly into the cubby by my bed. I felt like I had won the lottery. It was as exciting as getting the tapes.

I spent hours sitting on my bed listening to the tapes over and over. I memorized the lyrics to all my favorite songs. Soon my collection expanded to include *Saturday Night Fever* and a mixed tape that one of the group leaders gave me titled *More for the TC Crazies*. TC stood for the Therapy Chambers, where the groups took place. It was a compilation of dance hits, including several from Donna Summer like "On the Radio." My friends liked the music as much as I did and would often join me in my room where we would sing and dance, sometimes going berserk—jumping, shaking, and making crazy sounds—trying to imitate what we thought people did in groups, minus the hurting each other part.

The music gave me so much comfort and joy and was the seed for a lifelong love of singer-songwriters. The songs expressed so many things I felt inside that I didn't have words for. I played the tapes so much that my boombox would sometimes eat them. I would pull the mangled tape out of the machine, cut out the damaged part, and splice it back together with Scotch tape. Then I would clean the tape head, and voila, the tape played again, but with weird gaps in the songs. One time when my tape deck stopped working altogether, I borrowed a screwdriver and pulled the back off to find an intrusion of living, crawling, gross cockroaches. Once I got them all out and screwed the boombox back together, it worked again, like magic. I thought I was so clever.

CHAPTER ELEVEN

LIGHTS OUT; PLAY TIME

THE EVENING DARSHANS, where Bhagwan met with a select group of disciples, changed format. Now instead of just answering people's questions, he gave what was called "energy darshan." Devotees would be called up and would sit in front of Bhagwan in pairs. Several beautiful women, called mediums, all dressed in matching maroon dresses, sat or stood behind the subjects. Bhagwan had personally chosen these special women to assist him in transmitting his energy. Most of them were the maidens who lived in his house, plus a few other beautiful women.

The lights would dim, and the musicians would begin playing, as Bhagwan placed his index and middle finger on people's third eyes. He moved his fingers in sync with the music that grew ever more chaotic. As everything became more frenzied, someone flashed the lights on and off. The people Bhagwan was touching, as well as the mediums, swayed and shook, as if his energy surged through them like electricity. They sometimes appeared to not have control over their own movements, as if overcome in an ecstatic seizure. Everyone else in the auditorium swayed and raised their arms in the air too, moved by Bhagwan's energy and their devotion.

Receiving energy darshan was thought to be very special. It was the rare occasion to get a direct hit of Bhagwan's enlightened energy. It was so special that the lights were turned off in the ashram during these sessions. We were all supposed to sit silently and soak it up. But for me and my friends, "lights out," as it was called, was when an enchanted world emerged. While the whole ashram was dark and silent, with the exception of the music we could hear from Chuang Tzu, we goofed off and played. We ran down the open paths or huddled in one of our rooms telling stories and giggling. We would often be told to quiet down. We would for a couple of minutes and then venture somewhere else and get rowdy again. We often found our way to Lao Tzu gate to visit the samurais on duty. They were the only people in the ashram who weren't supposed to be meditating.

Devi and I thought one guard in particular was dreamy. We even rewrote all the lyrics to "Hey Jude," for him. When he was on duty, Devi, Kaya, Gita, and I took turns sitting on his lap as we joshed around. Devi was always the most adventurous when it came to interacting with people. She wasn't as shy as I was. Recently she had wanted to learn to French kiss and asked me to practice with her. When we did, it felt sloppy and kind of strange, and we weren't sure if we were doing it right. We were just trying to copy what we had seen the adults do. We still had a lot to learn.

One evening when we were hanging out with the dreamy samurai at Lao Tzu gate, we giggled and asked him to give us French kissing lessons. With very little prodding, he agreed. Devi went first. She sat on his lap, put her hands around his neck and leaned into him. Then their mouths met, and the samurai pushed his tongue into hers. She pulled back for a second, not knowing what to do with his tongue or her tongue. Then she leaned in again, this time thrusting her tongue into his mouth. Then they were both thrusting their tongues at the same time. After a couple minutes they stopped, and he rated her performance. As I recall the feedback was positive.

Next it was my turn. I was so nervous. I stood back hesitantly. I wasn't sure if I even wanted to kiss him. What I did know is that I wanted him to like me. I wanted to be his favorite, though I was already pretty sure Devi was. With the other three standing right there waiting for me, I went for it and climbed onto his lap. He put his arm around me, and then leaned down, putting his lips on mine. I could feel his breath on my face. His mouth was warm and wet. Our tongues mingled. I knew I was supposed to let go, not think, and be total in that moment. That is what we were told to do always, but it seemed even more important when it came to kissing or sex. I was scared of letting go. I didn't know where it would lead me or what it would make me feel. For a moment I was lost in the experience, and then I pulled myself back into reality, and quickly got off his lap. It was supposed to be fun and games, but my heart was racing. I felt something akin to excitement or fear. I could sense that kissing him, an adult man, had the potential to make me like him more, and that felt unsafe. When we all had our turns, we got back to our joshing. The samurai once again treated us like the ten-year-old sassy girls that we were.

We returned on other nights. Devi was always ready to practice kissing again. I don't think she felt the same reservation that I did. I kissed the samurai another time, but that time I was on guard and rigid. When we were done, he said, "What happened? Last time you were such a good kisser." I felt like I had failed. I wasn't open and receptive like we all were supposed to be. I was uptight.

*   *   *

Bhagwan spoke of the spiritual nature of sex. He called it "making love" and said it was a way to surrender and connect to the divine. But I was puzzled as to why something that was supposed to be so beautiful and spiritual often seemed so casual and even crude. I thought maybe I wasn't old enough to understand. Weren't people supposed to be in love to have sex? Not in the ashram, that's for sure. Or if people were in love, they still had sex with other people. If they got jealous or angry, they were taught to see it as another opportunity to face their hang-ups and grow spiritually.

One of the main features of the culture was to not repress your urges. Repression was the opposite of freedom. I believe this was one of Bhagwan's main teachings, or the one people most enthusiastically embraced. He didn't believe in marriage or traditional families. So unlike the outside world where people were like sheep and didn't feel free, here in the ashram, sex was to be explored without inhibitions.

There was a strong feeling of openness or looseness, like a collective flow in which everyone moved. Even people's bodies were free in the sense that many women wore clothes that revealed their braless breasts, and men often wore lunghis or robes with no underwear. Women who were in their prime physically were said to be blossoming. Men drooled over them. It wasn't unusual to walk in on people having sex, or to bathe in the co-ed shower with several adults who were sometimes making out. I saw many erections.

Sometimes as I walked down the row of rooms in Veggie Villas on the way to mine, I saw people naked or having intercourse. It was not surprising because there was really no privacy. Everyone had roommates. But it was more than that: people didn't seem to feel they needed privacy. In fact, some of those who slept around a lot had reputations. They were proud of their sexual juju and how freely they followed their sexual energy and seemed to want to show off. Even when I didn't see anything, I could hear loud orgasmic squeals coming from the surrounding rooms.

A man and his two children, a boy around seven, and girl about thirteen lived in one of the neighboring rooms in Veggie Villas. I sometimes played with the boy outside the back gate or at 35 Koregaon Park, a property that belonged to the ashram where there were abundant vegetable gardens. We usually ended up in his room after our adventures. The father had a loft upstairs in the room. I often saw him bring women with very large breasts home with him. I was told he had a thing for humungous breasts. His two children lived below. The girl had a boyfriend who was at least in his late twenties.

One afternoon when the boy and I returned to his room, his sister and her boyfriend were there and were making out. I got up to leave. But the girl said, "You can stay, you don't need to be shy." I sat down again. The boy and I continued to talk as his sister and her boyfriend made out some more. Soon the man was on top of her having sex right in front of us. I tried not to look, but the girl talked to us while it was all going on. I so wanted to feel comfortable, but I didn't.

On another occasion the girl's current boyfriend and ex-boyfriend were both in the room with us. They each took turns penetrating her. While one thrusted their penis inside of her, the other kissed her and fondled her breast. Amidst all the passion and moaning, we all chatted as if everything was normal. Despite being welcomed, I still couldn't shake the discomfort I felt watching them.

⋆ ⋆ ⋆

Now that I was eleven and my body was starting to change, I was more aware of men who had wandering eyes. I still only had small buds of breasts forming, but I guess that was enough to be seen as a budding woman. It was odd how I could feel it when I was being looked at that way. It always felt slimy, so I did my best to steer clear of the leering sorts.

One afternoon, Devi and I were in her room when one of her adult male roommates took off his clothes and laid naked on his bed. It wasn't even dark out. He started stroking his penis. I turned my back to him as Devi and I continued our conversation. After a few minutes, he called us over, "Come touch me." I froze.

Devi turned to me, "Should we?"

"I don't know," I said.

"Come on you guys, it's no big deal. All you have to do is touch me," he said. Devi and I looked at each other and shrugged our shoulders. We moved to the side of his bed. The very sight of his penis grossed me out. It didn't feel right to even look at it. Devi began stroking his penis as he moaned. She never had the inhibitions I did. I stood back, reticently watching. I was leery but didn't want to appear like a sissy. So after a few minutes, I took my turn and started stroking his penis tentatively. It was smooth and snake-like with slime coming out of its tip. I thought it was gross, so I stopped. Devi and I looked at each other. Neither of us wanted to continue. As we got up to go, the man urged us to stay. "Come on I am so close, don't leave me hanging. That would be cruel," he whined. I guessed that finishing meant having an orgasm, though I had no idea what that would look like.

We sat back down and continued. I didn't want to be cruel to him by not finishing. I heard other men say that if they didn't finish, they would get blue balls, which sounded painful. Finally, his penis throbbed, and gross white goop erupted from the slimy hole. Devi and I stood up and ran from the room. I felt a little sick to my stomach, but I tried to ignore it. I didn't want anyone to see that I wasn't carefree like we were supposed to be.

CHAPTER TWELVE

SHENANIGANS

It HAD BEEN over two years since my mom and I arrived at the ashram. Our six-month visa had long since expired. That didn't seem to be a concern since we had no plans of leaving. I still didn't see her much. She let me be, and I didn't seek her out. However, I did go looking for her when I got my first period. I was eleven and was shaken when I saw blood on my dress. While I knew it was my period, which I thought shouldn't have come for years, I knew almost nothing about menstrual cycles, puberty, or even my own anatomy. Nobody had prepared me, and I didn't know what to do. I felt ashamed, like it was something dirty. I didn't know why—maybe I thought it made me a woman, and I didn't want to cross that threshold.

I found Shreya near Buddha Hall, not far from her room that she shared with several others. When we were standing close, I whispered, "I got my period." I didn't want anyone to hear. She wasn't alarmed at all. The only thing I remember her saying is "there are some tampons in my room on the little shelf by my bed." She walked off in one direction, and I in the other. I found the tampons and figured it out on my own. I was pretty good at figuring things out on my own. Usually I didn't feel lonely, or all alone, but at that moment I did. I think I wanted a mother to reassure me everything would be okay. Once again, I just felt like my mom didn't even try. The next day, Ira congratulated me. I was horrified and blushed with embarrassment. My mom must have told her.

* * *

As I entered adolescence, or what I thought was adolescence since I was barely eleven, I started testing boundaries. They were pretty much nonexistent. I started getting more mischievous and wild. I think being so well behaved in the office left me longing for fun and adventure. I was always concerned about getting things right and not upsetting anyone, especially Vidya. I hadn't upset her before, but I had witnessed her when she was upset with others, and that was scary enough. I couldn't lose her or the other women in the office. But, when I left the ashram, or played with my friends, I was a different girl.I started visiting the Blue Diamond more frequently. One afternoon as I sat by the pool, instead of ordering fresh lime soda as I usually did, I ordered a beer and a fresh lime soda. I did it in part to see if the waiter would serve me, and because I was curious what drinking alcohol would do to me. When my order came, I mixed the fresh lime soda and the beer together and drank the concoction through a straw. As I sat there, the world started looking fuzzy. I felt giddy. When I got to my feet, I wobbled, so I sat back down. I was drunk. I stared at the sky for a long while, until the haze lifted. Eventually I crab walked back to the ashram. At the front gate, I stood up straight, pulled myself together and walked in looking alert and focused.

Back in my room, I met Gita and Kaya and announced, "I ordered beer at the Blue Diamond!" They both looked surprised.

"No way! They let you order alcohol?" Gita said.

"Yeah, I just acted casual, and the waiter didn't hesitate at all," I said.

"Well, you're taller than us, so you can probably get away with it. I don't think they would serve us," Kaya said. It was true, I was tall for my age.

"Well, then I can order for all of us," I said.

The next afternoon Gita, Kaya, and I skipped out of the office and made our way to the Blue Diamond. We sat down at a table by the pool. Instinctually, we all sat up straight and proper trying to look like ladies. We couldn't slouch around like kids if we wanted to order alcohol. The waiter approached.

"What would you like," he asked. Again, with my very best acting skills, I stayed cool, as if I was doing nothing out of the ordinary and said, "We would like one fresh lime soda, and two beers, please." He looked at me suspiciously.

"Beer?" he asked.

"Yes, please. Two beers," I said. He walked away and a few minutes later returned with our order. We mixed the beer and the fresh lime soda, just as I had the day before, and then drank it through straws. We figured if we were drinking through straws nobody would suspect we were drinking beer. It was glorious to feel so floaty and free, and more than that, it was thrilling that we were getting away with it.

We all got a little tipsy, and meandered on the streets near the hotel until we sobered up. We returned on many hot afternoons and drank together. We would get loud and clumsy and loiter at the wallahs near the hotel. Sometimes we'd buy an ice cream or practice giving each other hickeys.

One night when I wasn't with my friends, I got dressed up in one of the new silk outfits I had made by a tailor on MG road. Also, I somehow got my hands on some makeup. I put on heavy blush, lipstick, and mascara. I then made my way to the bar inside the Blue Diamond hotel and ordered a pina colada. I left after one drink, but I returned on a semi regular basis. I felt so independent, and I liked to test the boundary of what I could get away with without anyone noticing. Plus, I wanted to try all the different cocktails. In time I concluded that rum and Thumbs Up was my favorite. It was the sweetest of them all. Thumbs Up was India's version of cola, only sweeter—imagine that. The bartenders always served me, no questions asked. I don't know what the legal drinking age was, but there was no doubt that I didn't meet it. Maybe they served me because I was from the West and couldn't tell my age. I was concerned about a manager coming in, or worse yet, running into a sannyasin.

In time, Devi joined our shenanigans and the four of us girls got increasingly reckless. We started leaving the ashram in the evenings, not just in the afternoons. We would get drunk, and then skip, run, and goof around either along the busy road near the Blue Diamond or the quieter streets near the back gate. We would often belt out Supertramp songs. Sometimes we would stop and buy Moore cigarettes from the wallah near the hotel. We thought they looked sophisticated and went well with our silk clothes. We would light them up, inhale the smoke, and think we were so cool.

On one night in particular, we got very drunk. We were carrying on, stumbling down the street near the back gate when a bicycle rickshaw stopped next to us. "Rickshaw?" he asked.

"Yes, yes," we said. We all piled in. The rider stood and moved us forward. We squirmed around in an uproar of laughter.

"I have to pee," Kaya said.

"Me too," Gita said. We didn't want to stop the rickshaw.

"Let's pee off the back of the rickshaw," Kaya said. Next thing we knew, she was squatting off the back of the rickshaw peeing into the street. We all laughed hysterically. Then we each took our turns precariously squatting and peeing. The rickshaw driver kept on pedaling.

When we arrived at the back gate, we got out and paid the man. We swayed to and fro as we approached the gate. "We have to act normal," I said as sternly as I could. The guard at the back gate was a serious English man, all prim and proper. He would not take kindly to seeing us as we were. We tried to act normal, but it just wasn't possible without breaking into laughter. When we entered, the guard was indeed stern.

"What have you been up to? You all look drunk!" he scolded. Whatever else he said, I don't remember. We just ran past him. On our way to Veggie Villas, we stopped at the communal showers, where we proceeded to turn on all six showerheads. Fully clothed we got under the water and splashed each other. Someone had left their full tube of Close-Up toothpaste on the counter. We each squeezed it into our hands and spread it all over each other and the shower walls. We were having a great time. Then an adult, nobody I knew well, entered and shouted, "What are you doing?"

The next thing I remember was waking up naked in my bed the next morning. I didn't know how I got there. I didn't know if I walked there on my own, or if someone carried me there, removed my wet clothes, and put me in my bed. I worried we would be in trouble.

CHAPTER THIRTEEN

ENERGY DARSHAN

KAYA CAME to find me. "Sheela wants to see us," she said. Her words rattled me for a second. I had never been summoned before. Being called in to the big office, the one where Laxmi and Sheela sat, usually meant one of two things: To be honored with a special recognition, like receiving a gift from Bhagwan, or to be sternly scolded. Sheela was Laxmi's secretary, and Laxmi was Bhagwan's secretary. Laxmi was just one notch below Bhagwan. In my mind she was almost a holy woman herself. I never approached her or talked to her; I only admired her from afar. Sheela was very important too but was more accessible than Laxmi. Though Indian, she had spent several years in America and was westernized. She was energetic and could be lots of fun, but she was also intimidating. I had seen her yell at people before, like Vidya did. I did not want to stand in their shoes.

Kaya and I made our way to the big office and stood before Sheela, waiting for her to get off the phone. My arms were plastered to my sides, as we waited for our fate.

As soon as she hung up the call, she smiled. Whew, everything was okay! "Bhagwan has chosen both of you to get energy darshan in a few days," she said. That was not at all what I was expecting. What a relief that we weren't getting a scolding for drinking, or for making too much noise, or for kissing samurais. "Stern, a magazine from Germany, is going to film it," she continued.

"Wow. Thank you," I said. But I was confused. I had never made any effort to be close to Bhagwan. I didn't think Bhagwan even knew who I was. I was fine just living in the ashram. I didn't care about being spiritual. Nonetheless, I felt so lucky that Kaya and I were chosen, because it meant we were really the special office girls. My mind was racing: What if I didn't feel the energy? What if I didn't feel the ecstasy? What concerned me the most, however, was what I would wear. I ran back and told Vidya the news.

"That's fabulous!" she said.

"But I don't have anything to wear," I said.

"Not to worry, I'll call Samya at the boutique and ask her to make you a dress," she said. I was so excited. The ashram boutique had the nicest clothes, but I never had anything from there. I bought my clothes on MG road where they were much cheaper.

The next day I went to the boutique and met with Samya, the woman who ran it. She seemed excited, and together we designed a dress. Two days later it was ready. I went to try it on. It was pink, with an embroidered flower appliqué at the neckline, and dolman sleeves. It fit me perfectly. I felt like Cinderella.

The night of our energy darshan arrived. Kaya and I were sniffed into Chuang Tzu Hall. When it was our turn, we were called up to sit at Bhagwan's feet facing each other. The mediums took their places behind us. The lights dimmed. Bhagwan put two fingers on each of our foreheads. I leaned back, reaching my arms into the air, like I'd seen others do. I swayed with the mediums. Then the lights pulsated on and off to the music. I don't remember what I felt, but I don't think I was enraptured. Nonetheless, I tried really hard to focus on the moment—to let the current of Bhagwan's energy wash over me and purify my ego. I did my very best to be blissed out—it would be embarrassing if I wasn't. When it was over, I did feel kind of shiny and sparkly, as if I had been sprinkled with fairy dust. I wasn't sure if it was just Bhagwan's energy or if it was the heartfelt joy everyone in the auditorium was feeling.

★   ★   ★

The next day, Vidya told me to go see Vivek in Lao Tzu House. I was so excited I would finally get to meet her. I didn't know why she wanted to see me, but I knew it was for something good—Laxmi or Sheela were the ones who did the telling off, not Vivek. Being allowed to even enter Lao Tzu was a big deal. Not many were given such a privilege. I skipped along the Zen wall to Lao Tzu gate. The guard said hi to me, probably assuming I was just passing by, as I often did. When I was still standing there, he finally asked, "Do you need something?"

"I'm here to see Vivek. I got a message to see her," I said. He looked at me curiously.

"Let me see if she's available," he said, and called her on an intercom system. After a few seconds, he said "Okay, you're clear to enter. She's waiting for you in the kitchen." I knew where I was going, since I had delivered messages to Lao Tzu once or twice.

The house was quiet, as if nobody was there, or if they were, maybe they only whispered. I walked quietly down the hall, arriving at the kitchen to see the top half of the door was open. "Hello," I said softly. Vivek emerged from the far side of the room. She smiled and waved. Then she picked up a small rectangular box and walked to me.

"This is for you, Sarito, a gift from Bhagwan," she said, handing me the box. I nervously took it from her. My shyness was in full force. Vivek was the sight of beauty. Her sweetness and purity reminded me of the Virgin Mary, or at least how I imagined Virgin Mary would be.

Atop the box was a little note with my name written in brown ink. Vivek stood waiting for me to open the box. I was starstruck, but then realized she was waiting for me. It was a fancy gold Parker pen.

"Oh wow, thank you," I said.

"Bhagwan wanted you to have it," she said, reassuring me. There was nothing more to say, but I didn't want to leave. I wanted to know her. Though she smiled, there was sadness in her eyes. She seemed somehow solitary and circumspect, qualities I understood. Maybe she was a little shy like I was. But it was more than that—her presence conjured a deep sadness in my heart, as if the sadness in my own heart recognized the sadness in her heart. It was clear there was much more going on inside of her than I would ever see or know. Later that day, Kaya was also summoned to Lao Tzu and was given a pen just like mine.

CHAPTER FOURTEEN

WAS ENLIGHTENMENT A JOKE?

As MUCH as I played and goofed around, I was always observing and try-ing to make sense of things. I think I had always been on the lookout for danger or trickery. What people said often didn't match what I saw. I remember at eight years old doubting if God existed since I couldn't see enough proof. Maybe God was another deception like the tooth fairy or Santa Claus, I thought. So, when I overheard a swami say, "Enlightenment's a joke!" to another swami, I was so shocked that I stopped in my tracks. Both swamis laughed. My first thought was that those men weren't gen-uine seekers. I assumed that if you were Bhagwan's disciple, then achiev-ing enlightenment was the ultimate goal. Thus, I concluded, these swamis were slacking off.

But was enlightenment a joke? I hadn't heard of anyone getting enlight-ened, despite Bhagwan saying it was easy. And once people finished their groups, I didn't see them meditating much either. Mostly I saw people working, laughing, and making out. Then it crossed my mind that maybe for some, enlightenment wasn't really what people were here for. I don't know why, but I thought enlightenment was a serious thing even though I heard Bhagwan say never to take anything too seriously. He said life was leela, play.

I figured the only way I could diffuse my confusion was to ask Bhag-wan himself. That afternoon, I submitted the following question: "Beloved Bhagwan, why does everybody think enlightenment's a joke?" I signed my name and put it into the question box that sat in the reception area. I had submitted many questions before. If Bhagwan didn't answer your question in discourse, you would usually receive a little note in response. I asked him all sorts of things but never anything as serious as this.

One time I even got annoyed by his answer to one of my notes. It was when I was in Ruby Hall, the city hospital, sharing a room with a swami who lived two doors down from me in Veggie Villas. We had both come down with chicken pox, so we were put there to be isolated. Nobody could visit, but we could send and receive messages. I wrote Bhagwan a note asking him why nobody loved me. When his response came, I excitedly opened the little piece of paper. It said, "You love yourself; that is true love." He was wrong. I didn't feel like I loved myself. In fact, his statement made me feel bad, like I shouldn't need anyone to love me.

But this time, Bhagwan answered my question in discourse. However, I wasn't in Buddha Hall that morning. I stopped going to discourse most of the time. Nobody seemed to mind or even notice. If I thought things through, I could do whatever I wanted. On those mornings, I enjoyed a sense of peace and privacy that was so hard to come by.

After discourse, when people were dispersing from Buddha Hall, I headed to the office. Those that I passed were smiling at me more than usual. I had no idea why. Eventually, someone who must have known I wasn't there stopped, "He answered your question!" they said.

"Oh wow, I missed it," I said. I felt like people would see me as a bad disciple for cutting discourse. Having your question answered, having Bhagwan say my name, was just as special as getting energy darshan. But I didn't really care if I got special attention from Bhagwan—I just wanted to be special in general. I was more concerned if I would be in trouble for not being there.

When Vidya arrived at work, I impishly admitted that I wasn't at the lecture. She wasn't angry. She just said I should try to attend. She said I could listen to the recording at the front gate pagoda later that afternoon. I couldn't wait to hear what Bhagwan said. I hoped I would understand his answer.

That afternoon, I sat in the pagoda with a couple of other people. I closed my eyes and listened. A woman read my question: "Beloved Bhagwan, why does everyone think enlightenment is a joke?" There was a long silence. Then Bhagwan spoke:

> "Sarito, it is! But only a child can ask such a beautiful question
> — Sarito is only twelve years of age. Enlightenment is a joke
> because it is not something that you have to achieve, yet you have
> to make all possible efforts to achieve it. It is already the case:
> you are born enlightened. The word 'enlightenment' is beauti-

ful. We come from the source, the ultimate source of light. We are small rays of that sun, and howsoever far away we may have gone, our nature remains the same. Nobody can go against his real nature: you can forget about it, but you cannot lose it. Hence attaining it is not the right expression. It is not attained; it is only remembered."

As I listened to him speak, I still didn't really understand. I heard his words, but if we were all born enlightened, why was it so hard to remember? I also noticed that he said I was twelve, but I was eleven. I would turn twelve in a couple of months. I believed Bhagwan was supposed to be all-knowing.

As he continued, I sat there flustered and frustrated. He went on to tell several stories to illustrate his point, and then praised me again, saying, "Sarito, your question does not look very relevant, but it is relevant, more relevant than any grown-up person can ever ask." I didn't think my question was all that profound; it was just a genuine question. Sure, it was nice to be praised, but I was still confused. Why did enlightenment have to be so complicated? I figured all I could do was not try to figure it out. Maybe it would make sense when I was older. For now, I would just put it out of my mind.

CHAPTER FIFTEEN

SUDDEN DEPARTURE

I HEARD THE news when I was walking along the Zen wall. People gathered in clusters, crying, talking, and hugging. The usual exuberance and joy seemed to have drained out of the place. "What happened?" I asked.

"Bhagwan is gone, he's gone!" they said. What? My body contracted with dread. What would happen now?

Just moments earlier, Bhagwan was driven out of the ashram's front gate, destination unknown. None of us were informed in advance. He was just gone. It was June 1, 1981, a date cemented into my mind. Everyone was in shock and none of us were prepared.

When I arrived at the office, Vidya told me that Bhagwan, Sheela, and fifty or so others had left and weren't coming back.

"Where did they go?" I asked.

"To America," she said. "Sheela will look for a new commune. Bhagwan needed to leave for his health," she added. Bhagwan had been in silence recently—maybe it was because he was sick, I thought.

"When can we go there?" I asked.

"I don't know. In due course, but for now people will return to their home countries and wait." This was horrible news. Where would I go? The bond I had with Vidya was like that of a mother and daughter. The thought of leaving her made my heart clench. I stared at the shiny marble floor, leaving the scene for a moment. Then the faces of the people I had come to love in the office flashed before me. Would I see them again? I hated change. Things were fine as they were. I had friends, I had people I loved and who loved me. I could feel that my life was about to wobble again.

"Darling, you know how much I love you, right?"

"Yes," I said.

"If you like, you can stay here with me. I'll be here for a while helping to tie up loose ends," she said.

"What about my mother?" I asked.

"I could adopt you, and once Sheela finds a place for our new commune, we'll move there together," she proposed. Though I longed to stay by her side, the ties of biology bound me to my mother. I couldn't bear to hurt her by choosing Vidya. Somehow, I felt my mother needed me. Either option would be unbearable. With Vidya, I had fun, and I felt special and adored. With my mom, I never knew what would be next, and I felt I never did anything right. Even though it hurt, I loved her and was deeply attached to her—she was my mother. And even though I knew being with her meant I would feel emotions that were confusing and intense, I knew I had to leave with her. But I didn't know how I would survive without Vidya.

A week or two later, my mom had our visas fixed so we could leave. I wondered how we would be able to leave since my mom didn't have any money, but she said somebody left some money on her bed, enough to buy our tickets back to Hawaii.

I said goodbye to Vidya, Ira, and my three dear friends. I felt like I would collapse with sadness. While Vidya accepted that I needed to leave with my mother and reassured me we would see each other soon, I had no idea when we would all be united again. What if I never saw her again?

CHAPTER SIXTEEN

BETWEEN TWO WORLDS

WHEN MY MOTHER and I arrived in Honolulu, we walked down the open concourse. People passed by in an orderly fashion. Everything was so clean. The familiar scent of plumeria flowers coming from the leis of people passing by offered a pleasant welcome. I remembered living in Hawaii before we went to India. I thought of Island School and of Jack's land. I wondered what my life would have been like if we had never left. Would I have been happy? Now, though, as I walked through the airport skinny and dressed in orange and a mala, I felt profoundly out of place.

Shreya found us a temporary place to stay with some other sannyasins on the island. I felt anxious with uncertainty. I knew we were broke because my mom said so, and I could feel her tension about it. I didn't know if we even had enough money for food. I hated being poor and not knowing where we would live, or what we would do. My mom was good at asking for help and finding a way, but that embarrassed me. I didn't want us to seem like beggars.

In many ways my mother and I were now strangers, which only made things more uncomfortable. And as before, I felt her unrest and knew that having to worry about me as well as herself added to her strain. I think she was trying since we weren't fighting. I was trying too. But what I really wanted was to be with the community I had come to know. It didn't even matter how beautiful Hawaii was, I just wanted to be with my friends.

As the days passed, I became more withdrawn and listless. I found some comfort at the beach, where I would walk for hours. A few months before we left India, somebody gave me a Sony Walkman. I was so happy to have it now along with all my cassettes. As I walked, I listened to Elton John's *Greatest Hits* over and over. The lyric "goodbye yellow brick road" provided some melancholic comfort. At moments the music and the vast open sky transported me to a place inside of me that fostered hope. I felt that only nature understood my heartache and longing. I wondered where Vidya was and if there would actually be a new commune.

★ ★ ★

Amongst the sannyasins on the island, rumors were circulating that Bhagwan and Sheela were living in a castle in New Jersey. Who knew that New Jersey had castles? I certainly didn't. Not long after that, we went to a sannyasin gathering in a smoothie factory. I only recognized one man from Pune.

When he approached me, I just looked down and tried to avoid eye contact. What did he want? He'd always been nice to me, and it always felt creepy, even though nothing creepy happened. I could feel him still standing there, so I eventually looked up. When I did, I saw kindness in his eyes. "You look so sad," he said. "I'm sure you want to be back in the commune." He seemed to know exactly how I felt.

"Yeah, I wish I could go to the castle," I said.

"Maybe you can," he said with a big smile on his face. He then handed me a little piece of paper. "Here's the phone number for the castle, why don't you give Sheela a call?" I looked up, surprised.

"How did you get that?" I asked.

"I have my ways," he said jokingly. "But seriously, you worked with Sheela, and she might let you go there." I half wondered if the number was real. Everything about Bhagwan's location and plans were so hush hush. Plus, only "special" people would be privy to such coveted information. I didn't think this swami was in the upper echelons, but maybe he gave the commune money or now had something Sheela needed.

"Thank you," I said. I felt bad that I ever thought he was slimy. Maybe my radar was wrong. I ran back to Shreya to tell her. She saw my excitement.

"I got the number for the castle," I said. "I want to go there, can I call them?" "It's long distance, but we will see if someone will let us use their phone tomorrow," she said.

The next day, I called the number. Someone answered immediately. "Hello, this is Sarito, can I speak to Sheela or Vidya?"

"Just a minute," the voice said. I was stunned, surely it couldn't be this easy to get through. A few seconds later, Sheela's voice greets me.

"Hi Sarito, this is Sheela, where are you calling from?" she said.

"Hi Sheela, I'm in Hawaii. I'm not happy, and I'm wondering if I could come to the castle?"

"We are full here," she said.

"Oh, okay," I said, disappointed.

"But we just purchased a property for the new commune in central Oregon. A few people have just gone there to start getting things ready for us all to move there. You can go there now, and we'll meet you there soon," she said. That was the first I had heard of a new property. I felt relieved. There would be a new commune after all.

"Oh, that would be great," I said. "How do I get there? What about Shreya?"

"You come first, and your mom can come a little later."

"I don't think we have any money for tickets," I said.

"Gather the money for your ticket and come as soon as you can. Then once Shreya has the money, she can come too," she said.

"Ok," I said. She then gave me a phone number and told me to call and ask for Padma when I knew my plans. Padma, whom I'd never met before, was the woman in charge and was already at the new ranch. Lastly, she told me that I would need to get to Madras, Oregon, where someone would be sent to pick me up.

Within a few days we had the money. I don't remember where we got it from, but I think someone gave it to us. I was so relieved. I called Padma and told her when I would arrive in Madras. She assured me someone would be there to meet me.

A few days later Shreya and I were back at the airport. As it turned out, the bus I needed to catch to Madras didn't leave until the morning after my flight arrived in Portland, so I would need a chaperone and a place to stay for the night.

At the gate for my flight, my mom scanned the people waiting to board, and then approached a middle aged couple. She introduced herself and me, and then asked if they were going to Portland.

"Yes," the man said.

"My daughter needs to catch a bus to Madras tomorrow morning; would you be willing to put her up for the night and then take her to the bus station tomorrow?" she asked. I was horrified. These people were strangers. I wasn't worried for my safety; I was embarrassed that she was asking for their help. They probably thought my mother was wacko. I remember the puzzled looks on the couple's faces. I think they felt cornered. They looked me over, a veritable waif clad in orange. I am pretty certain they had never seen people like us before. Shreya assured them that I would be no bother, and that they would really be helping us out. The couple finally agreed. I think they felt empathy for me and knew that if they didn't help me, I might be on my own.

I hugged my mother goodbye and boarded the plane. My feelings towards her were all knotted up in a tangle of love, hate, and rage. How could she put me in the hands of strangers? But, at the same time, I wanted to get away from her and be back in the commune. I found my seat on my own. I stared out the window trying to convince myself everything would turn out okay.

When we arrived in Portland, the couple stood waiting for me at the gate. I didn't know what to say; I didn't know how to interact with regular people. I walked self-consciously through the airport, keenly aware that I didn't look like everyone else. Plus, orange gets people's attention. I could feel that the kind couple were searching for a way to interact with me. Finally, the wife asked me what awaited me in Madras. "I'm going to a new commune near there," I said. They looked confused but didn't press further. I didn't think to ask them about themselves. The only thing I knew about them is that they weren't hippies. They seemed like a nice "straight" couple, just the type of people my mom normally would avoid because they were too conventional.

The next morning the kind couple took me to the Greyhound bus station and helped me buy my ticket. Once I boarded, they stood by the bus and waved goodbye as it drove away.

* * *

I found a seat alone where I could stare out the window and listen to my Walkman. Soon we were out of the city and the scenery changed from lush green to dry desert. I didn't know anything about where I was going, nor what to expect when I got there.

After a couple of hours, the bus stopped in front of a cowboy clothing shop. The driver announced that we had arrived in Madras. I grabbed my bag and stepped off the bus, scanning the street for someone dressed in orange. Then a boy, maybe eight years old, dressed in orange and a mala, came out of the shop and walked towards me. He was hard to miss; everyone else wore Wrangler jeans with shiny belt buckles and cowboy shirts.

"I'm Rishi, Padma's son," he said. "My mom let me come to pick you up." Who did he come with, I wondered. I didn't see anybody else that looked like a sannyasin. Then a blond woman and her two teenage girls approached us and introduced themselves as Glenda, Becky, and Kim Harvey. I soon learned that they were the wife and daughters of John Harvey, the ranch foreman who stayed on after Sheela bought the Big Muddy Ranch. I was surprised that non-sannyasins were part of the community, and even more surprised that the new commune was smack in the middle of the Wild West, where ranchers and cowboys lived.

We all got into Glenda's dust crusted blue Ford Bronco and set off. I sat in the back seat with Rishi and Kim, the younger daughter. I stared out the window wondering if I would recognize somebody's face when we got to the ranch. I needed something familiar. Rishi sat next to me stuffing one piece after another of Big Red gum into his mouth, as if it was his last chance to indulge. He offered me a piece telling me that his mom had given him a few bucks to buy himself something. If the food at the ranch was anything like it was in India, candy would not be part of the menu; it would be a treat that you would have to buy yourself.

Although Rishi wore red and a mala, and was one of us, not one of them, he felt like a complete stranger. I don't think he had a clue how unsettled I felt. I traversed my mind to find something to say. I didn't know how to break the awkward silence. Finally, I blurted, "Is Vidya there. How many people are there?"

"No, she's not" he said. "My mom's in charge; there are just a few of us." I was sad that Vidya wasn't there. I wanted nothing more than to once again be under her wings of protection. I sat stiffly holding in my tears, telling myself it was going to be okay, though I didn't really know if it would be or not. I hoped there would at least be somebody I knew.

After thirty minutes, we arrived in a small wisp of a town. The sign read, "Entering Antelope, population 40." I could very well have missed the town entirely if I wasn't paying attention. It was quiet, run down, and looked deserted, except for a few cars parked in front of the Antelope Café. Glenda agreed to stop for a bathroom break.

We pulled into the parking space between two dusty trucks, one with a gun rack mounted at the back of its cab. As we entered the cafe, the few people sitting on the vinyl swivel stools at the bar turned to look at us. A man stood and tipped his cowboy hat, saying "Hi Glenda, another new arrival?"

"Yep," she said. The cowboy looked me up and down with a blank stare, doing his best to hide his judgement about how I looked. I couldn't really blame him—I did stand out. I looked like a child who just arrived from Woodstock or, dare I say it, a hippie cult. I figured he probably held his tongue because I was young and looked like a scared fawn. I sheepishly walked past him and the others at the bar to get to the bathroom.

Back in the Bronco, Glenda proclaimed: "Next stop Big Muddy Ranch!" As we descended the long solitary dirt road, all I could see was a dry withered landscape flecked with sage brush and twisted pine trees. It was beautiful in an empty, stark kind of way. I liked how peaceful it felt, especially in contrast to the chaos in India. As we thrashed down the winding road, we didn't pass a single car. We were in the middle of nowhere.

PART THREE
The Ranch

CHAPTER SEVENTEEN

THE BIG MUDDY RANCH

Finally, a homestead came into view: A old white house, a red barn, and some other outbuildings, including a second smaller house. Glenda pulled up in front of the small house. Rishi and I got out, and Rishi rushed inside to tell his mom we arrived. I waited outside as Glenda then drove over to the big house, where I assumed the Harveys lived. It was all like a strange, dusty dream.

A few minutes later, the front door swung open again. A plump woman with olive skin and thin eyebrows plucked into perfect arcs appeared. She smiled and then leaned in to give me a momentary hug. Hugging was always how sannyasins greeted each other; we never shook hands.

"Hi Sarito, welcome, I'm Padma," she said warmly. I liked my first impression of her. She seemed jolly and friendly. But as nice as she seemed, I could tell she could be tough if she needed to be. There was no way that Sheela would have put her in charge if she didn't "have her head screwed on," as she and Vidya liked to say. I always took that phrase to mean someone who was solid, not spacey or flaky.

"You'll be living in Howdy Doody," she said. What a funny name, I thought. I liked it, though I didn't know who or what Howdy Doody was. She grabbed my bag, and we walked towards an outbuilding just between the two houses. Inside, ten single beds lined the floor perpendicular to the wall, leaving just enough space to walk down the middle of the room. Two platforms flanked either side of the room, providing space for six additional beds. Padma pointed to the first bed up on the platform to our right. "Here's your bed, right across from Rishi," she said. I guess she thought since Rishi and I were the only kids, we should live together. I put my bag down and followed Padma outside again.

First, she showed me the bathroom that was attached to Howdy Doody.

It had one toilet, one shower, and one sink. Everyone who lived in Howdy Doody had to share it. I guess there would be no privacy.

Back at the small house, Padma introduced me to the women who were busy working in the kitchen. They all looked up from what they were doing to smile and say hello. I didn't know any of them, but they seemed really nice. Before heading back to Howdy Doody to unpack my bag, Padma took a clipboard down from the wall near the kitchen door. I saw a list of names. She added my name to the bottom of the list. "What number am I?" I asked.

"You are the 32nd sannyasin to arrive at the ranch!" she said. That was really something. I felt so lucky to be amongst the first to arrive. But so far, I had only met about five people.

"Where is everyone?" I asked.

"They'll be back before dinner," she said. "It's at six."

Sure enough, in the late afternoon, those working out on the land returned to the ranch yard in pickup trucks. I sat on the steps outside of Howdy Doody and watched them arrive. They were mostly men. They were dusty and suntanned and looked like they had been out on the range all day. They all still wore red and their malas, but the robes and dresses we wore in India were now replaced with red jeans, red shirts, and heavy work boots. Some of them even wore cowboy hats and smoked cigarettes without filters. To me, they looked like cowboys.

I made my way to the small house just before dinner. I sat at one of the tables on the screened-in front porch, which was set up as the dining room. From where I sat, I could watch people come in. I wanted to see if there was anyone I knew. But, as everyone filed in, I didn't recognize a single face. I sat there feeling squirmy and uncomfortable, like I didn't know where to be. It was as if I was searching for shelter in a new unknown world.

When dinner was ready, everyone lined up and filled their plates with lasagna just out of the oven. It smelled amazing. Things got livelier as people came to sit at the tables around me. Everyone talked and joked with each other. Some people said hello to me. I didn't say much; mostly, I just watched.

After dinner, several people gathered outside the small house and sat on the ground. One of the men, who I thought looked most like a cowboy, returned from somewhere with his guitar in hand. His name was Sam. He pulled up a chair and sat with the others who had gathered. I joined them.

Sam started strumming his guitar and singing songs that everyone knew, like "Blowin' in the Wind" and "All You Need Is Love." He also sang songs I didn't know at all. Some of them sounded like country or folk songs. I liked how they told a story or expressed a feeling that I had felt too. As I listened and gazed up at the starry sky, it was beautiful. Music and the sky, two of my constant companions.

⋆　⋆　⋆

Padma said Rishi and I didn't have to work because we were kids. She said we could just play and have fun, but that we would have school for a couple of hours each morning. However, the sannyasin man who was to be our teacher hadn't arrived yet. For the time being, we were free all day. We explored the creek beds, read *Archie* and *Richie Rich* comics, and took turns riding a moped. Sometimes we visited the Harveys and hung out with Becky and Kim when they returned from school in Antelope.

Although I didn't have to work, I started hanging out in the kitchen. I would help with meal prep and cleaning the tables. I quickly became friends with the main cook, Marga, who took me under her wing. She always asked me how I was and made me feel welcome. She would show me how to do things and let me make melted cheese sandwiches between meals. I would cut slices of cheddar cheese, place them on the bread, and put them under the broiler. When the cheese just started to bubble, I would pull them out and snarf them down. We didn't have cheese in India. There was no pizza either. Now, I had a voracious appetite, and I could down four sandwiches in one sitting. I figured my body was trying to right itself after three years of living in India. Or maybe it was puberty. What was certain was that my body was changing. My breasts were filling in, and my body was fleshing out. Before long, I would be a little pudgy.

Meanwhile, our teacher arrived. He was really tall with dark hair. I liked how nice and fun he was. He even made math fun. He'd come to Howdy Doody each morning, rousing me and Rishi out of bed by impersonating Elvis and singing, "Up in the morning off to school." After hemming and hawing, we would get up and get dressed. We'd grab something from the kitchen and then trek up one of the nearby hills. When we found a good place to sit, we would stop, and our teacher would give us long division and fraction problems to solve.

After school in the morning, I spent my afternoons in the kitchen. Marga had already taught me how to knead bread and make enchiladas, but I was ready for something grander. When there wasn't much to do, I'd sit on the porch and page through the *Betty Crocker Cookbook*. I admired the luscious cakes with perfect frosting. One afternoon, when she didn't look too busy, I asked Marga if she would help me bake a cake. Her eyes lit up. "Sure," she said. She seemed as excited as I was. She thought it would be a nice treat for everyone after dinner. I agreed.

We methodically followed the directions, mixing all the ingredients together. Then we put the batter in the pan and put it in the oven. I sat on the floor watching it through the oven door, delighted to see it rise and transform. To me, baking seemed like magic, which only really smart people could figure out. But it turned out it wasn't as hard as I thought. I liked learning new things and being useful. The cake wasn't beautiful, and it didn't look like the picture in the book, but it was cake, and everyone scarfed it up. I felt proud.

CHAPTER EIGHTEEN

AMONGST THE MEN

THERE WERE new arrivals almost every day. Soon all the empty beds were full, and additional beds were crammed into every bit of free space, like on the Harvey's screened-in porch. In Howdy Doody, it was me, Rishi, and fourteen men. I didn't like being the only female. I didn't want anyone to see my body, especially since I was going through puberty. Since we all had to share one bathroom, it was difficult to avoid being seen. It was the sannyasin way to leave the door unlocked, and for people to share. So, while one person took a shower, somebody else would sit on the toilet, and somebody else brushed their teeth. Men walked around naked in the bathroom and in Howdy Doody without reservation. When I showered, some guy would usually walk in. I don't know if they looked at me since I didn't want to look at them to find out. I just froze and pretended I didn't notice their presence.

I felt ashamed about how uptight I was, so I never spoke of my discomfort. Even if I had, I'm sure I would've been told to loosen up. Instead, I started to shower late at night and use the toilet as little as possible. When everyone was asleep, I would sneak out of bed and tiptoe to the bathroom, careful to open the door slowly so it wouldn't squeak. After showering, I would return to bed with wet hair. When I woke in the mornings my already frizzy and unruly hair would stand on end like the bride of Frankenstein. I tried to tame it by patting it down with water, which only helped a little.

Sometimes I could hear the men chatting before bed. They seemed crude, and sometimes talked about things I'd rather not hear, like about a woman's breasts, or who was good in bed. It disturbed me that women were being compared based only on how they pleased the men. I usually listened to my Walkman so I didn't have to hear them, but I couldn't escape all of it. One night as I was drifting off to sleep, I heard one of the guys say,

"Did you see, Sarito's getting pubic hair and tits." I was horrified, but stayed perfectly still, pretending like I was asleep and didn't hear them. I wanted to disappear under my covers. On another occasion, I woke up to find a fully clothed swami holding me. I screamed and bolted out of bed. "What are you doing?"

"I was just trying to comfort you—you seem so sad and alone," he said. I wasn't sure I believed him. I didn't know what to believe. It was true I was lonely, and he hadn't touched my private parts, but I thought if men got close to me it meant they wanted my body—that's how it seemed to go with the men and the adult women. After the fuss I made, he never came near me again.

★ ★ ★

The evening music gatherings grew. They were our main form of entertainment. We didn't have TV, newspapers, or radios. Amongst the new arrivals was a musician named Milarepa who started playing with Sam each evening. He lived in Howdy Doody as well, though I barely noticed him at first. I knew which bed was his and that was about it, but when he played the guitar and sang, he captured my attention. He sang songs I didn't know, but that I liked. They were songs that told stories of romance and heartbreak. My favorites were "Lyin' Eyes" and "Peaceful Easy Feeling."

Milarepa didn't look like the handsome men on the Marlboro billboards that I'd seen. He was of medium build, with dirty blond hair and a beard. What I liked about him is that he seemed gentle and sang the songs with a sweetness. I had never heard him talk about women's bodies like some of the other guys did. In fact, as I watched him, he seemed like he was nice to the women, and they seemed to like him too.

I liked the songs so much that I looked forward to hearing them, and I soon memorized many of the words. I even asked Marga if she knew who wrote the songs. She said they were songs by a band called the Eagles.

Much to my surprise, Milarepa approached me a couple of days later. "I hear you like the Eagles," he said, smiling. Marga must have told him, or he saw me singing along.

"Yes! I love the songs you sing of theirs," I said.

"Do you have any of their albums?" he asked.

"No, I wish I did," I said.

"I like them too," he said. Then he walked off and returned with his guitar to play for our evening gathering. Later that evening, when he sang "I like the way sparkling earrings lay against your skin so brown, and I want to sleep with you in the desert tonight with a billion stars all around," I stared up at the stars and imagined he was singing to me. I pictured a romantic scene of a man and a woman gazing into each other's eyes. I wanted to be in love someday. I felt a hint of romantic longing I hadn't ever felt before. Was this puberty too?

The next evening, he approached me again, and handed me the *Eagles Greatest Hits* cassette.

"Here you can borrow this, I think you'll like it," he said. I could barely believe it.

"Thank you!" I said. Over the next weeks, I listened to the tape over and over. I escaped into the songs and learned all the words by heart. The tone of the instruments, and the stories the songs told, sparked my imagination. I could envision a man standing on a corner in Winslow, Arizona. I felt the sadness in the song "Desperado." And the music had a tinge of country that suited the ranch environment.

Milarepa started talking to me more often. He seemed to go out of his way to be nice to me and ask how I was. We talked about the songs I liked, and just things in general. I felt comforted by his company. I had never really been friends with a man before. I felt like he cared about me and found me interesting.

One evening after dinner, he approached me at the table where I sat alone. Most people were moving about washing dishes and clearing tables. "Some guys are going to play poker; do you want to come watch?" he asked. I felt honored to be included, especially with the cool guys like him. He drove a backhoe and often ate dinner with a few of the other men who drove heavy equipment. I could tell that women liked them by their body language around them. Maybe the women were drawn to them because they were nice, or maybe because they had a cool, kind of unreachable vibe about them. But he didn't ask any of the women to accompany him, he asked me, which made me feel like a special friend. Plus, it would be a nice change from lying on my bed listening to music or reading comic books.

"Okay," I said sheepishly, too shy to look him in the eye.

"Great! We are meeting in the silo at 8:00 p.m. I'll see you there," he said.

"Okay, see you later," I said.

That night I entered the silo feeling bashful. I didn't know how to behave around men. They weren't old like I imagined a father figure might be, and they were not young like comrades either. They all sat around a barrel, which served as a table, drinking beer and acting macho. I was the only female. I really must be something, I thought to myself.

When Milarepa saw me, he gestured for me to come sit next to him. As I sat down, one of the other guys passed me a beer. I hadn't drunk alcohol since India. I took the beer and sipped on it as they continued their game. Between turns, Milarepa moved closer and closer to me, until the sides of our bodies were touching. Then with the utmost casualness, he put his arm around me and slowly reached up my shirt, resting his hand on my breast. I didn't move. Was this good? Was this gross? What did it mean? Did it mean he loved me?

But I was twelve, and I knew that it wasn't normal for a man to touch me that way. I knew it was sexual. But I wanted him to like me, so I settled on the notion that he only touched me like that because I was special to him. Somehow, I did not put two and two together to realize that all the open sex I had witnessed would one day pertain to me.

The other men didn't say anything, or even raise an eyebrow. They just carried on playing and bantering with each other. When it was Milarepa's turn, he would remove his hand from under my shirt, play his turn, and then put his hand back on my breast, sometimes squeezing my nipple between his fingers. I tried to sit still, though inside I was tangled up in all sorts of mixed feelings—fear, excitement, confusion.

Over the next several weeks Milarepa would invite me to other poker games. Each time I would sit next to him and sip beer, while he fondled my breasts. I was sure that his sustained interest meant it wasn't casual—it was genuine interest in me.

CHAPTER NINETEEN

ARRIVALS

THE SUMMER was hot and dusty. On some afternoons, several people would take a break from the heat and hard work and head down to the river. Whenever possible, I would jump into the back of the pickup truck and join them. It was on these afternoon drives that I got to see some of the ranch. We'd thrash down the washboard road through the valley. Along the way, I saw the work that was being done. First, I noticed that the road was widened and graded. I also saw places along the road where some of the guys were digging and moving dirt around with heavy equipment. Down by the river, the barren brown expanses were being plowed. After a few weeks, the fields turned to green, and by summer's end, yellow sunflowers exalted the sun.

At the river, we all splashed around in a swimming hole away from the current. I was told that the John Day River marked the border of our property. The other side of the river belonged to the man who founded Nike.

Though I saw all the work that was being done, I didn't stop to think about what was going to be built. I didn't have any idea of what the plans for the ranch were. I assumed it was for houses. I think I naively or wishfully assumed we would remain a small community, maybe a few hundred people. And I assumed that once we built houses and we were settled, the focus would turn back to meditation and the pursuit of enlightenment. That was, after all, why most people followed Bhagwan. For the time being, it seemed enlightenment and meditation were on the back burner. Nobody seemed to mind, though. Everybody wanted to work hard to create a nice place for Bhagwan.

★ ★ ★

The reality of what all the digging and dirt moving was for became clear early one afternoon. I was outside skipping around the ranch yard when I saw billows of dust welling up along the road from Antelope. I could always tell when someone was coming from the dust signals. But the dust stirred in this case was like a big cloud, much more than even a big pickup truck could rouse. I watched the dust cloud move closer. Then several large semis came into view. They were hauling halves of beige prefab houses. The trucks had big "Wide Load" signs on their bumpers. They were so wide that I was amazed they even made it down the road. I felt a sense of dread in my stomach. I could feel that things would be changing fast, faster than I could even process them.

Over the next several days, trucks delivered at least ten mobile homes, which were placed in clusters of three or five at the various groves in the valley that had been prepped with water and electricity. Each grove was named after a mystic or someone Bhagwan admired. There was Heraclitus Grove about halfway to the river and Subhuti Grove in the other direction. Each trailer had four bedrooms, a kitchen, and two bathrooms. With two to three people per room, and an additional six in the master bedroom, each prefab home could house about thirteen people.

One of the very first double-wides to arrive was placed a couple hundred yards behind the small house, an area that had been named Jesus Grove. It was where Sheela would live. Word came that she would be arriving soon to get things ready for Bhagwan. I learned that Sheela was now Bhagwan's personal secretary because she was the one who brought Bhagwan to America. Laxmi was still in India and not even part of the group who traveled with Bhagwan to New Jersey. I thought Laxmi must have felt hurt that she lost her position. I felt bad for her.

★ ★ ★

I was in the small ranch house when somebody told me my mom had arrived. I wasn't expecting her. We hadn't spoken, nor had I heard anything about her, since we said goodbye in Hawaii several weeks earlier. All I knew was that she was supposed to come once she had enough money to buy a ticket.

Just moments later, I heard the front door open. There she stood, alone. My first instinct was to tuck into one of the back bedrooms and hide or to run out the back door. I thought I was doing fine without her. I had already found my way, for the most part. I had a routine, a bed, and Marga looked out for me. But I knew that avoiding my mother wasn't an option. Then she saw me. Here we go, I thought. I tentatively waved at her, but she was already walking towards me, smiling with her arms held out to hug me. I hugged her stiffly.

"Hi, I made it. What a journey," she said, seemingly proud of the accomplishment.

"Hi," I said. On the outside, I was cold and stoic; on the inside I could feel the heat of rage rise in my chest. How dare she just approach me as if everything was okay. Things had never really been okay between us. I felt like a nostril-flaring bull ready to charge, but I pushed down my feelings, as if securing a lid over a pressure cooker. After a couple of minutes of despondent monosyllabic answers to her questions, she got a clue and said goodbye and told me she would see me around.

As I watched her walk away, I felt guilty. I could see that she felt hurt. Being around her stirred feelings of rage, grief, and disgust that lingered from the past. I hated myself for how I behaved around her. Maybe I really was the tyrannical girl she so often told people I was. Now that I was older, I couldn't scream and throw tantrums. We were all supposed to live with joy. Negative emotions were bad, and we were always positive. There was nowhere to put my feelings except to hold them inside. Plus, all my tantrums never helped me feel better anyway. Now, I would do the opposite: I would stop talking to my mother for the next four years, with a few exceptions.

CHAPTER TWENTY

SO LONG, HOWDY DOODY

THE TRAILERS were ready to live in. The now fifty or so of us were moved away from the ranch yard and into our new homes. By this time, there were a few other kids, including a couple close to my age. I had said hello to them, but little else.

One afternoon, I came home to Howdy Doody to see my bed bare and my belongings gone. I only got word that I had been moved after the fact. I had been moved to Subhuti Grove, a group of three trailers that sat along the road that headed north towards Patanjali Lake. I was to share a room with other kids.

Later that day, someone dropped me off at my new home, which was well away from the ranch yard. I could walk, but it might take half an hour. The trailer sat in a beautiful location surrounded by low hills and the serene valley. When I arrived, I was in awe of the wall-to-wall beige carpeting and brand-new bathrooms, though I didn't love the fake wood paneled walls. A deck outside of the living room overlooked the valley. It was all so fancy. It was the closest thing to a real house that I had lived in since Dixon, New Mexico. The master bedroom was set up with six beds on the floor and an attached bathroom. I was happy I got there early so I could claim one of the beds against the wall. I would feel more protected there than being smack in the middle of the room.

I was nervous to meet my roommates. I was shy and unsure of myself around other kids. I didn't know how to act, but if I was to share a room with five others, I had to buck up. I had to wrestle with my fear that I was different, weird, and that they wouldn't like me.

When the others moved in over the next couple of days, it was much better than I imagined. At first, there were just three girls and one boy. Later, another boy and girl moved in too. We were all civil and mostly just came to the room to sleep at night. I was pleased that I wasn't teased or given the cold shoulder. We all even managed to share the en-suite bathroom without any catfights. I think we were all mature for our ages.

The first girl I befriended was Jutta. She took the bed next to mine. She had recently arrived from Germany with her parents. She was kind and seemed so mature, even though she was only a couple of years older than me. I think she was fourteen. We were all generally friendly and often sat up at night laughing and goofing around. It had been a while since I could let my guard down and have fun like a kid. Now I had more people to sit with at dinner too.

CHAPTER TWENTY-ONE

WORK AS WORSHIP

SHEELA ARRIVED. She moved into the trailer in Jesus Grove, which served as both her residence and workspace. From the comfort of her living room couch, she took charge. Very quickly everything felt different.

Her first order of business was to call a general meeting, where she joked around and laughed with us. Then her demeanor shifted, and her tone became serious and focused. She told us that we were going to build an oasis in the desert. We were going to fulfill Bhagwan's vision and build a place where the "new man" would celebrate and live life to its fullest, setting an example for all of humanity. She said our work was to be our worship and that we needed to put our all into it. It sounded amazing. Yet, I couldn't quite imagine the barren landscape transforming into an oasis, at least not without extreme effort. We were told that we would now need to worship twelve hours or more a day, with no days off. I could tell that many thought it was an honor to be chosen for the task at hand. They were all in—anything to show Bhagwan how much they loved him.

All effort was turned to completing the construction at B Site, a secluded grove where Bhagwan's compound was being built. The sooner it was ready, the sooner he could join us. That sure motivated people to work with enthusiasm and joy. Being reunited with the master would be the ultimate reward for all the effort.

Hard work and the concept of work as worship weren't new. The Moms in Pune always insisted that everyone work with totality and to perfection, but that wasn't for twelve to eighteen hours a day, and the tasks weren't as demanding. In discourse back in India, Bhagwan often said that every moment of every day was supposed to be meditation or worship. He said you could attain enlightenment at any moment, even when doing something ordinary like cooking or cleaning. To illustrate this point, he sometimes told the story of the Buddhist nun Chiyono. As the story went, Chiyono had meditated for years with great dedication, yet she hadn't attained enlightenment. Then one evening, when she had all but given up, she took a water pail outside to fill it up. As she carried it in the moonlight, it broke. The reflection of the moon she saw in the pail a moment before, suddenly vanished. It was at that moment she became enlightened. Bhagwan called it the "ultimate accident."

With the new mandate, the days of slacking were over, at least officially. I could no longer drift around; I had to work too. I kept working in the kitchen, and since more kids had arrived, we all spent part of our time in school. The eight or so of us would meet in the small house. Everyone would talk and scream and not pay attention. I got up on my high horse when people didn't behave or follow the rules. I was a good girl. Some of the new arrivals stepped in as our teachers. I don't think they knew how to deal with us since were all different ages and at different academic levels. I was still on long division, while others my age did higher math. I was ashamed of how behind I was, surely something was wrong with me. Trying to do schoolwork only made me more aware of what a loser I was, so I hated school. The only part that was fun was learning French. It was a new topic for all of us, and the teacher found that the only way he could get us all to pay attention was to teach us dirty French bar songs that made us giggle.

Much to my relief, school was canceled after a few weeks. I'm not sure why. Maybe we were too much to handle, or maybe Sheela and the Moms needed the teachers and us to work on building the commune. I never seemed to need to do math or read anything besides cookbooks and comics anyway. Plus, Marga sometimes gave me reading lessons, much like Ira did in Pune. Maybe that was all the schooling I needed.

* * *

By late August, just a couple of weeks after Sheela arrived, Bhagwan's compound was almost ready. The grove was renamed Lao Tzu, after the Zen mystic. All that was left to do was plant trees and shrubs and roll out four thousand square feet of vibrant green sod. As a final touch, a pride of peacocks was set on the grounds to roam. Anything for Bhagwan.

On August 29, 1981, Bhagwan flew from New Jersey to Redmond, Oregon, on a chartered Learjet. Sheela then drove him and Vivek to the ranch in one of the two shiny Rolls-Royces that were recently purchased for him.

All sixty or so of us gathered at Lao Tzu Grove to greet him when he arrived. We found our places on the new grass facing Bhagwan's empty chair and meditated as we waited. Then, when we heard the crunch of gravel under car wheels, we all put our palms together in prayer position in front of our hearts. Once the Rolls-Royce pulled up in front of the house, Sheela, beaming with pride, got out of the driver's seat and walked over and opened Bhagwan's door. In Bhagwan's presence, Sheela seemed shy and nervous like a little girl. At all other times, she seemed tough and bold.

Bhagwan slowly, almost feebly, got out of the car and to his feet. He put his hands together in prayer position in front of his mouth, grinning widely as he spanned his eyes across us all and the landscape. I wondered what he thought of the ranch. I couldn't tell from his facial expressions. He always looked the same when he greeted us: a smile, his hands in namaste, and a distant look in his eyes. Perhaps it was because his state of enlightenment made him a hollow bamboo, a metaphor he used often. He said, "A hollow bamboo becomes a flute, and the divine starts playing it. Once you are empty, then there is no barrier for the divine to enter in you." Maybe that was one of the joys of being enlightened—maybe it meant life's stresses didn't affect him like they did me and others. I really didn't know, and I still didn't understand.

Everyone beamed with joy, feeling blessed to be in Bhagwan's presence again. He slowly made his way to the chair, sat down, and closed his eyes. We all sat at his feet meditating for another half hour. He then rose, put his hands in namaste again, and walked into his new home. We all lingered on the grass a little longer, taking it all in and enjoying a respite from our usual duties. It would be the last time we would sit with him for several months.

★   ★   ★

A month or so before he left India, it was announced that Bhagwan was entering a silent phase. He had often spoken of how silence was a more direct way for him to commune with us. Awakening, he said, was beyond what words could convey or the mind could understand. Most disciples accepted his silence, and even saw it as a blessing, and an opportunity for deeper spiritual understanding. If someone didn't like it, they kept it to themselves; otherwise, they would be told to surrender and stop being negative. Truth was, Bhagwan was unpredictable, and I sensed that no matter what he said or did, most devotees would take it as a spiritual opportunity and yet another way to surrender.

During those last couple of months in Pune, Bhagwan still came to Buddha Hall each morning, but instead of giving a discourse, he sat silently. That hour that we were in his presence was punctuated by devotional chants and passages from one of his books that someone read aloud. After an hour or so, he would rise from his chair and exit the hall.

But now at the ranch, we didn't even sit with him. It wasn't clear if and when that would change. He remained sequstered in Lao Tzu Grove, where only Sheela, a select few of special sannyasins, and the women in his household, the same fair maidens who lived in his house in India, had access to him. Lao Tzu Grove was protected by guards and an electric fence. Nobody was allowed to enter except the special few.

A few weeks later, Bhagwan was spotted taking afternoon drives in one of his Rolls-Royces. He was usually accompanied by Vivek or, on occasion, one of the other women from his compound. When people noticed him passing by at around the same time each afternoon, they started gathering at the side of the road just to get a glimpse of him as he passed.

Soon, standing on the side of the road became a daily ritual that we called "drive-by." As he passed, he usually slowed down and held his left hand up to the window in half namaste. On rare occasions, he would stop and say a few words to somebody. That person would be on cloud nine. Even if Bhagwan didn't stop, people were elated to be in his presence, if just for a couple of seconds.

I often skipped the whole thing. I didn't dislike it. I just wasn't drawn to all the hoopla and standing around. Bhagwan hadn't captured my heart like he had for so many others, and I didn't feel blissed out when I saw him. Plus, he never seemed to notice me anyway. I didn't have a special relationship with him like a few of the other kids did. Plus, I was still skeptical of the concept of enlightenment. I did believe in some kind of oasis, though. I believed we were the chosen ones.

I was confused by the inconsistencies that I observed. I was frustrated about Bhagwan's assertion that he was just an ordinary man, but he clearly wasn't. Did people believe him when he said he was ordinary? If he was ordinary, why was he untouchable to most of us, and why was he living like a king? So, watching him drive by in his glimmering Rolls-Royce was just a reminder of the mixed message. He didn't live like an ordinary man in India, and now he seemed like a god. Some rebellious part of me didn't want to play into it. I don't think I fully trusted Bhagwan. Maybe I was still clinging to the idea that truly spiritual leaders had to be simple and give up all luxury. I don't know where I even got that idea because Bhagwan had never said that. He didn't think you had to give up any comfort or pleasure to be a seeker—he said to embrace it all. Anyway, I wasn't there for Bhagwan. I was there because of the community, and because it was where I just happened to be.

CHAPTER TWENTY-TWO

DEFLOWERING

ONE AFTERNOON in mid to late October or early November, I was walking through the ranch yard towards the small house, when a pickup full of people stopped. Milarepa called out to me, "Hey, we're heading to Desiderata for a party, wanna come?" I never hung out with the construction crews and didn't even know most of them, but I knew Milarepa. I hadn't seen him as much since we all moved into the trailers. He waited for my response. "Okay," I said. He reached out his hand and helped me in.

Desiderata was one of the newest construction sites. It was tucked away from the rest of the building projects along the road heading out of the ranch. I held onto the side of the truck as we thrashed along. Twilight was approaching. A soft dusty-orange hue shone warmly on the jagged rock outcroppings as we passed. I felt joy as I took in the beauty. I was happy to be doing something different and to be included with everyone else.

At the build site, we all piled out of the truck and greeted the others who were already there. They had started a small fire and stood around drinking beer and listening to music blaring from a boom box. I didn't know where to stand or who to talk to. I was out of my comfort zone. Was I supposed to mingle and talk to others, or was I Milarepa's guest? I couldn't think straight in Milarepa's company. I was nervous and just stood still a few steps behind the group that had formed. Then Milarepa came and stood close to me, our sides touching. I felt more at ease in his shadow. Since he was popular and friends with everyone, I thought I would be seen as cool too since I was with him. He moved even closer and gently rocked into me, which was comforting.

Others gathered around us, talking and joking. Everyone was loud and having a good time. I don't remember any of the conversations; I was only half listening. The other half was wholly focused on the warmth of

Milarepa's body next to mine. When there was a gap in the conversation, he took my hand, leaned towards me, and whispered, "Let's go for a walk."

As we stepped away from the gathering, the Foreigner song "Waiting for a Girl Like You" blared from the boombox. Milarepa sang along, "I've been waiting for a girl like you to come into my life," as if serenading me. I felt a rush of excitement—my heart felt buoyant. We found our way amid the sagebrush, far away enough that the others couldn't see or hear us. He put his arm around me. We stood side by side looking up at the stars emerging in the dusk. I thought what was happening must be destiny—the beginning of a love affair. Maybe Milarepa was my Prince Charming. I felt a little embarrassed at my presumptuousness and innocent hopes, but giddily hoped anyway. I wanted to feel loved.

He guided me to sit on the ground. I sat there next to him, my heart pounding. Whatever was happening felt romantic and also a little on the sly. We were, after all, hiding in the bushes. He leaned over and kissed me, first softly and then passionately. I bashfully kissed him back. I didn't know what I was doing. The only other time I had ever kissed a man was when my friends and I kissed the samurai ages ago. I brought myself back to the current kiss. It seemed sweet at first, but when he came on with such force, I was thrown. It didn't feel tender. Then he stopped for a moment and looked at me. "You're beautiful," he said softly. He was tender after all. I could barely breathe. I felt so flattered and excited. We lay down on the ground. Then he pulled up my shirt so he could see my breasts in the moonlight. He looked at my body as his hands stroked my stomach, breasts, and neck. He then started kissing me again, first gently and then lustfully. I felt flushed. The excited part of me thought it was such an honor that he chose me, but the cautious part of me manifested as tension and a knot in my stomach. I sensed that what was happening was not above board, but my longing for love and attention won out. I told myself that our budding secret love affair was something special. If I protested or told him to stop, I would seem like a prude, and he wouldn't like me anymore. We kept kissing as he stimulated my nipples. I knew that next he would be putting his hand down my pants. I froze at the thought. Then, the sound of a truck's ignition broke the spell.

Someone yelled, "Milarepa, we are leaving now." He stood up. "We better go," he said. I got up, pulled my shirt down, and we walked hand in hand out of the brush. I was worried that somebody would notice, and we would get in trouble. But when we hopped into the truck together, no one said anything or even looked at us suspiciously. Maybe I was just too uptight; maybe I just wasn't good with going with my energy like Bhagwan had always said we should. I knew Bhagwan said sex was sacred. Even so, I couldn't shake the notion that sex was dangerous, crude, and gross, unless you were in love.

I sat close to Milarepa in the back of the pickup. His body bumped against mine as we rode along the road. We stopped at several of the housing sites to drop people off. As we approached the site where Milarepa lived, he leaned towards me and said, "Stay with me tonight." I was tongue-tied. I didn't know what to do. It was all happening so fast. I hadn't even digested what had just happened, but I felt an urgency to respond. If I didn't say yes, I thought, then our love wouldn't grow. This was my chance to take a leap.

He turned to look at me, waiting for my response. His eyes were kind. "OK," I said softly. I felt shy and unsure of myself. I think I was blushing, thankfully in the dark.

The truck stopped. With purity and hope in my heart, and a scramble in my head, I hopped out of the back of the truck. Milarepa put his arm around me again. By the light of the moon, we walked in silence over the bridge that crossed the creek to the cluster of trailers where he lived. I remember the quiet and the crisp air. I wondered, does this mean we will be together? Is he going to be my boyfriend? I knew my life was about to change. It was just a few weeks before my thirteenth birthday. Maybe I was the girl he'd been waiting for, just like the song said.

We arrived in his room. Two mattresses sat on the floor, as was customary. Much to my relief his roommate wasn't home. While Milarepa was in the bathroom, I sat on the end of his bed, fidgeting. Part of me wanted to get in the closet and close the door. But I didn't move, I just counted the seconds until he reappeared in the doorway.

"Are you going to get undressed for bed?" he said. I stared at the floor, and then at him. I already felt naked. "Take a look at my cassettes to see if there is anything you'd like to listen to," he said pointing to a shelf in his open closet.

He left again—I guess to brush his teeth. I took off my clothes, trying to act like I was at ease, but my body stiffened. I sat stark naked in front of his closet holding my knees to my chest, trying to focus on the cassettes. I could feel my heart pounding. What now? I kept telling myself "This is good. This means he loves you." But I was conflicted. Another wiser voice said, "Run home." I tried to ignore that voice, the side of me that wanted to fit in and please others compelled me to stay, insisting: *Don't be difficult.*

Milarepa came back into the room and got into bed. "Come here," he said reaching his arms out. I stood up and slowly walked toward him, as his eyes wandered over my naked body. He smiled. I lay down with my back to him. He pulled me close. I didn't move. I could feel his naked skin against mine. I felt so connected to him. I had never been skin to skin with anyone. It felt soothing. Maybe we would sleep intertwined. Then he started to softly stroke my belly, the crest of my hip, my breasts. My body felt electrified and frozen at the same time. I told myself to be receptive and open like I was supposed to be. I didn't do anything; I just let him touch me all over as my body quivered. Then his hand moved between my legs. I willed myself not to clench my legs together. He thrust his tongue in my mouth more vigorously, as he climbed on top of me. I still didn't move. I felt like I was only half there, like I was observing the scene from outside of my body. He spread my legs, and with a push, slowly thrust his hard penis into me. It hurt a little and I moaned. "Are you okay," he asked.

"Yes," I said tentatively. He continued to thrust his penis in and out of me. I waited for the feeling of connection I felt when he held me, but it didn't come. I thought I was supposed to feel some kind of ecstasy, but I didn't. I felt like an anonymous body. I couldn't see his face in the dark. Was it supposed to be so impersonal? I thought sex was supposed to be a beautiful union. *When would this be done?* I didn't complain, I didn't make a sound, but he moaned and then moaned louder as he pushed into me hard. Then he was done. After a few moments, he rolled off me, kissed me goodnight and went to sleep.

I was wide awake—wired and confused. I had let him take my virginity. The fullness I had felt in my heart, the excitement and anticipation I felt just an hour earlier, morphed into heartache and loneliness. I felt stupid and soiled in a way that couldn't be undone. But maybe, I hoped, I just felt this way because it was my first time. Maybe it would get better as our love affair unfolded. And maybe I should be proud since I was the youngest girl at the ranch to have a boyfriend. That in itself was an honor that I took to mean I was desirable.

As the sun rose and light glinted through the window and onto our faces, I looked over at him. For a moment I just saw a man—an undeserving man whom I let get inside of me. I kind of hated him—I couldn't get his residue out of me. He hadn't even used a condom. I felt so shaky, and now that the deed was done, I wanted, I needed him to reassure me that he would treat my delicate heart with care.

When he awoke, he quickly got up and took a shower. He then got dressed, gave me a kiss goodbye saying, "Stay as long as you want." What? He barely even said good morning. He didn't even ask me how I was. Did he forget that he took my virginity just hours earlier? Weren't we going to have breakfast together and plan our next meeting? I stood in his bedroom bewildered as he walked out the door. I put on my clothes and snuck out of his house hoping no one would see me. I walked home feeling heartsore and ashamed.

★　★　★

Over the next week, Milarepa invited me to sit with him at dinner a couple of times. I felt uncomfortable sitting next to him as he and his friends joked around. I took our connection seriously and found it crude when his friends laughed and congratulated Milarepa for "popping my cherry." Those words made me feel ashamed, like taking my virginity was a sport. Each time I ate dinner with him, Milarepa invited me home with him. And when we were alone together, the macho demeanor vanished, and he became loving. I drank in his adoration and tenderness, and the tension in my heart melted when our bodies pressed into each other.

Not more than a week after I lost my virginity, I received a message to go see the nurse practitioner at Pythagoras, a newly set up clinic in one of the trailers. When I arrived, I was surprised to see three other girls my age were already present. The nurse practitioner came out to greet us and told us all to come with her into the examination room. We looked at each other perplexed. Why were we here?

"It's time for all of you to be fitted for diaphragms," she informed us. I was taken aback, realizing that news of my lost virginity had evidently spread quickly. The Moms must have been concerned about the possibility of unwanted pregnancies among girls my age, something they surely wished to prevent.

The nurse proceeded to explain that each of our bodies were unique, and she would examine each of us to find the appropriate size diaphragms.

"Alright, Sarito, let's begin with you. Please remove your pants and underwear and climb onto the examination table," she instructed. Feeling a mixture of shock and vulnerability, I undressed from the waist down, got onto the table and draped a sheet over my crotch. "Okay, now put your feet in the stirrups," the nurse said. Nervously, I positioned my feet in the stirrups, bracing myself for the unfamiliar experience. It was my first gynecological exam, and the sense of exposure was distressing. I took a deep breath, held my composure, and remained still. The other girls stood behind the nurse, observing with curiosity.

Gently, the nurse inserted a cold speculum into my vagina and proceeded to provide the others with an impromptu anatomy lesson. "Notice that bump in the back? That's her cervix," she explained. She pointed out other relevant structures too.

Intrigued, the other girls leaned in for a closer look. After taking the necessary measurements, the nurse removed the speculum. I felt an immense sense of relief. I jumped off the table quickly and put my pants back on. Each of the other girls went through the same procedure, and the nurse emphasized the differences among our bodies, noting that one of the girls had a longer birth canal compared to the rest of us.

I never learned who arranged for us to receive contraception. None of the Moms approached me or explicitly discussed my sexual activity. Nevertheless, clearly someone in a position of authority knew; perhaps they all did.

That gynecological exam marked the first time I truly learned about my own anatomy. We didn't have a formal sex education program; I guess we were supposed to learn from experience or by observing the adults. And while the infamous word "orgasm" often entered conversations, I didn't know exactly what it meant. All I knew was that it was when men ejaculated and that it was when they moaned with ecstasy. I only had a vague notion that women could have orgasms too. I had heard women scream with ecstasy, but I was oblivious to the specific anatomy involved. I had yet to feel that kind of pleasure.

CHAPTER TWENTY-THREE

MAGDALENA

WINTER WAS COMING. We had long since outgrown the kitchen in the small ranch house, but nonetheless, for the time being, it was where we all gathered for dinner. To have enough seating for everyone, we set up plastic tables and chairs outside. Now frost and ice coated the outdoor furniture. The women in the kitchen and I would go outside before dinner and scrape it off. Fortunately, we had all recently been given identical boxy down coats in the shade of rust. At the end of the day, everyone would migrate to the small house and line up to be served piles of hot lasagna or enchiladas. All bundled up, we huddled outside and ate dinner with steam rising from our nostrils and our plates. It was not fun, nor was it sustainable.

Now all effort was put towards building an operational, heated cafeteria and dining hall by December 11, Bhagwan's birthday. It was just a few weeks away, but it was already clear that the work crews were a force to be reckoned with. Fueled by Bhagwan's vision, the crews could move mountains. Plus, Sheela promised that if the cafeteria was done on time, Bhagwan would come and have Satsang in the cafeteria to celebrate his birthday. The opportunity to once again sit at Bhagwan's feet inspired people to work even harder, and for sixteen or more hours a day.

The site for Magdalena—the name given for the cafeteria—sat in a valley along the road to the river, about a mile and a half from the ranch house. Within a few weeks, the land was cleared, a concrete slab was laid, and then voila, a large beige tin building was erected. The monstrosity looked like a warehouse and seemed out of place in the barren landscape. Inside the vast space was divided into a kitchen area, a bakery, and a huge dining room. The kitchen had numerous stoves, a walk-in cooler, and commercial dishwashers. The bakery had industrial ovens, large racks for the fresh bread, and broad tables where we could prepare the bread. The dining hall had gleaming linoleum floors and high ceilings. It was how I imagined a high school cafeteria might look, though much cleaner. Cleanliness was close to godliness, so our saying went.

We filled the dining hall with cheap white tables and chairs. Next all the equipment arrived—large pots, slicing machines, and hundreds of unbreakable Corning plates. Everything was ready ahead of schedule. Bhagwan would come celebrate his birthday with us. It was high time to dance.

*   *   *

Celebrations were a big deal, at least they were in India. We didn't celebrate any of the traditional holidays. Instead, we celebrated Bhagwan's Enlightenment Day in March, and Guru Purnima, also known as Master's Day, in July, and of course Bhagwan's birthday. I would venture to say that the celebrations were the highlights of our communal existence. Back in India, we would all gather in Buddha Hall. Bhagwan would sit on his podium while Anubhava and an array of other musicians led us in songs of devotion. When we all sang together, it felt magical. As the celebration unfolded, we all went wild. Some people danced at the back of the hall; others remained seated swaying their arms in the air. There was so much bliss and joy. I don't know how it happened exactly, but the high was undeniable.

Now, at the ranch our first celebration would be the perfect reward for all the hard work. But the feeling on the ranch was different than India— the vibe was less carefree. Plus, the musicians who would play weren't the same either. I didn't know what to expect, but if devotion was the key ingredient, that had not changed.

The day arrived. We prepared the dining hall for Bhagwan's visit. We moved all the chairs and tables to one end of the hall to create a large open space so we could sit on the floor. Others set up a podium with Bhagwan's chair at the opposite side of the hall. Then everyone arrived, clean and with beaming smiles. There were a lot more people than I realized—maybe two hundred. We all sat on the floor in silence with our eyes closed, as if creating a spiritual space.

Then Bhagwan arrived. Sheela brought him in through a side door. The band which included Sam and Milarepa, began to play. As Bhagwan made his way to his chair, we all sang "sweet, sweet Bhagwan, happy birthday to you." He sat there for about an hour as we sang him the devotional songs we all knew, as well as a few new ones. I didn't feel the same abandon as I did in India. I'm not sure why. Maybe it was because I was older now. But I sang and swayed along. It was still nice to be with everyone.

CHAPTER TWENTY-FOUR

CHEAP CHAMPAGNE

WHEN MAGDALENA first opened, I worked in the bakery with Marga and the other women I knew from the small house. I loved the tactile feeling of the dough and the air bubbles popping under the pressure of my hands as I kneaded. We baked enough bread, and an assortment of other things, for the whole commune.

I liked doing something practical, and taking the loaves out of the oven was always exciting. Plus, the other women and I had fun as we worked. We had a boom box. We played a rotation of Sally Oldfield, Gerry Rafferty, Christopher Cross, and Chris Williamson as we worked. If there was a lull, I entertained myself by studying *The Tassajara Bread Book*. I learned how to make plaited loaves. I loved how fancy they looked when they came out of the oven, as they could be served for a special occasion.

Magdalena quickly became the hub of our social lives—a place where nearly everyone, except the Moms, converged for a hot meal, a couple of beers, and a sense of connection. Working there meant I got to see everyone more than if I just showed up for dinner. In those early days, I sometimes met up with a couple of the teens and goofed off for a little while before getting back to work. In the evening, I watched people come in, welcoming those that I knew with a smile.

I was always on the lookout for Milarepa. Sometimes when he saw me, he smiled warmly and invited me to sit with him and his cool friends. Other times he didn't seem to notice me lurking in the corners watching him. I wanted to see more of him. I didn't want our relationship to be a secret. It puzzled me how different he was with me in public than in private, especially given that we spent at least two nights a week together. That was when I had what I thought was a brilliant idea. I would have a party at my trailer. I thought it would be a way for me and my roommates to hang out and have fun and for me to summon more of Milarepa's attention. And since I was so shy, I figured if I provided drinks I would loosen up and that would make my roommates like me.

The next morning, I retrieved a twenty-dollar bill, the only money I had, from where I had stashed it in a cassette tape, and put it in my pocket. When I got to Magdalena, I found Marga, as I knew she sometimes went shopping in Madras, or at least knew who did. We hugged, as we always did. "How are you doing?" she asked warmly.

"I'm fine. I want to have a party," I said excitedly.

"Oh cool!"

"Do you want to come?"

"No, not my kind of thing."

"Okay, well I want to get drinks. Do you think you could buy whatever is affordable?"

"Sure."

"Get as much alcohol as you can with this." I handed her the twenty-dollar bill.

"Okay. I'll do my best. Come find me Wednesday to pick up what I got."

"Thank you! See you later." And I was off.

I told my roommates that I was getting alcohol for a little party. They didn't seem terribly excited, but they all agreed to come. Then I worked up my courage to invite Milarepa. He agreed to come too, though he seemed blasé about it. I was a little worried he wouldn't actually show up.

On Wednesday afternoon I found Marga. She gave me a box with five bottles of André Champagne.

"It was the cheapest I could find," she said. They were just over three dollars each."

"Thank you," I said, hugging her.

"No problem. I hope you have fun."

The next night we all gathered at our trailer. I opened the champagne. My roommates and I hung out on the porch sipping away, slowly becoming goofy and giddy. I still wasn't sure if Milarepa would show up, but he did. By that time we were well on our way to being drunk. I approached him and gave him a hug. He hugged me back, kind of. He seemed withdrawn and cold. My heart sunk a little. I thought maybe he was uncomfortable meeting all my roommates, though I was pretty sure he already knew most of them. I tried to brush off his aloofness, hoping it would shift once he had a drink.

As we all got crazy drunk, Milarepa continued to pretty much ignored me. I talked with my friends, trying to act like I wasn't hurt, but when I saw him leaning in on Jutta at the other side of the porch, my heart clenched. It was plain as day that he was coming on to her. I couldn't stop watching them. I felt humiliated and crazy jealous. I knew that he was following his energy, as Bhagwan said we should. However, to me it wasn't freedom, it was agony. I wanted to collapse or do something like insert myself between them or make a scene. But then I would look like a fool who had made the tragic error of becoming attached. The feelings were so intense that I just quietly left the scene and went into the bathroom, where I sat on the toilet collapsed over myself, crying. I thought myself weak and pathetic.

After a while I felt calmer. I splashed my face with cold water and opened the bathroom door to rejoin the party. I had hardly taken two steps when I saw Jutta lying naked on her bed. Milarepa's head was between her legs, bobbing. Jutta saw the look of pain in my eyes, but Milarepa's head was in her crotch, and he didn't see me at all. I ran from the room. It was now dark, and everyone had moved into the living room. I bolted past and went onto the porch and curled into a ball. I felt worthless and beyond humiliated. All my roommates had heard me go on and on about how special I was to Milarepa, and now I felt like the laughingstock.

I stayed on the porch until everyone left. Jutta came and found me. She said she didn't realize that I would get so upset. She said she didn't know what to do. She assured me she didn't like him the way I did. I believed her, but I still felt like a worthless piece of trash. Our friendship was forever scarred by that incident.

A couple days later Milarepa approached me at dinner and invited me to sit with him. He said nothing of what happened. It was as if it didn't happen at all. He was back to his loving self, showering me with adoration. His sweet talk lured me back into his bed, as it would for the next three years.

CHAPTER TWENTY-FIVE

JESUS GROVE

M Y STINT working at the bakery was short-lived. Unexpectedly, Sheela plucked me from my routine to serve as her receptionist at Jesus Grove. I didn't know why since I hadn't interacted with her that much in Pune. I wondered if she was keeping an eye on me for Vidya. Maybe it was just that Sheela knew I was eager to please and was very good at keeping secrets. Whatever the reason, I embraced the opportunity to be closer to Bhagwan's inner circle, a seemingly special privilege.

Perched on a couch against the living room wall, Sheela fielded a constant influx of visitors—from those giving her updates on projects, to those meeting for advisory sessions—and occasionally those being called in to be reprimanded. My designated spot was across the room, about ten feet away, on a second couch. Next to me was a side table with the phone. My primary job was to answer it: "Hello, Jesus Grove, how can I help you?" and then tell Sheela who it was. Several others worked at Jesus Grove too. There was an Italian man who cooked for Sheela; an Austrian man who took care of her Mercedes, which was always shiny despite the pervasive dust; a woman who took care of Sheela's clothes; and yet another who did the cleaning. Answering the phone was hardly enough to keep me occupied, so I helped in the kitchen or doing laundry.

Those early days at Jesus Grove were laid back and fun. All of us who worked there got along well. When Sheela was in a good mood, she was fun and playful. She'd joke around with us with a mischievous bent. She could tease and pick on people in the most charming ways. She called one woman "spic" and another "shrink." I thought they were just funny nicknames, but later learned that spic was nasty, and that she called the other woman shrink because she was small in build and also too often gave unsolicited advice, apparently like a psychiatrist or shrink would. Nonetheless, everyone laughed at her jokes and prodding. I figured if Sheela thought something was funny, then it must be funny.

Sheela had a strong presence and was always engaging and the center of attention. She seemed like a solid pillar that didn't sway under the pressure of her numerous responsibilities. I imagined her confidence was borne of Bhagwan's trust in her, and in turn her dedication to Bhagwan and fulfilling his vision. I saw her as an example of devotion and dedication; she tackled every task with her all; she was "being total" like Bhagwan encouraged.

In addition to overseeing Bhagwan's mission to build a utopia, as his personal secretary, she oversaw the entirety of the Rajneesh movement. This encompassed keeping sannyasins globally connected, overseeing the distribution of books and discourse tapes, and serving as the public face of the movement. On top of that she was responsible for making sure Bhagwan was comfortable and had the things he wanted. One thing he wanted was more Rolls-Royces. Two was not enough. I didn't understand why he needed more cars, but I knew better than to question his desires.

Sheela met with Bhagwan each evening to talk things over. She said she told him about everything—not just spiritual matters, but about the building projects and the various challenges that arose. Whether everything was being directed by Bhagwan or not, Sheela asserted herself as the one in charge, wielding the power Bhagwan bestowed upon her.

She directed everything that was happening at the ranch and said that everything she did was for Bhagwan. She quickly morphed into a tough, albeit charming, authoritarian. We all said yes to whatever she wanted. Now surrendering to Bhagwan really meant surrendering to Sheela too, since she was the one relaying the directives.

Padma now reported directly to Sheela, as did several other women whom Sheela pulled into her inner circle and put in charge of various work departments, which we called temples. We worshiped at temples, which seemed a lot better than working in departments. Some of the new temples included Chang Tzu, the construction department, and Raidas, the cleaning department. The Moms drove around in pickup trucks, talking over a Motorola radio system, as they coordinated and barked orders at their crews.

*   *   *

As our building frenzy continued and new people arrived in droves, the neighboring ranchers and Antelope residents took notice. They were growing suspicious of what we were doing. They accused us of violating land use laws. The ranch was zoned for agricultural use and nothing more. I don't know if Sheela had considered the zoning laws when she bought the ranch, or if she just didn't think it would be an actual issue. I could tell Sheela was aggravated that anyone questioned what we were doing. She thought it was none of their business, but the complaints were mounting.

In an attempt to appease the rancher's doubts, Sheela invited some of them to come meet with her and see what we were doing for themselves. In preparation for these visits, all of us who worked at Jesus Grove would polish the fancy glasses, make exotic fruit punch with frozen melon balls as ice cubes, and make delicious appetizers like stuffed mushrooms and puff pastry shells filled with spinach and gruyere cheese.

When the guests arrived, Sheela welcomed them with her bubbly charm. The others and I would serve the food and drink with beaming smiles. The guests always loved the delicious food and drink, and surely the fancy presentation too.

Most were enchanted by Sheela's quick wit and fun demeanor. She didn't miss a beat. For every question they asked, she had an answer. When asked why there were so many people, she assured them that the new arrivals were here to help restore the land. She'd follow up by alluding to all the land restoration projects we were undertaking. By the time the guests left, I had no doubt that she had convinced most of them that they had nothing to worry about—that we were here to work the land and live in peace and harmony.

It was true that work was being done to restore the land. Thousands of willow trees were being planted as part of a creek restoration project. And the fields down by the river had been plowed and were ready for spring planting. But saying we were farmers was a lie. While we were farming the land, we weren't here for farming. We were here to be with Bhagwan and to be part of the commune, and everyone was working madly to make that happen.

In addition to building housing, we were building warehouses for Bhagwan's books and tapes, and the world headquarters for the Rajneesh movement—a for-profit business that was prohibited under the ranch's agricultural zoning. Our task was to build a self-sufficient spiritual commune. Farming was merely one small fraction of that vision.

Any assurances the neighbors and Antelopians may have had were short-lived. As new structures popped up, so did the tensions with the neighbors. The latest new buildings were two large tin structures in the valley close to the road that led to Antelope. One was for the Rajneesh Buddhafield Garage (RBG), where the heavy equipment could be serviced; the other was an office building named Socrates. Sheela insisted that the buildings were for farm related activities. That was only partially true. Before long another warehouse-like structure was erected in the valley near where I lived. It was soon full of Bhagwan's books and tapes. Storing and shipping Bhagwan's books and tapes was clearly not a farming activity.

As the weeks passed, Sheela's demeanor became more serious and focused. She now seemed stressed and easily agitated. On top of everything she had to do, she now had to figure out how to deal with the ever-mounting tensions with the neighbors, who were banding together to take legal action. She was mad. Her playful and agreeable demeanor took a back seat, while her fierce determination took the wheel. She would not back down. She now spent hours on the phone, trying to arrange for certain sannyasins to come to the ranch, like lawyers and planning engineers, who could help deal with the land use challenges.

★ ★ ★

On occasion, Sheela invited me to join her when she drove to Antelope. Why she needed to go to Antelope wasn't clear to me, but it seemed it was to make phone calls, or to visit the couple of properties the commune had just purchased for some reason. Though we had phones on the ranch, it seemed that she preferred to conduct business from Antelope.

First, we stopped at a trailer, called the "communication center." While Sheela talked on the phone, I just sat in the other room, occasionally doing the small tasks she asked me to do. Much of the time I sat daydreaming or doodling. I did not pay too much attention to the conversations, but I heard enough to realize that in addition to inviting American sannyasins who had the skills she needed, and she was also playing matchmaker. She was making arrangements for certain American disciples to marry certain foreign disciples. The goal was for the foreign disciples to obtain green cards so they could come and live at the ranch. The people at the top of the list for an arranged marriage were those who Sheela, or possibly Bhagwan, felt were important and integral to the community.

On my second or third trip to Antelope, my ears perked up when I heard Sheela mention Kaya's mother. She was telling whoever she was talking to that it was important for Kaya and her younger sister to get green cards too. When Sheela hung up the phone, I gathered my courage and entered her office. She looked up at me, waiting to hear what I had to say.

"Will Kaya be coming soon?"

"Yes, I am making arrangements," she said. I smiled and went back to my seat. I was excited at the thought that Kaya would join us. Having a good friend my age could make things much more fun. Maybe she would even work in Jesus Grove too, I hoped.

CHAPTER TWENTY-SIX

THE DANCE

Most nights I joined the rest of the commune for dinner at Magdalena. I liked being amid everyone else and visiting with some of the teens or my adult friends. On most nights I was on the lookout for Milarepa. I was evermore smitten with him. At least two times a week, he would take me home with him. I wanted to see him more than that, like a real boyfriend and girlfriend would, but he never made plans with me. I didn't know why not, and I didn't ask. I was too bashful around him to ask questions. I was clearly the follower, not the initiator. To get his attention, I had to be at the right place at the right time and hope he'd notice me and choose me. I would walk by his table in the dining room to casually indicate I existed. Then I'd linger after dinner, hoping he would come find me. I was so starry eyed that I didn't even consider what he might be doing on the nights he wasn't with me.

On the nights we were together, we'd walk down the road from Magdalena to his trailer holding hands or arm in arm. It was magical—I felt giddy as my mind raced with romantic notions, or lyrics to romantic songs. We didn't talk much—I was tongue-tied around him. My heart pounded, and I became shyer and more timid than I was already. When he did talk, it was to tell me how beautiful or sexy I was. I was beyond charmed. My heart burst with love, but it wasn't just love, it was equally a desperate yearning. His adoration temporarily quelled all my insecurities and loneliness. I didn't realize it at the time, but I innocently put my worth and my heart in his hands.

In his room, I would lay naked on his bed. After gazing and stroking my body, he would lean in to kiss me. He was tender and loving. I soaked it all up, innocent and malleable, there for his taking. I felt as fragile as a China cup that could shatter into a million pieces. I was scared to let go, but I pushed through my fear, as I could feel it was a barrier to connection.

Connection was what I craved more than anything. It's what made me feel like I belonged.

I didn't know much about sex, only what he and I had done together. I followed his lead. Things progressed from kissing and stroking to him kissing me all over. He'd linger between my legs for a little while, before finding his way back to my lips. And then we would make love. As his passion exploded, I remained contained. When he moaned and drove his penis deeper into me, I stayed perfectly still. The few moments of silent union after he orgasmed was my favorite part. I felt so close to him—just us—skin to skin, heart to heart.

★　★　★

Milarepa and several other musicians often jammed in the Magdalena dining hall after dinner. They had even acquired microphones and amps. I enjoyed the music, but what I liked even more were dance nights. We'd all set loose to songs by the Pointer Sisters, Madonna, and Michael Jackson. It was our fun time—a time of joy and frolic. We all danced freely and with everyone else. It was about freeform movement, not dance steps. On occasion, when Milarepa would come dance with me, I felt like a blushing bride.

On one of the dance nights, I spotted Marga standing on the sidelines. I went and joined her to say hello. After giving each other hugs, we watched the people on the dance floor and caught up. Then I spotted Milarepa dancing with another woman—none other than one of the fair maidens from Lao Tzu House. I couldn't stop watching them. Seeing how fixated I was, Marga turned to me calmly and said, "Since you're sleeping with Milarepa, I'm not going to sleep with him anymore." I was startled. I was caught completely off guard. All I managed to say was a feeble "Uh oh, thanks." I felt sick at the thought of them together. And how on earth did she know I was sleeping with him anyway? I had never told her. She must have heard it through the robust gossip mill.

Marga and I stood side by side a bit longer. I was using all my energy to stay calm. I still didn't know what to say and was trying to decide if I was mad or hurt by Marga or not. If I followed the general status quo, then I should've been fine with it. Everyone slept around, it was not a big deal. I realized I wasn't mad— I was jealous. The thought of Milarepa and Marga together was weird. Finally, I rationalized that maybe he slept with a couple of people before he was with me, but now he was with me—the past was the past. I couldn't hate Marga. She was my friend, and I knew she cared about me. She was doing me a kindness that many others wouldn't do.

I glanced out into the dance floor again. Milarepa was now slow dancing with the same woman. Her name was Chetna. She was Bhagwan's laundress. The only time I saw her was when she accompanied Bhagwan, instead of Vivek, on one of his afternoon drives. The Lao Tzu women didn't often come to Magdalena, so seeing her amongst us was unusual. All I could figure is that she must have wanted to dance. She was a beautiful, sophisticated English rose. She had perfectly straight dark hair, dark eyebrows, and high cheek bones. I'm sure she had many swamis vying for her affection—both because of her looks and her status. I had admired her in the ashram the few times I got close enough to see her.

What was Milarepa doing with her? I wondered. How did he even know her? As I watched, I saw them smiling and soft eyed, entranced with each other. I kept looking at them, while tension formed in my body. I couldn't bear to watch anymore. I said goodbye to Marga and walked into the kitchen to get myself together and try to brush off what I had just seen.

A few minutes later, as I was heading back into the dining hall, Milarepa and Chetna were walking in my direction holding hands. I silently gasped. They walked past me as if neither of them knew me. It was clear they were going home together. I felt like I would collapse into myself, but I continued walking, acting like I was okay. I had taken a blow to my heart. Thoughts flitted in my mind: I'm nothing, I hate him, she's much prettier than me. I felt so hurt, and desperately worthless. I hated myself for caring.

I saw them together more frequently. They often sat in the cafeteria snuggled up to each other like love birds. I soon learned that they had married a couple of months earlier when he and I lived in Howdy Doody and wasn't even on my radar. During that time, he had left briefly for California where he married her so she could get a visa to live in the US. People who were joined in arranged marriages often established residency in a town or city and play acted as if they were married for real. I don't know exactly how the locations were chosen, except that for the most part they were in states other than Oregon—probably so their unions wouldn't look suspicious. All couples learned each other's habits and idiosyncrasies so they would be prepared if and when the INS called them in for an interview. As such, the mock couples often spent time with each other. I hoped that Milarepa and Chetna's romantic expression was just a charade, but the signs blatantly confirmed they were actually together, at least partially.

I was wickedly jealous and swallowed it like poison. I berated myself with sharp lashings: I wasn't special enough, I was invisible, I was too fat, and the list went on. I didn't say a word.

On the nights that Chetna didn't come to Magdalena to meet him, he often sought me out and asked me to go home with him. He never mentioned her. Instead, he wooed me and told me how special and beautiful I was, just as he always did. His full attention was on me, and I was plugged back into my fantasy that our connection was a deep secret love. But when he left and went back to Chetna, my worth drained out of me again.

I tried to accept that it was just me and Chetna. Maybe I could learn to accept that he had only one other lover. Even if I could accept such an arrangement, in my mind's eye I could never match her attractiveness. Surely, she was a good conversationalist, a good lover, and had special charm because she was part of Bhagwan's inner circle. But Milarepa kept coming back to me, and anticipating our next night together kindled my hope that one day he would choose only me.

CHAPTER TWENTY-SEVEN

BUILDING TENSIONS

Vidya arrived sometime in the late winter. Strangely, I don't remember it, probably because so much was happening at once. By the beginning of 1982, not only had the population swelled to several hundred people, but several new temples were created, including a legal department. Sheela's proclamation to the outside world that we were just a peaceful group who wanted to farm the land and live in harmony with our neighbors came crashing down. The neighboring ranchers and the citizens of Antelope had now joined forces with a watch group called 1000 Friends of Oregon. Together they alerted the Wasco County Planning department of our land use violations.

The commune was now embroiled in numerous legal battles. Whatever charm Sheela wielded just a couple months earlier, morphed into contempt. She now referred to those that opposed us as bigots and rednecks. She seemed to take it personally that anyone would challenge us—as if whatever she wanted was above the law since she was fulfilling an enlightened master's vision.

Vidya dove right back in, resuming her place just below Sheela in the Moms' hierarchy. She set up office in the new Socrates building where she oversaw the rapidly growing legal department, as well as Ramakrishna, the personnel department. She was the one who decided which temples people worked in, and the one to tell people off if they were "negative" or were goofing off too much. Before long the whole upstairs area of Socrates was full of desks with people diligently working away.

I left my post at Jesus Grove and went to work with her—if you can call it that. I just did menial tasks and tried to stay out of the way. I knew Vidya still cared for me, but she no longer watched over me with the same maternal dedication. It was as if she was so focused on running the commune that she only saw me out of the corner of her eye. She still seemed to like having me around, however, and praised me for my maturity and appearance, saying things like "come sit with me my beautiful girl." I would go and sit next to her while she talked on the phone or spoke to people who came to see her. I felt lucky to be near her, and thought it was a blessing to be so close to the inner circle. The Moms must've liked something about me, which boosted my confidence and sense of worth.

★   ★   ★

Over the next couple of months many things happened at once. First, the commune bought several commercial properties in Antelope. If the locals didn't like us doing business from the ranch, Sheela decided we would run the commune's businesses in Antelope instead. This tactic only riled Antelopians further. They felt invaded and wanted us gone. To try to keep us out, they refused to issue Rajneesh Foundation International, the spiritual branch of the Rajneesh movement, a business license for its book sale operation. By March 1982, the Antelopians decided the best way to stymie our invasion was to put forth a vote to disincorporate the city of Antelope. If they succeeded, there would be no city to give us the business licenses we needed, and we wouldn't be able to do business. This inflamed Sheela and her gang further. They weren't going to let that happen. They had access to money and a large workforce at their command—they had the power to bully.

Half of Antelope was for sale anyway, so the commune bought up even more properties. Within days, sannyasins were moved from the ranch into the newly purchased houses so they could establish residency. Antelope's population of forty more than doubled overnight.

Now, red clad disciples walked the empty streets of the once almost ghost town, while the original residents, mostly retirees, stayed inside their homes, contemptuously avoiding us. When voting day arrived, the Rajneeshee residents voted against the disincorporation. The measure failed. One hurdle overcome.

The situation was so bizarre that hundreds of journalists and TV reporters swarmed Antelope to cover the story. We, the Rajneeshees, were suddenly notorious. We were the "red people" who followed a strange Indian guru who loved Rolls-Royces—a clan who invaded central Oregon and terrorized the small town of Antelope.

Over the next months the commune purchased even more properties in Antelope, including the cafe. We were well on our way to taking over the town. Eventually we would rename Antelope the City of Rajneesh.

* * *

Meanwhile back at the ranch, building continued even though permits were being stymied by the county planning department. But Sheela and the gang were not deterred, they just had to be more creative when stating what buildings would be used for. They got a permit to build a school, but I never saw a school. They also got a permit to build a massive 2.5-acre greenhouse right in the middle of the valley, at the mouth of Lao Tzu Grove. It was used as a greenhouse temporarily, but soon would be converted to a large auditorium.

The legal team looked at every and all options we could use to bypass the zoning laws. Before long, the lawyers had found a solution: we could incorporate our own city. It promised to remove all our land use issues and would allow us to govern ourselves. To incorporate, we needed approval by the Wasco County Board of Commissioners, and for 150 ranch residents to vote in favor of it. That wouldn't be a problem. To ensure our freedom and our future, sannyasins would vote in any way they were told to. The lawyers petitioned the state, and it was approved.

On May 18, 1982, 154 ranch residents voted in favor of incorporation and the city of Rajneeshpuram was born. We had our own zip code, 97741.

CHAPTER TWENTY-EIGHT

FIRST ANNUAL WORLD
CELEBRATION – 1982

JUST A MONTH or so before the incorporation of Rajneeshpuram went through, Sheela dropped a bombshell on us. She announced that we were going to host The First Annual World Celebration. Devotees from around the world would all gather at the ranch to celebrate and sit once again at Bhagwan's feet. It was slated to take place from July 3–7, and we were expecting 6,000-7,000 devotees to attend. We only had three months to prepare. In short order, brochures were sent to Rajneesh meditation centers in Europe and beyond.

Organized mayhem ensued. Crews throughout the valley built hundreds of tent platforms. Large yellow and white circus tents went up that would be used as kitchens and bathing facilities. Semis arrived hauling hundreds of Porta Potties, which were arranged in rows at numerous intervals between the tent platforms. Extra-long picnic tables were quickly built and placed under white canopies. A fleet of yellow school buses arrived for our public transportation system. As with everything at the ranch, all aspects were attended to. The Moms were master organizers, and most of us loved to work.

A couple of days before the festival was to begin, eighteen hundred or so beige tents sprung up on the tent platforms, each to sleep three to four people. And then, on July 2, 1982, busload after busload of sannyasins descended on the valley, full of awe and ready to celebrate. Each person was given a pamphlet with a schedule of the daily meditations and meals, and a map of the valley with a bus schedule. Those with money could pay for a plane tour, rent a bicycle, or buy all sorts of Rajneesh-branded mementos and books at the Noah's Ark boutique, a kind of general store set up in one of the old barns in the ranch yard. I was overwhelmed. I kept a smile on my face, but secretly couldn't wait till everyone would leave. I felt like we had been invaded. I was already struggling to adapt to all the new permanent residents. I could only imagine that the Antelopians were in shock as they got wind of what was going on.

On the first day of the festival, the seven thousand visitors, as well as the rest of us, dressed in shades of red, orange, pink, and purple, lined the road. We were all heading to the greenhouse, now fitted with a linoleum floor and a podium for Bhagwan to sit on. It was christened Rajneesh Mandir and would henceforth be used for meditations and communal gatherings. Inside the hall, we took our seats and waited in silence. For all seven days of the festival, Bhagwan would join us for Satsang—a heart-to-heart communion—a chance to bask in the master's sweet nectar, transmitted to us without words. After Satsang, the visitors had a few hours to do meditations, tour the ranch, and have lunch. Around 2:00 p.m., everyone lined the road again for drive-by.

Drive-by had become an increasingly exuberant ritual of devotion. But during the festival, the daily event reached new heights. It turned into a colorful and exuberant parade. Anybody who had an instrument brought it, forming impromptu jam sessions along the line. Everyone would clap or dance to the thump of the drums and the embellishments provided by the maracas, tambourines, and guitars. When Bhagwan's car slowly proceeded down the line, the musicians would amp up their playing, while others danced and flailed about like frenzied Maenads. Everyone hoped that their enthusiasm would inspire Bhagwan to stop in front of them and give them some extra energy. More often than not, the rapturous joy worked. Bhagwan would stop his car, take his hands off the wheel, and thrust his arms to the music as if emitting electricity. Everyone jumped, clapped, swayed, or trembled with even more vigor. Then, after a few minutes, he would put his hands back on the wheel and continue his slow drive down the line.

While most others vied to get as close to Bhagwan as possible, I didn't even try. I didn't like being in crowds, and I found myself thinking it was all a little nuts. But when I caught myself questioning Bhagwan or the hysteria I saw around me, I would quickly correct myself. Such thoughts were unacceptable. I may not have been devotedly in love with Bhagwan, but I was devoted to the commune, and I wanted to be accepted by the others, so I never voiced my doubts.

The festival culminated with Guru Purnima Day, also known as Master's Day, an Indian tradition where devotees show their gratitude for their guru. It was the highlight, the big shebang to close the festival. Bhagwan would come sit with us while we all celebrated in his presence.

On that evening, we all gathered. I could feel the joy and the sadness of those who knew they would have to leave soon. The band was poised and ready to rock out. As Bhagwan approached the hall in his limousine, the musicians began to play. Wearing a fancy robe and a hat, he walked from his car to the podium, thrusting his arms in the air in time with the music to the excitement of the crowd. Then he sat down on his throne, put his hands in a delicate position in his lap, and closed his eyes.

At first, the musicians played beautiful and soothing instrumental segments, punctuated with spans of silence. As the hour progressed, the music became more dynamic. Singers belted out devotional songs, backed by a full band. We all sang along, raising our hands in the air and swaying to the beat. At the back of the hall, people danced with abandon. When the music ended, a unique feeling befell the hall, one that I have only ever felt when a large group gathers together in song and celebration. It felt like a transcendent, shiny quality that is hard to describe. I didn't know how it was created, but my best guess was that it was a kind of alchemy that happened when so many people sang, meditated, and celebrated together in singular devotion. Most would say it was Bhagwan's energy. I wasn't so sure. What I was sure of is that total surrender and devotion could elicit all sorts of feelings and actions.

Over the next few days, the visitors, barring a few who were invited to stay on, left the ranch. The valley felt eerily empty, like a tent ghost town. The festival was a huge success that revitalized people's devotion to Bhagwan and made a lot of money to help fund our projects. Many of the participants expressed that they wanted to stay longer. Sheela promised more opportunities to visit the ranch in the future, including a Second Annual World Festival slated for the same time next year.

CHAPTER TWENTY-NINE

REUNION WITH FRIENDS

O
F MY FRIENDS from the Pune ashram, Gita was the first to arrive at
the ranch after me. She arrived a couple of months before the festival
and settled into one of the spare beds in our room at Subhuti Grove. Our
living space now buzzed with the energy of five teenagers—three girls and
two boys. Jutta, Gita, and I spent our evenings drinking beer that we swiped
from the cafeteria. Nobody seemed to mind that we drank—it was kind of
a "don't ask, don't tell" thing. We sang and goofed around. The two boys
were more reserved, probably overwhelmed by our sassy behavior and our
budding bodies.

Devi, whom I knew had been in Germany with her mother, arrived
some months later. As for Kaya, just before the festival was to commence,
Sheela gave me the heads-up that she would soon arrive. She didn't share
any specific details. A couple of days later, amid the throngs gathered along
the road for drive-by, someone told me they had just seen her. A surge of
excitement propelled me through the crowd to find her. I looked for a little
while with no luck, so I took my place and waited for Bhagwan's car to
move down the line. Afterwards, as everyone dispersed, I spotted her a little
way off. I ran over to her, "Kaya, Kaya!" She turned around. "Hi," I said. I
reached out to hug her.

"Hi," she responded, her tone somewhat subdued. Our hug felt tentative
too, and I couldn't help but notice the changes in her demeanor and appearance. Puberty had transformed her, which was evident by her shapely figure and large breasts. We just stood facing each other for a minute, looking
at each other, as if trying to find the familiar behind our changed bodies. It
had been less than a year, but in that time, we had become teenagers.

Right after the festival, Kaya, Gita, and I moved in together. This time
it was just the three of us in a room in Heraclitus Grove, a new cluster of
trailers across the road from Magdalena, up a steep hill. We fell back into

a rhythm with each other. While Kaya's silly side emerged again, she still seemed sort of bitter. I figured the hormones of puberty were hitting her hard. Puberty was affecting all of us, but it showed up in different ways. While Kaya was more angsty, I was a brooder, and Gita swung from cheerful to moody from one hour to the next.

Our teenage antics—strutting around, listening to music, and acting silly—were confined to the privacy of our room. When we were amongst the rest of the commune, we adopted a more adult demeanor. Though not spoken, it seemed we were expected to shed our childhood innocence and act mature. We weren't seen as kids any longer; we were young women now. As such, we no longer skipped around holding hands, or generally acting carefree. I was dismayed, and I clearly remember the day I reached for Gita's hand as we walked to breakfast, and she pushed it away. "We can't do that anymore," she said.

"Why not?"

"People will think we're childish," she said. I felt a little rejected. I didn't think anyone would even care. I was sad that we had to grow up and that our playful and spontaneous intimacy with each other was being replaced with self-consciousness. We were each traversing the precarious edge between childhood and adulthood in our own ways, trying to find our new identities. It was confusing and lonely, and I wondered how we were supposed to somehow know how to navigate this new stage of life with little to no guidance. I didn't feel like an adult, even though I was having sex. I still had all sorts of fairytale notions about true love and happily ever after. Even Vidya treated me like a little grown-up much of the time and rarely asked me what I was up to or what I was feeling. Did the Moms just overlook the fact that we were in a time of transition? Did they figure that since we were having sex with adults, we knew what we were doing? Don't get me wrong, most of the adults were nice to us, but there was no personal mentorship. We were all but abandoned to navigate the choppy waters on our own.

As our bodies changed, we now had the attention of men. It wasn't just the slimy glances I sometimes got from swamis in Pune when my body was still that of a girl. Now that I had hips and breasts and had grown tall, men asked me if I wanted to go home with them on a regular basis. "No!" I would say and walk away. Yuck! I wasn't interested, I was only interested in Milarepa. He was the only man I had ever slept with. With him, it wasn't just about sex—it was about love.

Oddly, even though I didn't sleep around, somehow my breasts were popular. They were apparently my best feature. A particular group of men often asked me to flash them, saying, "C'mon Sarito, show us your tits. Don't keep them to yourself. C'mon make our day." I blushed and thought the men were crude, but I usually just obliged to shut them up. Plus, I didn't want to seem too uptight and repressed, even though I was sure something was wrong with me for having hang-ups about sex. Fortunately, most men weren't as vocal, which in my mind made them seem sensitive and caring by contrast. I could still feel their subtle glances at my body, and in time it just seemed normal, and I didn't even notice when it was happening.

★ ★ ★

Sheela put Kaya to work at Jesus Grove, just like I thought she would. Kaya always seemed to have a special place in Sheela's heart. But after just a couple of weeks, Kaya was gone. She told Sheela she wanted to work somewhere else, and surprisingly, Sheela let her go. By this point, hardly anyone dared challenge Sheela. She and the other Moms had become even more authoritative. It was as if there was so much on their plates that they couldn't stand anyone stepping out of line or having personal needs. We were all to work in the temples where we were assigned and not complain. Those who did complain would usually be scolded and be told things like, "If you can't accept the job you were given, you're welcome to leave," or "Shape up or ship out." If Sheela or Vidya was in a playful mood, you might be lucky and be told, "tough titties." But, in Kaya's case, Sheela let her work somewhere else. I'm not even sure where.

When I asked Kaya why she left, she said, "It was boring, I want to be out in the community with everyone else." I was a little envious of her courage to break away from her special role as Sheela's sidekick, yet I didn't have the gall or the desire to break free myself. Despite often feeling invisible in the midst of the office chaos, I relied on Vidya and the other women for reassurance and a sense of place. I didn't realize it at the time, but I think Kaya didn't want to feel stifled by the pressure to be mature and well-behaved. She was embracing her teenage rebellion, whereas I was repressing mine. Maybe she realized that being "special" was a kind of curse.

CHAPTER THIRTY

RAJNEESHPURAM

BEFORE THE dust had even settled after the festival, Sheela announced that we would begin building the city of Rajneeshpuram. She said it would be a place "where people would live in harmony and love." The irony wasn't lost on me. Sheela didn't exactly exude love and harmony. It was strange seeing her say those words with a straight face. I was starting to see how well she could wield and manipulate her personality to get what she wanted. And it wasn't only her. Those in her inner circle also didn't exude love and harmony. They mimicked Sheela's managerial style and dished out orders with fierce authority. What would ensue was like a charade.

As a city, a group of sannyasins, all handpicked by Sheela, were sworn in as officials. Swami Krishna Deva (KD) was our mayor. Before long, we had an airstrip, a police department called the "Peace Force," a fire department, and a fleet of gray Oldsmobiles. Only Moms and important people had cars of their own. The rest of us got around on our busing system that remained in place after the festival.

Now that we were a self-governing city, we could issue building permits to ourselves, though I don't know exactly how that all worked. Building a city, even a small one, was a massive operation. To start with, we had to draw up blueprints, procure supplies, buy more heavy equipment, and increase the workforce. Plus, all the new arrivals needed housing and to be fed.

On the whole, sannyasins were highly trained professionals who had abandoned their affluent careers to follow Bhagwan. Now those with the specialized skills, like planners, lawyers, and engineers, which were needed to bring the vision to life, could once again apply their training. But this time for Bhagwan, not the unconscious masses that we were told included everyone but us. Those with specialized skills put their heads together to actualize Bhagwan's vision of the new commune. Most of the other people in the commune worked to implement the plans, like worker bees.

Work had already begun to erect a dam alongside a portion of the county road descending from Antelope to Rajneeshpuram. Heavy equipment moved tons of dirt from dawn until the sun sank behind the hills. At the same time, a complex called the Rajneesh International Meditation University (RIMU) was being built near the mouth of the valley. Once complete, a number of therapy and meditation groups would be offered for a fee. It would be a way for sannyasins from around the world to be in the Buddhafield. I don't think any of the group offerings were cheap. I am sure Sheela knew people would come, and because of their love for Bhagwan, they would pay the high prices. This endeavor would bring in money for the commune.

The future RIMU participants would need housing separate from the permanent residents. To this end, someone had the ingenious idea to use the tent platforms left over from the festival to make little A-frame cabins. They were quick to build, and in no time, an A-frame village sprouted up in a side valley not far from RIMU.

When the dam was complete just a couple of months later, it was filled and named Krishnamurti Lake, after another of Bhagwan's favorite mystics. When full, it held 350 million gallons of water and spanned a 40-acre area. The face of the dam was planted with flowers in the shape of the two-bird logo—a white bird overlaying a red bird, symbolizing Bhagwan leading his flock.

Even those who opposed us couldn't deny our ingenuity and the skill it took to build the dam and create a lake, especially in such a short amount of time. Some even called it an "engineering masterpiece." And the dam was not our only feat—our agricultural undertakings, sewage reclamation system, and land conservation practices were all state-of-the-art.

But the window of unbridled freedom to build was ever tenuous. The 1000 Friends of Oregon, the citizen group who opposed the incorporation of Rajneeshpuram in the first place, along with the neighbors, and an increasing number of angry citizens, were doing everything they could to have the courts reverse Rajneeshpuram's incorporation. I even learned that many of those who hated us "red people" had created a bumper sticker that said "better dead than red." People not only plastered the stickers on their bumpers but also on the windows of their houses. Needless to say, we were in a perpetual tug-of-war with the law, so when we had the advantage, everything had to happen at warp speed.

CHAPTER THIRTY-ONE

RAJNEESHISM

A NEW DIRECTIVE came down: we were to recite a devotional chant, known as the Gachchhamis, twice daily—before commencing work and at day's end. Regardless of our roles, whether working in the fields or in the office, we were all to gather, take a seat on the ground or floor, orient ourselves toward Bhagwan's house, and engage in the recitation. The Gachchhamis weren't unfamiliar; we had recited the chant in Pune when Bhagwan entered his period of silence. Back then, the morning Satsangs in Buddha Hall were bookended with the resonant voice of Taru Ma, a rotund Indian devotee and one of Bhagwan's original disciples. She led us in the chant. With each verse she intoned, we reverently echoed, bowing our heads. The chant had three verses:

Buddham sharanam gachchhami, I bow to the feet of the awakened one.

Sangham sharanam gachchhami, I bow to the feet of the commune of the awakened one.

Dhammam sharanam gachchhami, I bow to the ultimate truth of the awakened one.

This daily ritual exalted Bhagwan in a new way. It was a constant reminder to surrender and that our work was our worship. Similarly, Bhagwan still being in silence seemed to only create more reverence for him, not less. It was as if the void created by his silence allowed for key precepts to be recited, repeated, and elevated to dogma. Instead of sitting with him in person, except for special occasions, enormous pictures of him hung on the walls of all buildings, seemingly deifying him. Disciples would even quote Bhagwan if they saw someone else step out of line, saying things like "be total," "leave your ego at the door," and so on.

The motto at the ranch was: Life, Love, Laughter. We were to live to the fullest, follow our energy, and be total in everything we did, especially our worship. We were to be open-hearted and surrendered. We were to celebrate and laugh, since after all life was just leela, play.

Bhagwan was most certainly not living like an ordinary man. Nothing about the way he lived or the way we worshipped him was ordinary. He was the beloved master. He spent his time cloistered away in his gated and guarded compound. His household staff took care of his every need. He wore custom-made robes and hats that grew ever more lavish. His flock of Rolls- Royces grew by the month—at this point, he had about fifty. When he came to Rajneesh Mandir for one of our celebrations, he looked more like a guru rockstar than an ordinary man.

While being a sannyasin meant surrendering, being positive, and living life to its fullest, it was also about being authentic. But you had to be authentic in just the right way—in the acceptable way. Purporting to be free of societal conditioning and inhibitions, being authentic was often expressed by unfiltered blurts of whatever was on someone's mind. It rarely felt like people considered how their words would affect anyone else. Sometimes these expressions of one's "truth" stung or were shocking. For example, someone would just yell at you out of the blue, or criticize you by saying things like, "Drop your ego trip, Ma." Or, if someone was cranky, a friend or coworker might say, "You need a good fuck!"

Again, opposing teachings were at odds. Bhagwan taught us not to repress our feelings, but at the same time, we were to be positive and would be called out by the Moms if we weren't. What I came to understand is that it was okay to feel your negative feelings—be it jealousy, sadness, or rage—but it had to be short lived, and then you had to drop it. It was just our egos that created problems anyway.

However, I'm not sure if the "feel it and then drop it" approach always worked. It certainly didn't for me. Maybe this practice was more effective in India, where there was a greater focus on reflection and inner growth. This was markedly different at the ranch, where the emphasis was more on devotion and outward focus and less about "being a light unto yourself," as Bhagwan often said. Nevertheless, there was a general atmosphere of goodwill and kindness. People who hated each other one day could be seen laughing together the next. If they were carrying grudges, they were at least able to put them aside and carry on. In my case, I did often find joy and levity when I interacted with others and had learned to hide my "negative" feelings. Having bad feelings and being told I should drop them was far worse than just not sharing them.

*   *   *

Bhagwan had come to America on a medical visa, citing health concerns including back pain, diabetes, and asthma. His visa had been extended once, but now was about to expire again. The lawyers and the Moms brainstormed the best way to ensure Bhagwan could stay in America. They determined the best option would be for Bhagwan to apply for permanent residence status as a religious leader. The application was filed.

I thought deeming him a religious leader was all for show. It was in complete opposition to Bhagwan's teachings—teachings that were so blatant and repetitive that they were etched into my brain. It was impossible to miss how often he condemned religions. He was anti-religion and didn't like any kind of "isms." This new label was clearly just for show so he could get a visa. I was starting to see a pattern—the powers that be wanted what they wanted, and the means of getting it didn't matter.

And it didn't stop at the declaration that Bhagwan was our religious leader; the name of our religion was declared to be "Rajneeshism." Soon the book, *Rajneeshism,* was published. It was touted as our own bible. At the same time, Sheela started wearing a lavish red satin gown with a matching head scarf. The iconic two-bird logo, now a religious emblem, was embroidered onto her lapel. If Bhagwan was the master, she was the high priestess—the ambassador of Rajneeshism.

And then, a three-tiered spiritual hierarchy, called a Sansad, was formed. Bhagwan named the people for each tier. Being on the list was a high spiritual honor. The cherry on the cake was that Bhagwan declared that some of the people within the esteemed hierarchy were already enlightened. And if they weren't yet, he promised they would be in this lifetime—specifically within three months of his own death. After the announcement, we all speculated about who was or wasn't enlightened. I thought it was all a joke. I'm not sure how seriously others took it, but my sense was that most saw it as yet another example of Bhagwan's spiritual farce. Religion or not, enlightened or not, things went on as usual—Sheela and her inner circle still ran the show.

* ★ ★

On October 14, 1982, Bhagwan was summoned to Portland to be interviewed by the INS. Sheela and her gang made it a spectacle. A group of about thirty—Moms, women who took care of PR, a couple of musicians, and me as a tagalong—traveled to Portland in advance of Bhagwan's arrival to prepare. In front of the INS building, Sheela directed us to roll out a red carpet leading from the curb to the front steps. We then flanked the carpet with greenery, or maybe it was flowers.

When Bhagwan's car pulled up at his appointment time, a flutist and guitarist started playing an instrumental version of one of our devotional songs. The sannyasin cameraman maneuvered in front of Bhagwan like a paparazzo, capturing the significant event. Those of us present stood alongside the red carpet with our hands in prayer position. Once Bhagwan entered the building, everyone, including me, got down on our knees, faced the INS building, and chanted the Gachchhamis. As we bowed our heads with each verse, a group of press and non-sannyasin bystanders gathered to watch our pageantry. I felt embarrassed that we were making such a scene. I averted my eyes away from the bewildered stares.

As outlandish as our display was, I believe its purpose was to try to convince the INS that Bhagwan was our religious leader. After the interview, Bhagwan returned to the ranch. A ruling on his visa was promised within sixty days.

In mid-December, word came that the INS denied Bhagwan's application, claiming that his health problems, and his self-imposed period of silence, rendered him unable to lead a religion. The verdict infuriated Sheela and everyone, including sannyasins around the world. The lawyers, fronted by the compelling Swami Prem Niren, vowed to the press that we would appeal the case all the way to the Supreme Court if necessary.

Days after the INS's denial, sannyasins were bused from the ranch to Portland to protest outside the INS offices. The swath of colorfully dressed devotees held up signs proclaiming, "Silence is his way," "Stop modern crucifixion," and "America needs Bhagwan." At the same time, sannyasins from the meditation centers throughout Europe took to the streets in solidarity. Over the next months, the Moms rallied sannyasins to write letters to the INS in support of Bhagwan as a religious leader, urging people to emphasize that his silence didn't diminish his spiritual potency, it only enhanced it. The INS received around 2,700 such letters.

For the time being, as the lawyers appealed the INS ruling, Bhagwan could stay in the country. His immigration battle, however, would continue well into the future. The threat of his deportation was ever looming.

CHAPTER THIRTY-TWO

TWINKIES AND THE PRESS

THE ESCALATING conflicts in Antelope, the incorporation of Rajneesh-puram, and Bhagwan's immigration battle drew a swarm of media attention, as well as many curious visitors. When neighboring ranchers and Antelopians complained about all the traffic, Sheela deflected the blame onto them, asserting that it was their opposition to us that made us infamous. In other words, if they hadn't challenged us and just let us do what we wanted, we wouldn't have received so much attention. Our new-found notoriety, and by extension the huge influx of visitors, was thus their fault. By the end of the year, the Associated Press would name Rajneesh-puram one of the top stories of 1982.

Sheela abandoned all diplomacy. Anyone or any law that stood in opposition to her, and by extension Bhagwan's vision, fueled her contempt. She reveled in her power, brazen and unfettered. It was as if Bhagwan putting her in charge went straight to her head, making her think she was invincible. The stance she put forth, and that her deputies echoed, was that we, the Rajneeshees, were in the right no matter what. She accused anyone who couldn't or wouldn't see it that way of religious intolerance and bigotry. She seemed like a politician who was quickly forging a public reputation as a vitriolic, albeit sometimes charming, tyrant.

She said all publicity was good publicity. She, in fact, seemed to relish it. Visitors and the press were welcome—the more, the better. As such, a PR department was quickly assembled, led by Isabel, an exotic and beautiful Chilean woman. She and her group of other attractive women greeted the press and other visitors with a smile. They were coined the "Twinkies." It was an allusion to the Hostess cakes that were filled with sweet cream. They were indeed the hostesses, and they could charmingly weave fluffy narratives that many ate right up.

Though the Twinkies usually had the perfect quasi answers in response to pointed questions, some of the more earnest journalists were less prone to back down or be swept up in the "everything is love and light" presentation. Ed Bradley of *60 Minutes* was one of the journalists that didn't fall prey to the charm. I didn't know who he was or what *60 Minutes* was, but from the buzz going around, I figured he must be a big deal. When very important people came to the ranch, Sheela stepped in and showed them around herself. When I saw her giving Ed Bradley a tour of Magdalena, he looked serious and cynical. He didn't appear to be charmed.

On the whole, it seemed like the Twinkies' charm worked wonders. They would drive the press and visitors around in a fleet of vans, explaining Bhagwan's vision while pointing out all our accomplishments: our organic farming endeavors, the six thousand trees we had planted, and our celebratory lifestyle were always emphasized. Plus, seeing so many happy people in one place must have impressed people too.

What we had accomplished in such a short time was impressive, even to our haters. It really irked the neighbors. They said we could only do all that we did because of a workforce of unpaid laborers. It was true, none of us were paid. By the end of 1982, the official population at the ranch was seven hundred, with an additional seventy sannyasins in Antelope. The real number was more like a thousand.

* * *

While the press reported about us, we also reported about ourselves. The first issue of *The Rajneesh Times*, our very own newspaper, was printed on September 3, 1982. The weekly paper became the best way for sannyasins at the ranch, and around the world, to stay abreast of what was happening in Rajneeshpuram and Antelope.

As I recall, one of the first issues donned the headline: "Bhagwan Flies to Portland—Permanent Resident Status Sought as Religious Leader." The headline on the December 3, 1982, issue read: "The Future Face of Fashion?" Below it was a photo of me dressed as a Bavarian peasant. The caption below the photo read: "The next time you see this face it may be looking at you from the cover of a glossy magazine." I guess it was a slow news week. To the left of my photo, the headline for the other leading story that week read: "Rajneesh Community Offers Deprogramming Courses for Cult Victims."

One morning, a couple of weeks earlier, I was leaving Milarepa's trailer after spending the night with him, when I struck up a conversation with a German Ma who worked in Lao Tzu. She looked me up and down, assessing my every curve and feature. "You know you could be a model," she said.

"Really?" I looked at her doubtfully.

"Yes, really!" she said. She told me she had been a successful model in Europe and had even graced the covers of many prominent magazines. I was impressed. "I think if I sent pictures to the people I know in New York, they would want to sign you. You could be the next Brooke Shields." I suddenly felt a burst of excitement and lapsed into a fantasy. Maybe I could go to New York and make money for the commune, I thought. Maybe I would get to wear beautiful clothes and be somebody. I had seen magazines with pictures of Brooke Shields. She was my age, and I thought she was so pretty and sexy.

Coming back to reality, I concluded the whole thing was a long shot. What was I even thinking? There was no way I would be able to go. And anyway, I couldn't compete with the likes of Brooke Shields. Nonetheless, I kept thinking about it, and I finally mustered up my courage and approached Vidya.

"What's up, my darling girl?" she said. She usually called me some term of endearment, and I soaked it up.

"Gaya, who was a model, says I could be a model too," I said anxiously. "She said if we take pictures, she'll send them to her contacts in New York." Vidya looked at me with curiosity, not the disapproval I half expected.

"Well, darling, you know I think you're gorgeous. If you want photos, I'll arrange for it," she said. I beamed at her and then got up and hugged her.

"Thank you, thank you!"

"I think it's a brilliant idea," she said.

A few days later, everything was set for the shoot. Gaya put together outfits, fixed my hair, and applied a little makeup. First, we headed to the barnyard to take some photos with the horses, then we made our way to the Lao Tzu compound for another set of pictures. It all took a couple of hours. When we were done, she declared, "You did great, Sarito! I think we got some great shots."

The next day, Gaya and I looked at the proofs. She selected her favorites.

The photographer then developed about ten larger prints that Gaya promised to send off to New York. The next thing I knew, I was on the cover of the *Rajneesh Times*.

Page three of the paper had three more photos of me and a short write-up. I started reading it and did a double take. It read, "Ma Prem Sarito was sitting on the front porch of her mother's house in Rajneeshpuram when the woman next to her smiled and said: 'Why are you here when you could be modeling in New York?'" Huh? Nobody had even talked to me, and I was most certainly not sitting on the porch of my mother's house. I didn't even know where my mother lived exactly. But, I suppose, the *Rajneesh Times* couldn't say where I really was, namely at the house of my adult lover. And surely, the powers that be wanted to present an image of Rajneeshpuram where kids lived with their parents.

Weeks, or perhaps even months, passed, and no word came back from New York. I finally asked Gaya, and she said something vague like, "They liked the photos, but didn't think you would be a good fit at the moment." I was sure it was because I wasn't pretty enough. I did feel let down but acted like I didn't really want to go to New York anyway. After that, some of my photos were used in ads for Chiyono, Rajneeshpuram's hair salon.

CHAPTER THIRTY-THREE

THE MEAT MARKET

DINNER AT Magdalena was the epicenter of our social scene, brimming with laughter and good times. It was where everyone unwound, had a couple of beers, and hung out with their pals. While a handful of people were in committed relationships, the predominant narrative was one of people choosing companions for the night. Open sexuality and casual encounters were still the norm. Following your energy was not just accepted; it was encouraged. Doing so was a sign of how spiritually liberated you were. As such, instead of pussyfooting around too much, people flirted unabashedly or just walked up to someone they'd been eyeing and asked them to go home with them. It was all very open and fluid.

I covertly cringed at the notion that people were just hooking up for sex. I was still rooting for love. Clinging to my romanticism, I imagined that when people left the cafeteria together, all nestled into each other, they were falling in love. The idea of engaging in sex with no emotional strings attached seemed not only distasteful, but also hurtful. Sometimes I heard women saying how they liked a man they'd slept with, but he was already off with somebody else. Yet, any kind of attachment was seen as a weakness. We were taught that if we felt jealous, possessive, or hurt, it was our issue—an ego hang-up. So, if you were hurt by somebody who was just following their energy, the onus was not on them for hurting you but on you for feeling hurt.

After standing in line to get my dinner, I would scan the dining hall to see who I could sit with. I'd often sit with the other teens, or if I was lucky, with Milarepa and his friends. Milarepa's friend group included two Brits, Vish and Mutribo. Vish, though an actor by training, worked driving heavy equipment. Mutribo worked in Edison doing audio-visual stuff. A fourth member of the group, who also drove heavy equipment, was an American man named Rama. He was the guy who pressured Devi and me to give him a hand job in Pune. I didn't like him and felt gross when he leered at me through his tiny glasses.

Together, the men bantered and told tasteless jokes reminiscent of an all-boys boarding school. It made sense since Mutribo had attended a school called Eton, which I was told was known for such humor. Their confidence and cool air, as well as their off-color humor, was magnetic to many women. Milarepa and Mutribo were particularly popular. Women often stopped to say hello while others sauntered past their table in some kind of flirting ritual.

When women flitted around Milarepa, I felt threatened. Though I hoped he and the many women I saw him with were just his friends, I sensed it was more than that. I was still gripping to my delusional belief that he just rotated between me and Chetna. But now the pool of women to choose from had grown by leaps and bounds. The more I saw Milarepa interacting with other women, the harder it was to believe that loyalty and love would prevail. Reality kept smacking me in the face, leaving no room for denial.

It all played out before my eyes like a bad dream. Milarepa was sitting at dinner with a woman, all cozied up. I watched from a little way off as they got up and walked out of the cafeteria arm in arm. I felt like the breath had been kicked out of me. It left me with a crushing sense of humiliation. It felt like a betrayal to my very core.

I watched the same scenario play out night after night. The only thing that changed was who the woman was. Each time I watched, my heart clenched again. I shamed myself that Milarepa was just following his energy, just like Bhagwan said we should, so I shouldn't be upset. But while he was being liberated, I was quickly becoming a basket case. I was sure if I let my feelings spill out, I would be a laughingstock for believing in love and romance.

Milarepa had lured me in, my heart full of innocence and hope, and then duped me. All the while I believed in the fairytale and fell in love, or at least that's what I thought it was. I opened my heart to him. Now I could see all his sweet talk and seduction were hollow. I had walked right into the trap. How was I supposed to have known that I shouldn't be vulnerable and open my heart, especially when our entire way of life was to have an open heart? Nobody had warned me that attachment was to be avoided. Now my open heart was broken. I couldn't rewind time and undo the injury.

As it turned out, Milarepa always followed his energy. Over time, he came to be known as the commune's most notorious womanizer. He didn't sleep with dozens of women; he slept with hundreds, probably multiple hundreds. That is not an exaggeration. Other men even envied his seductive prowess and saw him as some kind of idol, wondering what his secret was. As a tongue-in-cheek way of teasing him about it, his male buddies took to calling him the "rapist." They thought it was hilarious. That name, or some version of it, stuck, and many others referred to him by that name. Some of the teens, the boys in particular, called him "Milaraper."

Yet, the dance between him and me continued. I was still in his rotation, but less and less. I took his sleeping around to mean I wasn't attractive enough—if I could only be sweeter and more appealing, I rationalized, then he would choose me, and only me. I berated myself incessantly for not measuring up to the other women. I started worrying about how I looked, about my weight, and how I could win his love. Other times, I gave myself hope by reassuring myself I was special to him because in the larger picture of his conquests, he had still slept with me more than most of the others. I even took to counting how many nights we had spent together. At that point, it was close to one hundred times.

Despite all the mind games I played with myself, I felt tortured and stuck. I held it inside and acted cool, at least the best I could, as that is what our culture mandated. I didn't know how to unhook myself, and I found the best remedy for my anguish was to be with Milarepa again. When he chose me, my self-flagellation and heartache evaporated as if by magic, only to return a day or two later. This cycle played out over and over.

CHAPTER THIRTY-FOUR

BUSINESS VENTURES

IN THE spring of 1983, the commune purchased and opened a 120-room hotel in downtown Portland, aptly named Hotel Rajneesh. At the same time, we launched "Zorba the Buddha Rajneesh Restaurant and Night-club." The concept of "Zorba the Buddha" was Bhagwan's vision of the ideal modern human being—someone who embraces life's pleasures like Zorba, while also pursuing the inner peace and awareness of Buddha. It's also a fitting name for a business aiming to balance profit with a sense of deeper purpose.

The hotel was open to the public but also served as a base for the increasing number of sannyasins who traveled to Portland for business. In fact, the Moms, the lawyers, and those involved in procuring supplies needed to build and run the city frequently commuted between Portland and the ranch.

Around the same time, we acquired three DC-3s and a Convair, all branded with the two-bird logo on their tails and "Air Rajneesh" inscribed in big letters on their sides. Soon, the runway that ran along the main valley was widened, and Air Rajneesh was open for business, offering flights between Portland and the ranch most days. Those needing to travel back and forth could now do so efficiently. Plus, the commune could make money by selling tickets to visitors coming to the ranch.

The pilots wore maroon suits and ties, pink shirts, and maroon captain hats. I and some of the other teen girls became the flight attendants, or "air hostesses," as we were called. Our uniforms were mauve polyester pants, pink shirts, a floral pink scarf, and a clip-on flower.

One or more times a week, I was assigned to a flight. Our departure time was early, so at 5:30 a.m., the pilots would stop to pick me up. I'd be awake and ready in a flash. The startle response I first noticed years earlier in the Huerfano valley, when I felt like I was always on alert, had only gotten worse. I was always on guard to some extent, so much so that when I heard the sound of a car pulling up or a hand on the doorknob of my room, I would bolt up in bed.

The rides to our airport in the dawn light were silent. We were too tired to talk. In preparation for the day's flight, I and the second air hostess would clean the plane, stow the food, and make coffee, with just a few minutes to spare before the passengers arrived. I was often paired with Kaya or Devi, and once we were more alert, we would joke around and have some good laughs.

When it was time to begin boarding, we welcomed each passenger, acting all poised and mature. Once everyone was seated and we were ready to go, came the best part: making the announcement. The script was stored in a plastic sleeve in a cubby at the front of the plane, but I had memorized it. As we started taxiing down the runway, I would stand at the front of the plane, the PA in my hand, and recite the script: "Welcome to Air Rajneesh flight 101 to Portland. Our flying time will be fifty-six minutes. Once in the air, we will serve drinks and a brie plate. If there is anything we can do to make your flight more comfortable, let us know. Now, please buckle your seatbelt in preparation for takeoff. And remember, there is only one sky to fly with Air Rajneesh."

The passengers always smiled, and sometimes even clapped, when they heard that line: "There's only one sky to fly with Air Rajneesh." It seemed to calm people's anxiety about flying on an old plane. I never knew why that line had such an impact, until I learned that one of Bhagwan's most cherished books was titled *Only One Sky*. Sometimes the flights were turbulent. At such times, I kept a calm veneer, smiled, and handed out barf bags. I actually didn't know if we were safe, but I knew better than to show my own anxiety.

I liked being away from my lonely perch in the office and amongst more people. Maybe Kaya was right in thinking it was better to be out in the commune with everyone else. After we arrived in Portland, we often had several hours to kill before we flew back to the ranch later in the afternoon. It was my only contact with the outside world. Sometimes the crew would hang out in the airport lounge and watch TV or go to the main terminal for rum raisin Häagen-Dazs. I rarely had any money, but the pilots must have been given an allowance, as they always paid. But, more often than not, we'd go to Hotel Rajneesh, and venture out from there.

I often walked the streets in Portland alone, mesmerized by all the products I saw in the shops. I wanted to buy things. I was keenly aware of how I stood out with my red clothes and mala. I felt ashamed and didn't like the stares I got, nor the honks and whistles from cars passing by. A favorite place to window shop was a small indoor mall called the Galleria. I'd peruse the beauty supply shop, smell shampoos, and then leave.

Zorba the Buddha Disco and Lounge was within walking distance of the hotel. It quickly became hugely successful—a hotspot not only for the delicious vegetarian food but for the celebratory dance scene. There was no denying that sannyasins' effervescent zest for life enlivened the dance floor. Even those who thought us odd couldn't deny that we knew how to create an environment where people could let their hair down and dance the night away. Soon, live music was added to the bill, with weekly performances by the newly formed Rajneesh Rock Band and the Rajneesh Country Band, fronted by Milarepa. His being the front man for the band only increased his appeal and popularity with the women.

Zorba the Buddha became the Rajneesh movement's quintessential brand. We had since bought the Antelope Cafe and renamed it Zorba the Buddha Cafe. Soon, Rajneesh meditation centers throughout Europe would open Zorba the Buddha restaurants and discos that quickly became hugely popular and highly profitable. By 1984, the Rajneesh communes in Germany alone operated fifteen Zorba the Buddha restaurants and thirteen discos. The discos in Berlin and Cologne reported having close to 250,000 customers each in their first year of operation alone.

It seemed that the communes in Europe were being ever more styled after the commune at the ranch. In fact, it seemed they were now linked to the ranch, and as such gave a portion of their profits to us to keep it running. The enterprises at the ranch required a lot of money. Sheela said the commune was spending a million dollars a month. That would not have been sustainable without money coming in from the multiple new business ventures, as well as the continuous donations from wealthy disciples.

CHAPTER THIRTY-FIVE

THE "TEENIES"

B Y EARLY 1983, there were about twenty-five teenagers and thirty or so kids at the ranch. The other teens also worked in temples alongside the adults, doing jobs ranging from construction and cleaning to working in Edison, the electronics department. Some of the smart boys had a propensity for technology. They excelled and learned on the job. In fact, the Moms said that instead of going to school, we should all learn from experience instead. Some learned more than others. I, for one, didn't learn much, except how to type and do calligraphy. I'm sure I picked up a few other skills too, but there was no formal schooling. Mostly I learned from watching and listening.

I was thankful we didn't have to go to school. Adults who had been to high school told us how lucky we were not to go through the same drudgery they endured—the cliques, the boring hours sitting in classrooms being taught useless garbage, and most of all, the lack of freedom.

I wholeheartedly adopted the belief that schooling was a bad thing—a kind of conditioning that would tarnish my soul. But more than that, I knew I was way behind, and avoiding school meant I didn't have to face that reality. I also believed I would be in the commune for the rest of my life and had no use for writing and arithmetic. However, sometimes I felt that the Moms had just forgotten about us or didn't know what to do with us, so they just put us to work. We were not a priority, especially not in the face of the larger challenges at play. Putting teens to work was in many ways a win-win: we didn't have to go to school, and we could also contribute to the workforce.

It was a different story for the twenty-five or thirty younger kids who ranged in age from six to twelve. They all bunked together in Howdy Doody. They were looked after by a few adults. Their parents lived elsewhere in the commune; I don't know how often they even saw their kids.

The younger kids were rarely in our midst. I strain to remember even see-ing them. I don't know if they had school or what they did all day. I would occasionally see a couple of them in the ranch yard, but that was about it.

As for babies, there were none, nor were there to be any. Birth control was mandatory. In addition to having a nurse practitioner who fitted peo-ple for diaphragms, as she did with me and the other girls, condoms were in ready supply in all housing facilities. Plus, in India, on Bhagwan's and the Moms' urging, many women had been sterilized and many men had gotten vasectomies. Having children was still not part of Bhagwan's vision. If that longing arose, they only had to remind themselves of his stance on the matter: children were a hindrance on the spiritual path. They also knew that getting pregnant and wanting to keep the child would mean having to leave the ranch. It would mean abandoning the unique and extraordinary opportunity to live in Bhagwan's Buddhafield.

I never did hear anyone express a desire to have kids, but I did hear peo-ple allude to how absurd it would be. And yet, despite the general stance about children being a hindrance, I didn't feel like one. We teenagers, or "teenies," as we were called, were loved by many. We were praised for our maturity, lack of conditioning, and free spirits. Some even emulated us as living examples of Bhagwan's "new man," free of societal hang-ups. What-ever teenage angst we had was not, for the most part, within the adults' purview. All focus was on charging forward with positivity and surrender.

*　*　*

Most of us teens banded together in our own little sub-tribe after work. We'd put aside our adult-like personas of the day and revert more fully into the teenagers that we were. We were sassy and playful and gossiped up a storm. We watched movies like *Fame* and *Grease*. After seeing pictures of Madonna and Cyndi Lauper, not to mention watching *Flashdance* for the umpteenth time, many of us girls cut the necklines out of our sweatshirts and wore leg warmers to be fashionable.

We all bonded over music. We listened to many of the popular '80s bands like Culture Club, Duran Duran, Blondie, the Eurythmics, and The Police. And we loved to dance to the music of Prince, Madonna, Marvin Gaye, and the Pointer Sisters, to name a few. How the current music infil-trated our community, which was essentially in the middle of nowhere, still baffles me, but thank God it did. It was a huge part of our lives. I know it was for me.

Soon, a whole slew of slang entered the teen vernacular. Sloping, meaning goofing off, was a favorite. It meant ducking out of work or stretching the fifteen-minute mid-morning tea break to an hour. There was also groping, meaning making out. Sloping and groping were often used together, as in "Sarito was sloping and groping during the tea break." Another popular term was "boned," meaning being told off, as in "a mom caught me sloping and boned me good." Then there was "hangdog." You were hangdog if you were moody or mopey. It was not a compliment, though it could be neutral. If someone told me to "stop being so hangdog," I would feel ashamed about my lack of positivity. But if one of my friends asked why I was so hangdog, I told them of my angst. Two other favorites were "wanker," essentially meaning loser, and the Valley Girl phrase "gag me with a spoon." There was a swagger that came with the use of this language. It was fun and playful but also a cool facade behind which we could hide our hurts and insecurities. Surely, we were all going through a lot, though I didn't know what was in anybody else's heart.

CHAPTER THIRTY-SIX

SEX APPEAL

It wasn't long until most of the other teen girls had also lost their virginities to adult men. Some of the girls were, or thought they were, in relationships or quasi-relationships with the men. It was rarer for the teen girls to sleep with, or have relationships with the teen boys, though it did happen. I had the distinct sense that the boys were not old enough yet, even though they were the same ages as us girls. Maybe part of it is that they didn't have the bold confidence that the adult men had.

For us girls, our newly curvaceous bodies made us objects of desire—ripe fruit. For me, the leering attention felt at once validating and uncomfortable. I gleaned a fleeting sense of value from the attention, even when I thought some of the men were gross and crude. Looking back, I think many of us were clamoring to belong and feel cherished, and having the ability to summon the male gaze was a kind of currency.

Some of the girls embraced their sexuality and adopted the sexual freedom that was modeled to us. It didn't come as easy for me. I envied the ease and comfort they had with their bodies. I don't know why I was so prim and proper, or where I came to see the sport of sex as something dirty. Maybe it was because, for me, the sexual act opened me up to being hurt, and I feared that I wouldn't be able to just have sex and not feel anything. My heart had already been broken. What if it broke again and again? Wasn't sex supposed to be sacred, like Bhagwan said? This kind of sex sure didn't seem sacred to me.

Nonetheless, I was jealous of the popular girls since they were so beloved. I didn't want to sleep with other men, but I wanted to be desired because it made me feel better about myself. Plus, I had seen more teens, including sexy girls, sitting with Milarepa and his gang at dinner more frequently. I could see him checking them out and bantering with them. I feared he would choose one of them over me.

How men saw us played a large role in our popularity. Who was the coyest, the sexiest, the prettiest, or had the nicest body were all at play. The more "liberated" and open you were, the better. Soon some of the adult men ascribed more attributes to us teen girls after they had slept with us: who had the nicest tits, who gave the best blowjobs, and who was good in bed. Within the teen scene itself, other factors also came into play in terms of popularity—mainly you had to be cool and liked by the other teens. The ones who seemed to be the most popular, at least from the sidelines from where I observed, seemed to have confidence, swagger, and a toughness. As for the boys, many of them were cool because they worked at Edison—not only were they smart, but they also always passed along their new music discoveries. It also seemed that having a parent who was important helped you gain "special" status.

Though I felt the need to compete and be desirable, the thought of flaunting my stuff or acting seductive left me shuddering. If I didn't want to be left in the dust, however, I'd have to push through my discomfort and come out of my shell.

I mustered my courage to wear a skimpy outfit. Before drive-by, as the throngs lined the road waiting for Bhagwan to pass, I quickly went to my room and changed into a maroon miniskirt and a pink tube top with shiny silver stripes.

Before I could change my mind, I returned to the drive-by mayhem. And sure enough, men looked me up and down, others smiled, still others said, "Looking good." The feeling of so many eyes surveying my curves felt uncomfortable. I felt ridiculous and like I was trying to inhabit a persona that didn't suit me. And though I felt the urge to give in to the gravity of my shame, I lifted my gaze from the ground to meet the eyes of the passersby. I tried to act casual—as if I had no idea I looked sexy, or perhaps even slutty—that I was just dressed normally.

As uncomfortable as I was, I thought maybe I just had to get used to it. Just recently, a woman commented to me that I should enjoy my sexuality. She said I seemed restrained and uncomfortable and wasn't letting myself blossom. I felt bad that I was seemingly stunted sexually—I didn't even have sexual desires. Did I just have to act as if? I would keep trying.

The next time I was in Portland, and was done with my air hostess duties, I put on my sexy outfit again. I ventured out and walked the streets to window shop. I didn't get far before men whistled at me, while others yelled out of their car windows, "Hey sexy thing." Was this a good sign? It didn't feel good, but what felt even worse was the way some people looked at me with disapproval, maybe even disgust. I must have looked like a hooker—a very young hooker.

I was quickly discovering that not only did I feel uncomfortable dressing provocatively, but I also didn't actually like the leering kind of attention it drew. And anyway, I'm sure my awkward discomfort wasn't sexy at all. The unwanted attention and propositions I received were already more than I wanted. Trying to compete with my peers wasn't worth it, especially since I wasn't even trying to seduce anyone—I was just hoping Milarepa would want me.

While I was growing resentful of being seen through a sexual lens, some of those who developed a little later felt left out. They were jealous of the attention those of us with breasts and hips got. Devi, my sweet friend from Pune, was a later bloomer, or maybe she just wasn't an early bloomer. She seemed eager for men to desire her. I would see her sitting on men's laps with her hands around them. Everyone adored her—she was sweet, open-hearted, and uninhibited. But much to her dismay, the men didn't ask her to go home with them. I guess since she didn't have breasts yet, she wasn't yet "juicy."

Though I didn't see Devi much because we worked at opposite sides of the ranch, the warmth between us always remained. When we did cross paths, we'd give each other a hug and hang out for a little while, divulging everything to each other, just like old times.

One day, not long after she arrived at the ranch, we were hanging out on my bed talking about the men she liked, and about my longing for Milarepa, who I felt was slipping away from me. She looked at me, dismayed, almost frustrated. "Sarito, you are so lucky that you have breasts; the men love you. Milarepa is not your only option," she said.

"Uh, I guess. At least men don't just stare at your breasts," I said.

"I'm jealous! I want men to want me. They don't notice me that way," she said. I didn't know what to say. I knew her day would come soon, and I thought developing late may save her from premature heartbreak. Maybe she could avoid growing bitter and jaded like I was becoming.

"It'll happen soon," I said. "I'm sure you will get breasts soon." She seemed a little reassured.

I was right; her plight didn't last much longer. Within a few months, her hormones endowed her with large breasts, much larger than mine, and a lean, sexy body. Lots of men wanted to enjoy her body. And unlike me, she liked their attention, and her open, innocent, yet unabashed demeanor lured men in. In time, I even heard that if she was attracted to a man, she would walk straight up to him and hand him a condom. Now that was brave. What if the guy said no? Wouldn't she fall to pieces? But she didn't, and the men usually didn't say no anyway. She seemed free and didn't seem to get jealous or anything. While it made me sad somehow, I was also in awe of her ability to enjoy, let go, and celebrate life. I envied her openheartedness. My heart was hurt, timid, and miserly.

CHAPTER THIRTY-SEVEN

THE DEVATEERTH MALL

CONSTRUCTION CONTINUED. The ranch yard was being transformed into a Wild West-style town. A two-story open-faced cedar structure, with an overhanging awning and a wood-planked walkway, popped up. It was named Devateerth Mall and housed a number of new retail businesses, open to ranch residents and visitors alike. The shops included the Chiyono hair salon, an ice cream parlor, a pizzeria, and a bank, to name a few. Across the yard, Noah's Ark Boutique and General Store offered an array of color-appropriate clothing and Rajneesh-branded tchotchkes. The neighboring Buddhaghosha Bookstore sold Bhagwan's books and cassette tapes of his discourses.

Some sannyasins still had some of their own money and could buy things, but many of us didn't have a cent. It was around this time that all permanent residents were given a monthly voucher worth ten dollars, I think. That was how we could have a meal in one of the restaurants now and then. They could also be used at the bistro in Portland.

The second story of the mall was for offices. The legal department, now called Rajneesh Legal Services (RLS), as well as several other administrative offices, now occupied most of the second floor. It made it convenient to go downstairs and get a treat, like a humongous chocolate chip cookie. By this time, Ira had arrived and worked in RLS too. Like in Pune, she often gave me a few dollars to go buy myself something. Sometimes she even bought me nice clothes from the boutique. She, like everyone, was busy, but she still occasionally took a little time to sit me down, pick out an article in Time magazine, and ask me to read it to her. I still hated reading but obliged. Nobody else ever tracked my education, and I knew that she wasn't doing it to torture me, but because she cared for me. While my reading had improved somewhat, I was far from reading at my grade level.

The new mall became an epicenter, second to Magdalena. When I went downstairs to the shops, I would often run into someone and chat for a while. Other times I would wander towards Jesus Grove and slip into the dry creek bed for a respite. Gazing into the vast sky, I watched the wispy clouds form and dissolve. The quiet reflection rekindled my hopes and dreams. I still had so much life ahead of me. Moments like this occurred from time to time, seemingly out of nowhere. It was as if a part of me emerged that still had huge hopes and dreams about my life.

By far, the best part of the new mall was the "teenie" disco that took place in the ice cream parlor twice a week. We let loose to the likes of Prince, Madonna, the Pointer Sisters, Marvin Gaye, and Michael Jackson. Though I felt increasingly separate from the other teens, the "teenie" disco was where I felt the most connected to my peers. When we all danced together, we danced off our personas for the night. While it was mostly us teenagers who gathered, there were a few adults who were especially friendly with the teens and joined us. By and large, they were the men and women who were sleeping with us—or hoping to.

CHAPTER THIRTY-EIGHT

SECOND ANNUAL WORLD CELEBRATION — 1983

THE SECOND Annual World Celebration was fast approaching. With the mall and Rajneesh International Meditation University (RIMU) complete, brochures were created and sent around the world. The brochure not only advertised the festival but also several extended-stay therapy courses led by some of the same esteemed "Rajneesh therapists" who led groups in Pune. The courses included things like Journey to the Heart of Hearts, Rajneesh Dehypnotherapy, and Rajneesh Neo-Vipassana. It all sounded like fluff to me. Those of us who lived at the ranch didn't do daily meditations or spiritual training. Our work was our meditation, though to me it still felt like work when I actually did anything useful. I had never read any of Bhagwan's books, and I still thought enlightenment was probably a joke, though I was on the fence.

Sheela in particular didn't have spiritual aspirations either. On several occasions, I heard her joke about how she slept through all of Bhagwan's lectures. She seemed to think all the woo-woo, arm-swaying new-age types were flaky kooks. Maybe I had taken on her and the other Moms' perspective since I lived in their world so much of the time. Since Sheela was a businesswoman more than a seeker, I assumed that offering self-growth courses was a business move more than anything else. It could be a profitable enterprise, and it would allow those who zealously wanted to be in Bhagwan's Buddhafield to do so for a fee.

Now that we had a downtown mall full of businesses, the festival brochure was chock full of ads promoting them. There was an ad for Air Rajneesh with the tagline "Traveling to the Further Shore? Contact Us!" There were also ads for the Buddhaghosha Bookstore, Noah's Ark Rajneesh Boutique, and Zorba the Buddha Rajneesh restaurants. We now had three Zorba the Buddha restaurants: the restaurant and nightclub in

Portland, the rebranded Antelope Cafe, and now one in the ranch house. The Harveys had been moved to a trailer.

Though it looked like we had numerous businesses, they were all really part of one entity—the commune, the religion, or the city of Rajneeshpuram. However you looked at it, Sheela, who was being directed by Bhagwan, was running the show. Dividing up our enterprises into multiple entities sounded fancy and probably helped for various legal reasons that I didn't fully understand. There were more organizations than I can even remember. The biggest ones were Rajneesh Neo-Sannyas Commune, of which Vidya was president, and Rajneesh Foundation International, of which Sheela was president. There was also a foundation that owned Bhagwan's Rolls-Royces and Rajneesh Investment Corporation that owned the ranch and the properties we acquired in Antelope. By my best estimation, there were at least ten different legal entities.

*   *   *

The week-long Second Annual World Festival in July 1983 drew fifteen thousand people, more than double the number of the first one. Like the year before, the main events each day were sitting in Bhagwan's presence for Satsang each morning and celebrating along the side of the road for the mid-afternoon drive-by.

Drive-by grew even more lavish. Now people could buy roses to place on Bhagwan's windshield as he passed them. Not only was it a way for spirited devotees to express their love and devotion, but it was also a way for the commune to rake in money. Each rose cost two dollars. As Bhagwan inched along the crowds that lined the sides of the road, the roses piled up on his windshield. The piles got so high, in fact, that Bhagwan would periodically stop his car while a few assigned people removed the roses, making space for the next round. On Guru Purnima Day, or Master's Day, the final day of the festival, the celebration reached its peak. Thousands of rose petals rained down from the sky, dropped from the Islander, Air Rajneesh's smallest plane, flying above. The crowd below erupted with joy, singing and dancing in a kind of Dionysian parade. "Drinking from your wine Bhagwan, drinking from your wine."

I was even less of a fan of the second festival than I was of the first. It was overwhelming, and so I often hid during the large events. On one day of the festival, I joined the Harveys in their new double-wide, where they served hot dogs. I had never eaten them before, and I felt so guilty not only for sneaking away but for eating meat. I had been a vegetarian my whole life. The reason I even remember the event is that not long after lunch, I was back at my trailer vomiting. I guess my body didn't know how to digest the likes of hot dogs, but at the time I thought it was instant karma for breaking the rules.

That afternoon was the last time I saw the Harveys. Soon after that, they left the ranch and moved to Madras. I didn't know why, but the rumor was that Bob Harvey found out adult men were making sexual passes at his daughters. I could surmise that Sheela no longer welcomed them once he complained about it.

CHAPTER THIRTY-NINE

THEN WE GOT GUNS

I N THE middle of the night on July 29, 1983, three bombs blasted Hotel Rajneesh in Portland. The staff and guests, ousted from their beds, ran in panic into the street. Barely dressed, they stood in shock, watching smoke and flames ravage the building. Nobody was killed, but several were injured.

When I arrived at the office the next morning, nobody was sitting at their desks. Instead, people huddled together in a hushed frenzy, saying things like "how could anybody do this to us—we, the chosen ones?" The circular arguments went from anger to disbelief and back to anger. As we learned more about the incident, reality sunk in. We had been targeted—there were people who actually wanted to terrorize us.

I had heard murmurs that we were under threat, but I thought it was an exaggeration. I assumed the Moms fabricated the stories to spin in the press, to emphasize the bigotry and discrimination we claimed to suffer. Now, their proclamations proved to be true. The violence of the bombs, and the fact that anyone wanted to bomb us at all, shocked me. There was virtually no crime at the ranch, and certainly nothing violent. In that sense, we did live in peace and harmony.

When the press questioned Sheela, she spewed rage. She said the bombing was an act of religious intolerance and vowed to protect her people. Now her convictions were backed by cold, hard facts; she had evidence to justify her vehemence. Combative and strident, she made it clear she meant business and wouldn't be intimidated by anyone.

It was determined that the man responsible for masterminding and detonating the bombs was a member of an extremist Islamic organization. He had fled the scene and failed to show up in court. Eventually, the law caught up with him, and he was tried for his crimes. In 1985, he was sentenced to twenty years in prison for the bombing, and an additional year for failing to appear in court.

★   ★   ★

Then we got guns. I didn't realize what Sheela meant when she said she would protect her people, but it became clear when we got Uzis—and lots of them. There were guard posts at the top of the road descending to Rajneeshpuram. Visitors and press were now searched for drugs and weapons upon arrival. Wherever Bhagwan was, so were two or more guards dressed in red uniforms carrying Uzis. When Bhagwan sat in Rajneesh Mandir for his birthday celebration in December, guards with Uzis in hand now stood at either side of the podium. During drive-bys, guards with wires in their ears like CIA agents strode beside his car, their stern faces a stark contrast to the celebratory crowd enraptured in song and dance. Apparently, even Bhagwan's car windows were bulletproof, though perhaps they had always been.

Oddly, I didn't feel scared. I believed Sheela when she said people hated us, and I believed that the guards were just protecting us, though it also crossed my mind that it was in part a theatrical ploy. I didn't know if those carrying the guns even knew how to shoot them. It was only later that I learned they all had been trained in military tactics, complete with target shooting.

CHAPTER FORTY

FACING REALITY

As the population grew, I felt smaller and smaller, like an indistinguish-able dot in an intricate mosaic. I now floated between the office, Jesus Grove, and Air Rajneesh. Much of the time, I felt like I existed in a netherworld of my own—not fully in the adult world or fully with the teens. Being the office girl turned out to be both a privilege and a curse. While the other teens were gallivanting around, working and goofing off together, I was sitting at a desk near Vidya or working at Jesus Grove, acting mature and obedient.

Though I shared a room with other teens, we weren't really friends, and I didn't hang out with them. I did see Kaya, Gita, and Devi on occasion. Devi had made new friends, while Kaya and Gita had become best friends. I'd sometimes sheepishly approach them, but I was no longer privy to their private worlds. I also sometimes joined in with the other teens but felt like I was getting the cold shoulder. Part of it could have been that I had grown more introverted and unsure of myself. At the same time, I assumed the teens saw me as stuck up because of my position with the Moms and my goody-two-shoes behavior. That was understandable—we all feared the Moms, and getting chewed out was hellish. While many were good at hiding their deviant adventures so they wouldn't get caught, I went the other way. I was well-behaved so I wouldn't get in trouble. I never stayed out late, I didn't drink anymore, and I followed all the rules. I clearly wanted the Moms' approval—it made me feel special. But when Sheela or Vidya used me as an example of good behavior in one of our all-teen meetings, I hated it. And I'm sure it didn't help the other teens like or trust me. It was lonely up on my high horse. I hid my hurt feelings by acting aloof—a coping mechanism that allowed me to at least appear like I didn't care what they thought of me. But I did care—a lot.

*   *   *

My two current roommates were an Australian girl, who was a couple of years younger than me, and an American girl, about my age. Though I was increasingly on the periphery of the teen scene, there was little animosity between me and my peers—just a kind of indifference. However, the American girl, who was now my roommate, was the one person who truly rubbed me the wrong way.

Lina exuded a sense of entitlement and self-confidence that most of us didn't possess. I believed that any kind of selfishness or self-importance was distasteful. In my mind, it was the opposite of surrender and dropping your ego. I believed that humbleness was close to godliness, something Bhagwan might have said.

I didn't know why Lina was so full of herself, but maybe it was because her father was one of the lawyers, which made her notable. Perhaps it was also because she recently arrived from California, where she had attended school. She was clearly well-versed in "mean girl" tactics.

While I envied her confidence, I hated her lack of consideration for anybody else's feelings, especially mine. She bragged about how men loved her because she was blonde, beautiful, and had brains to boot. I tried to just steer clear of her, but when I saw her strutting her stuff and flirting while wearing my clothes, which she borrowed without my permission, I was pissed. While we teens were creative in how we dressed, nice clothes were something special and hard to come by. When I confronted her, she would twist things around and argue, insisting I needed to chill out and be more generous. Eventually, I would give in, exasperated by her lawyer-like arguments.

She continued to wear my clothes, and worse still, I more frequently spotted her sitting with Milarepa at dinner. Unlike me, who didn't even have the guts to approach him, she teased and flirted with him. She told me they were friends and were having a great time. I worried she would displace me. I had found a little comfort in thinking I was at least the only teen girl Milarepa was having a relationship with, and that she was only a friend, but that now felt tenuous. She had his attention. I did not. In fact, he had pretty much ignored me for weeks.

* ★ *

Milarepa's birthday was approaching, and my romantic heart decided I would give him a rose and leave it in his room with a card. Hopefully, it would remind him of my existence.

On the day of his birthday, I asked the doctor, who had a practice in Madras, to buy me a rose. That afternoon, with the flower and a note in hand, I furtively approached Milarepa's trailer. The last thing I wanted was for anyone to see me being so idiotic. At this point, I knew my fixation on Milarepa was foolish. I worried I would be the laughingstock if someone saw me essentially begging for Milarepa's attention. It would be even worse if I ran into him, or worse yet, him and another woman.

At his trailer, I tiptoed to his room. I scanned his bedside table for a place to put the vase and note when I did a double take. There on his bedside table sat a gift and a note with hearts and kisses, signed "Lina." My heart knotted up. I quickly placed my note and the rose on the table and bolted out of his room. I hated myself. "You are so stupid! You're a pathetic, worthless loser," swirled in my head. Fuck! I had no idea they were involved. I thought it was just an unfounded fear rooted in my insecurity. Fuck them both! I fumed.

That night, back in our room, I was palpably ornery. I couldn't look anyone in the eye for fear of bursting into tears. When I didn't join in the chit-chat before bed, Lina asked, "Sarito, why are you so hangdog?" I didn't answer at first, but then I emboldened myself to confront her. Being blunt was a key sannyasin trait, and I thought it was the best way—direct and to the point.

"Have you been sleeping with Milarepa?"

"Yes, I have. We're in a relationship," she said blankly. I felt so small and deflated, weighted down by shame. I hated myself for caring so much for someone so cruel. I had been duped again, or even worse, I wasn't even memorable enough to consider. I stared at the floor, avoiding eye contact. Where could I even begin? The onus was on me for caring, for allowing myself to be vulnerable, for believing what Milarepa and I had was special and unique. His dalliances with other women were already torturous enough, and now he was pursuing someone my own age. I was evidently replaceable, just another fleeting fancy.

After a long silence, she continued. "We've been having fun." More silence. "He seems to really like me. He's so nice and showers me with compliments." He probably showered her with the very same compliments he had given me. She kept going, talking about the numerous things they were going to do together. When she finally paused, I responded.

"You know I'm in love with him, right? He's the only man I've ever been with."

"Oh, I never even thought of that," she said. "I knew you were with him, but I didn't think you still were." Then she walked to the closet and pulled out a picture, handing it to me. "Look, he just gave me this headshot that was taken to promote the Rajneesh Country band. You can have it—he means more to you than he does to me."

I stared at his black-and-white image—his broad smile, his bright eyes. The only words that came to mind were "I hate you." I tucked the picture away, hoping some glimmer of hope could be restored after a good night's sleep. But come morning, I couldn't construct any explanation or fantasy that made me feel any better. I felt powerless, and all I could think was that he discarded me because there was now riper fruit to gratify his needs.

Then came the self-flagellation: Maybe if I were more liberated, walked with a lilt to my hips, lost weight—maybe then I would be good enough. But there was no way I could do all that, and I was sick of trying to compete. Lina won. She was shiny and fresh; I was used goods.

I put on my mask of indifference, doing my best to hide my shame and pain. When Lina came into our room, I ignored her completely. In the privacy of the bathroom, I stared at Milarepa's headshot and wept. Then, in a fit of rage, I tore the photo into tiny pieces. That was it—I was done. Well, almost done.

★   ★   ★

I moped around as privately as I could. Inside, I was tortured, clinging to a tiny thread of hope. Maybe it was too painful to fully let go, or maybe I was just a glutton for punishment. I still wanted my belief in love to be restored, and I wanted to know why I had been forsaken. In true sannyasin fashion, I decided to express myself. I had never asserted myself to Milarepa before. Confronting him in person was too terrifying—so I wrote him a note, saying something like:

Beloved Milarepa,
I have enjoyed all the time we've spent together. Our love is something special. What we have is beautiful. Has something changed
for you? You haven't seemed as interested in me. It would be a
shame to dissect our love like a rose, petal by petal.
   Love, Sarito

Just remembering those words— "It would be a shame to dissect our
love like a rose, petal by petal."—makes me cringe with embarrassment. I
sealed the envelope, wrote his name on it, and gave it to one of his band-
mates to deliver. Then I waited anxiously to see what would happen next.

Several days later, I was hanging out at the dispatch hub in the middle
of the ranch yard. Amid the radio communications from the various construction crews and buses, a pickup truck full of men heading to work
stopped in front of our window. Milarepa waved to me from the back of
the truck. I walked outside. He reached out and handed me a letter. Then
the truck drove off. Not a word spoken. I stood there in the dust, staring at
my name, written in brown ink, on the envelope, tense with anticipation.
Whatever words he had written could make me feel like I was in heaven or
in hell. He had that much power in my universe.

I walked towards the ranch house and down into a ravine where I often
went alone for respite and to smoke cigarettes that I hid in the bushes. I
sat on the ground and opened the letter. It was a page long, written in the
same brown ink. I only remember bits of it. It started by saying that I was
a "beautiful woman" and that he had "enjoyed our time together." I didn't
feel like a woman. I felt like the fourteen-year-old that I was, pining for true
love. He then said it was important to be free, not tied to any one person,
to go with the flow. Then came the kicker, the line I remember verbatim:
"Hundreds of men would give up enlightenment to be with you." I read
that line over and over. It was an utterly absurd statement and complete
bullshit. He ended the letter with: "I'm sure we'll get together soon."

Although the letter was discouraging, I looked for anything I could inter-
pret as encouraging. I found it all so vague and confusing, yet I clung to
every word. It felt like he was trying to flatter me as he drove a dagger into
my heart. I guess he was trying to let me off easy. Maybe it was better to see
myself as an object that "hundreds of men" would want to sleep with than
to feel utterly disposable. My gut reaction was one of insult, but I didn't

listen to my gut. I hung on to the letter and read it periodically as a way of reassuring myself that he at least thought I was, at one time, attractive.

Several weeks later, he invited me home with him for the last time. As we had sex, tears rolled down my cheeks. "What's wrong?" he asked. Didn't he know? I couldn't speak. My heart ached. I knew it was over. One way or another, I had to pry myself away from him and at least try to move on.

CHAPTER FORTY-ONE

MOTHERLY ADVICE?

I HAD STOPPED going to Magdalena for dinner and mostly kept to myself. I avoided the other teens. I didn't trust them. Wasn't there supposed to be some kind of unspoken rule about loyalty, where girls didn't sleep with the men somebody else was with? Clearly not. I aligned even more with the adults, convincing myself I was better off that way.

For a while, my mask of indifference worked, and nobody noticed a thing. But then one of the women in the office looked me over inquisitively. "Sarito, are you okay? You look thin."

I did my best to brush it off. "Yeah, I'm okay, just been busy," I said, smiling as I held back my tears.

"Well, eat more!" she said, smiling and poking at my ribs.

"Okay," I replied, heading to sit at my desk.

Later that afternoon, Vidya summoned me to her room in Jesus Grove. When her chronic back problems flared, she often worked from her bed. I never liked being summoned; you never knew if it would be something minor or a major chewing out. Though I almost never got a chewing out, I was still nervous.

When I arrived, her door was open. She sat on her bed, with two other Moms sitting on the floor beside her. They were in the middle of a serious discussion and didn't notice me for a minute or so. Then Vidya saw me. "Oh, come here, my darling," she said, motioning for me to join her on her bed. I sat down, and she gave me a big hug. Then she put her hands on my cheeks and looked at me carefully with her undivided attention, just like she used to in India.

"You are getting thin. I hear you've been upset," she said. I had been found out. My friend in the office had clearly told Vidya. I must not have been hiding my angst as well as I imagined.

"Yes," I admitted. I felt awkward, like I had failed because I wasn't happy.

I needed to toughen up. I tried to hold it together and repress the sorrow welling in my heart. "I'm doing better now," I said, bursting into tears. She hugged me again.

"What happened?" she asked.

"Sarito is depressed and pining over Milarepa," one of the other Moms interjected. My stomach sank. Clearly my involvement with Milarepa was common knowledge. Vidya looked at me to see if I would nod in agreement. When our eyes met, she could see it was true.

"Oh darling, your heart is broken. No man is worth starving yourself over," she said. "You must eat!"

"Okay," I said feebly. Yes, I could eat, but would that make me feel better? We sat there silently for a few moments. Then Vidya's face lit up like it always did when she had an idea or a solution.

"The best thing you can do is sleep with somebody else," she said. She and the other women started listing names of men they thought would be good for me. I cringed.

"I'm not interested in anyone else," I insisted. But they continued.

"You know Bodha, right?" Vidya asked. Of course I knew Bodha. He was handsome like Superman, and I'd had a crush on Superman ever since I saw the movie. More importantly, Bodha was also sweet.

"Yes," I said.

"Well, you think he's handsome, right?" she asked.

I looked at her shyly. Even talking about men made me uncomfortable. It felt like a taboo subject, like we were plotting something deviant.

"Yes, I think he's handsome," I admitted.

"Okay, then how are you going to arrange to meet up with him? Do you want me to set it up?" she asked, looking me straight in the eye.

"Oh, no, please don't! No!" I said.

"Okay. You arrange it yourself. And by the way, he's well-endowed in the penis department," one of the Moms said. Yuck! What? Was that relevant? How did they even know that? I got the creepy crawlies talking about such subjects.

I had no intention to approach Bodha. But, days later, he approached me, probably on Vidya's urging. When we met up at his trailer, we just hung out, and he played his guitar. He had no interest in my body. I felt rejected and assumed he didn't find me attractive.

CHAPTER FORTY-TWO

SLEEPING AROUND

Maybe Vidya was right; maybe even Milarepa was right—I needed to broaden my horizons and be open to other men. As much as I recoiled at the idea, I was miserable enough to consider it. But my thoughts were muddled. On the one hand, a part of me thought that sleeping with other men would help me break my attachment to Milarepa. On the other hand, I had no desire to sleep with anyone unless we were in love. I wanted it to be special.

At this point, Milarepa was still the only man I had ever slept with but pining and being faithful to him made me feel pathetic. So, despite my instincts, I settled on trying to be more available. I didn't take to strutting my stuff at Magdalena, but if a guy showed interest in me and he wasn't repulsive, I would be agreeable. Over the next few months, I let several men take me to bed.

The first was a mild-mannered Englishman, or maybe he was Australian. He always drove a pickup truck. On the night we spent together, he was on duty at an old farmhouse away from all the hustle and bustle, down Mevlana road near Patanjali Lake. When we got in bed, I lay passive as he had sex with me. I felt no passion, just sadness. In the morning, he dropped me off on the side of the road just before we entered the ranch yard. I didn't want anyone to know I spent the night with him, and he didn't either. I remember the bright sun, mellowed by the crispness of the morning air against my skin. Although I was wearing a flimsy summer dress, I felt naked and exposed. What had I done? I didn't feel any better. I felt worse. I felt used.

Next, it was Milarepa's good friend Vish. I didn't even think he was attractive. When he first asked me to sleep with him, I said no. Then I felt bad for saying no. When he pressed me, I finally gave in, thinking it would be cold and ungenerous if I didn't. Again, I just felt passive through the whole experience. I felt my purpose was to relieve the men of their sexual burdens, with no regard for myself.

In the morning, I was relieved it was over, and we went off in different directions. A few days later, he approached me again. It struck me as odd, as I was sure he could pick up on my lack of engagement. I asked him, "Why do you want to sleep with me again?"

"Because fucking you helped ease my back pain. Really, my back felt great the day after we slept together. I'm worried it will flare again," he said. I rolled my eyes. I was catching on that men used various lines to try to get me in bed, but this was low. Usually, they would say how beautiful and special I was and how they would love to be close to me. This was just utility.

"Why can't you sleep with someone else?" I asked.

"I tried, but it's something about you that helped," he said. Then he added, "And Milarepa thought you would be open to being with me." What a blow. Was Milarepa pawning me off to friends to get me out of his hair? Was this his way of trying to help me move on? I took a deep breath and stuffed the pain, fury, and feelings of worthlessness deep down inside.

My instincts were tugging at me, telling me to say no and walk away. But I couldn't do it. I was so invested in being liked and fitting in that I finally agreed. At least Vish got his physical therapy.

The fourth man was a romantic Irishman, whose approach was much sweeter. We'd take walks together where he'd woo me with romantic poetry and shower me with compliments. But I didn't let most of it in. I had erected barriers around my heart. I no longer trusted sweet talk. So far, it had just been the language of manipulation. The Irishman persisted, wearing away at my resistance. He'd say, "Close your eyes." Then he would start reciting a poem and kiss me. As usual, I was confused. Maybe he really was enamored with me, I thought. Or was he just exceptionally smooth and charming? I didn't know how to read the cues. I played it cool.

Eventually, he took me to bed and had his way with me. When he was done, he said, "That was okay, but you didn't seem that into it." It was true, I wasn't into it at all. I just sort of took it, as it seemed to be the price I had to pay for his companionship. "I still like you, though," he said. That was something, I thought. At least being with me wasn't just about getting off.

A couple of nights later, I saw him going home with another woman, a woman who had been his lover on and off for a while. I figured he chose her instead of me because she was better in bed. Anyway, he had cheated on her by being with me—at least that's how I saw it. But I don't think anyone else saw it that way. There was no real concept of cheating—it was just going with your energy. After a few days he would come back to me, again and again telling me how enamored he was with me. I just followed wherever I was led, usually back into his bed. I didn't get attached; in fact, I wasn't even attracted to him. Soon we drifted apart but remained friendly.

While various men were taking me to bed, others just wanted to make out and fondle my breasts. Usually, it was just a one-off thing, like when one of the lawyers and I remained in the conference room after a meeting. He looked at me, "You are really something," he said. He then leaned in to kiss me as his hand wandered up my shirt, resting on my breast. Then suddenly he pulled back. "I shouldn't do this," he said. Why not, I wondered.

Others, like the Uzi-carrying guard who found me one day on a little back porch at Jesus Grove, didn't feel the same way. Guards often came back there after their shifts. I never really knew what they were doing. Strangely, I never even thought to ask. It just seemed normal, and it was implied that I observe and not speak. In retrospect, it's clear that they were there to load and unload the guns before or after their shifts.

The first time this particular guard found me on the back porch, I froze. I worried he would call me out for sloping or smoking, but he didn't. Instead, he sat down next to me and bummed a cigarette. He started chatting with me, cooing me with his charm. We sat there for a long while. It was rare to just hang out with someone in a quiet place and talk. After that first meeting, it became our thing, a slowly evolving secret tryst.

Each time we met, his sexual advances progressed. First, an arm on my shoulder, then his hand up my shirt. He fondled my breasts for ages as he whispered sweet nothings into my ear. "You are so sweet," "I adore you," "We should get together away from here."

I thought he was in love with me and was keeping our meetings secret because he had a girlfriend. He said he was thinking of leaving her, but if I saw him anywhere else, which was often at dinner with his girlfriend, he would not even nod hello. I'd feel angry at his two-faced deception and felt so dumb for falling for the flowery bullshit. It was the same old thing—I so often read meaning into things where there was none. I wanted love, but I was living in a world of lust and games. It was all smoke and mirrors, and I walked right into it.

As I tried to be liberated, I had a string of one-night stands. None of them were memorable, and I can't even remember some of their names. I felt disgusting, as if each new trespass further tarnished my body and embittered my heart. I had given myself away, or it had been taken away. There was no way to undo it, to remove the slimy shame that encapsulated me, nor to restore the innocence in my heart. With my purity irrevocably ruined, it no longer mattered what men did to me. I just passively went along with whatever came my way. It was a lust-driven culture, and my body, mostly devoid of me, was a plaything.

I even gave in to the smarmy Rama, with his beady eyes and little spectacles. He cornered me one afternoon up the hill in Heraclitus Grove. He begged and begged me to go to bed with him. I said no over and over again. "C'mon, it will be fast," he said. Finally, I gave in, feeling I should be more agreeable. He then undressed me, pushed me to his bed face down, and forcefully probed me anally. When he was done, he laid down beside me. He didn't touch me, he just stared at the ceiling with a grin on his face. I felt broken. Something of him was inside of me like a putrid poison. I missed Milarepa, who at least was loving and tender.

*   *   *

I was in the office when I got a message that Sheela wanted to see all the teens at Jesus Grove. It wasn't often that all of us were called to a meeting on such short notice. I left immediately. I joined some other teens in the ranch yard who were also making their way to Jesus Grove. "Do you know what the meeting's about?" I asked.

A girl with whom I was friendly responded, "It's probably about our party last night."

"What party?"

"You didn't know about it?"

"No," I said. There was a long silence. Maybe she realized I wasn't invited, and she wasn't supposed to tell me about it. Finally, she continued.

"Um, a bunch of us got together and got drunk. Then someone proposed that we play a game where we all wore blind folds and make out with each other, and then guess who it was," she said. That didn't sound like fun.

"Who was there?" I asked.

"Most of the teens, and a few adults," she said.

"Which adults?" I asked.

"Milarepa, Mutribo, and a couple of others," she said. My heart still panged hearing Milarepa's name and knowing he was part of it, but I wasn't surprised. Those were the men who often hung out with the teens. They were probably after a new conquest, trying to get some of the girls in bed.

"Was everyone into it?" I asked.

"At first it wasn't bad. We were all kissing each other and laughing," she said.

"And then?" I asked.

"Then people started having sex with each other all over the place," she said.

"Were you still blindfolded?"

"Yes. We didn't know who we were with," she said. I could sense her hesitation as she continued. "Then Priti removed her blindfold and went ballistic. She discovered she was having sex with Manu."

I gasped. That was way more out there than anything I had heard of before. Sure, I had heard about and seen adult men going home with the teen girls, but this was in a new stratosphere. I imagined Manu's humiliation. He was nerdy and unpopular amongst the girls; I think most of them thought he was gross. Priti was a budding Latin beauty. I imagined her horror when she took off her blindfold to find a boy she found repulsive penetrating her.

"What! That sounds horrible," I said. I felt sick as I ran the scene through my head again and again.

"Yes, it was pretty bad. When Priti freaked out, we all sobered up real fast," she said.

"So, it was like an orgy?" I finally asked.

"Yes," she said. Who in the hell came up with such a crazy idea, I wondered. Everything about it rubbed against my prudish leanings, and yet I was hurt that I wasn't even invited.

We arrived at Jesus Grove and congregated with the others who were already there. We sat and waited for Sheela; the room was devoid of the usual teen banter. I could see dread on many of the other's faces.

Then Sheela entered the room, her face was stone cold. I could tell she was about to spew fury. Without any preamble, she came to the front of the room and began her rant. "I know about the party you had. How could you be so irresponsible?" she said. She went on to scold us for drinking and being rowdy when others were trying to sleep. She hammered in the fact that we were underage and were not allowed to drink—if the word got out, it could cause the commune lots of problems. She told us that we knew better.

I thought the worst was yet to come, but she said absolutely nothing about the orgy, or about the adult men having sex with teenagers. There was a collective sigh of relief for not getting in trouble for the orgy. I was perplexed, but I guess the sex part was okay in her eyes—just a natural part of the culture. It didn't seem she or the other Moms ever wanted to address the subject. It was, in fact, a non-subject.

CHAPTER FORTY-THREE

NOT JUST ANOTHER PRETTY FACE

WHILE TRYING to be open sexually did help me get over Milarepa, it didn't make me feel empowered and free as I had hoped. Instead, I was mired in shame and rage. The more I slept around, the more exploited I felt. The joyful freedom and non-attachment enjoyed by so many adults, and perhaps some teens, clearly wasn't for me. Hearing of the orgy, and of the men who participated, nauseated me. It was bad enough that the other teens were playing the game with each other. It wasn't just that, however; more men had taken to sleeping with the teens. I hated how they seemed to have no consideration of how their "freedom" affected us.

One such example was when one of my roommates had spent the night with one of the men who lived in the same trailer as us. When I ran into him in the morning, he greeted me and then said, "Your friend was a pretty good lay for a teen." I felt my body tense, a wad of rage gathering in my throat. I wanted to punch him and spew words that would cut like daggers. Instead, I swallowed my contempt and said nothing.

I returned to my room to find my roommate curled up under her covers, sobbing. I sat down by her bed. "Are you okay?" I asked. She peaked out and looked at me. Her eyes were full of sadness. My heart swelled with sadness too.

"I did something so stupid," she said.

"Sleeping with Anand? I just saw him." I wasn't going to tell her what he said, that would be cruel.

"Yes," she said. "He had sex with me, and I felt like a piece of meat—like he didn't even know who I was." She paused, tears in her eyes. I understood how she felt. "At least with other men, I felt there was some kind of connection." I wanted to hug her, but I sensed she didn't want to be touched.

"I'm sorry. Stay away from him! He's a slime," I said. I sat at the edge of her bed a bit longer, hoping it would bring her comfort.

While some men were loving when they got us into bed, others were not. Either way, it felt like, more often than not, it wasn't about who we were, but the men "getting their rocks off" as they would say.

So much of the value ascribed to us was skin deep. I wanted to be appreciated for more than my appearance, the firmness of my breasts, or how well I satisfied a man's desires. I couldn't stand that my body and my appearance were what defined me. But who was I really? What talents did I actually have? I had no idea. What I did know is that under my obedient exterior, I had grown bitter and spiky. I resolutely decided I was done with men.

One day, when I was in Portland, I wandered into a shop that sold an array of knickknacks, including round pin-on buttons with all sorts of statements and slogans. For a couple of bucks, you could have a custom button made with your own text. I didn't have a cent, but I perused all the wares when the words "I am not just another pretty face you are trying to deal with" formed in my mind. That's exactly what I wanted to say, not just to the men, but to myself. I was not just a pretty face, and I was resolute that I would stand up for myself and ward off the men. They could try to deal with me, but I would stand my ground and push them away.

However, even if I had the money to have the button made, I doubt I would have had the courage to wear it. If anyone had asked me about it, I would either have played it down as a joke or erupted into a rage. All the fury I had willfully bottled up would come spewing out: You fucking bastards think I'm dumb and pretty. Do you even give a flying fuck about anybody but yourself and your dick?

Unfortunately, blowing up and causing a scene was never an option. The only place to direct my fury was inward. Any outward expression would lead to a reprimand, being told to check my ego and get in line. Or worse, I would be told I was being negative and was polluting the Buddhafield. If I didn't get my act together, I imagined, I could even be kicked off the ranch—the worst possible fate.

I didn't want to tempt fate. Though, sometimes when my anger rose up inside, I wondered what it would be like in the real world. I imagined it as rosy. I liked the idea of living my own life and having money so that I could afford to buy things when I visited shops. On the flip side, I imagined a grim and lonely life where I wouldn't fit in or have friends. Worse yet, I'd have to be among the unevolved masses, not the chosen ones. And if I did end up in the real world, I wondered how I'd survive without basic skills.

CHAPTER FORTY-FOUR

KIDS IN ANTELOPE

THE LATEST hindrance to our progress was accusations that the incorporation of Rajneeshpuram violated the separation of church and state. I had to ask someone what that meant. They said it meant that government and religion should not mix, and a city could not be run by a religion. As usual, Sheela and the Moms were up in arms, and now the lawyers worked non-stop to prove we weren't in violation. First, we claim we're a religion, but now we weren't run by said religion? Nonetheless, if the lawyers didn't succeed, Rajneeshpuram couldn't continue.

Meanwhile, efforts moved forward to take control of Antelope. The motivation, I assumed, was to have a backup city from which the commune could run its businesses if the courts overturned Rajneeshpuram's incorporation. With a majority, the sannyasins who now officially lived in Antelope elected sannyasins to the city council and the school board.

All the younger kids and some of the teens were moved to Antelope to attend Lincoln School. I wondered why. Was it to get them out of the way? Was it a ploy to make the commune look like education was a priority? Or perhaps it was simply to further irk the Antelopians. All the local ranchers withdrew their kids from the school and instead opted to drive them back and forth to Madras each day.

For the time being, I and several other teens slipped under the radar and continued to work on the ranch. The teens who were moved to Antelope were paired with the younger kids in a big brother or big sister arrangement. They were responsible for their little buddy when they weren't in school. They would wake them up in the morning, get them ready for school, meet them after school, have dinner with them, and put them to bed.

It was not an easy task. I know because I filled in for other teens a couple of times. Many of the younger kids were unruly and acting out. The houses where the kids lived were more like dormitories than homes. The living room floors were lined with ten or more mattresses where the kids slept. The six-year-old boy I was to care for was extraordinarily temperamental.

When I arrived in the morning to get him dressed and fed before taking him to school, he stood behind several other boys, seemingly trying to hide behind them. He wore only a t-shirt and no pants. His tow-blond hair stood on end. When I called his name, he froze and stared at the floor. I moved closer and reached out to him. "Come, we have to get you dressed. Can you show me your clothes?" He bolted and ran away from me, erupting into a full-blown wailing fit, tears and snot running down his face, screaming, "No, no, no." I chased him around the room, to no avail. I didn't know what to do, and admittedly, I had no experience calming a child. I only knew how to be bossy, just like the Moms modeled to me.

Telling the boy what to do didn't help one bit. I just sat still for a few minutes, and then approached him again more gently. He had calmed a bit, and I finally managed to get him dressed. Then he peed his pants. He was clearly miserable, and I was most certainly not the person he wanted or needed to see. I was a complete stranger, which must have been scary for him. While I was utterly frustrated and thought he was a brat, I felt sad for him. He needed his mom or dad; he needed to feel safe. There was nothing I could do about it.

Then the word came down from Sheela that all kids had to attend school in Antelope. I didn't know why. I hoped I could get out of it, but no such luck. I wasn't going to get any special treatment this time. Those of us who lived on the ranch were bussed back and forth each day. Now my ignorance would be on full display. I would flunk out, I was sure. Plus, something about having us all attend school seemed curious. Since when did anyone care about our schooling? It seemed like a hoax to prove that we were legit and could run a city and fulfill the municipal responsibilities. The powers that be even hired a non-sannyasin schoolteacher, Mr. Pearson. He looked to be in his early 50s with thinning gray hair and poor posture. He wore blue button-down shirts, khaki pants, and square glasses. He seemed like a kind man, but he was not assertive. I am sure he had never dealt with the likes of us before.

I remember sitting in class while he tried to teach us. He was met by a barrage of interruptions from the smart-asses. Many talked over him as if he didn't exist—as if the fact that he was a non-sannyasin meant he was lesser and didn't merit respect. I don't know why, but I empathized with him. He didn't deserve to be treated so badly.

In time, he managed to break us into groups. I remember being asked to work with others to design a city government. Sheela had just recently paid us a visit where she spoke to us about meritocracy—a society where people were assigned jobs that matched their aptitude. I went with that concept since I couldn't think of anything else.

Within a few weeks, Mr. Pearson was gone. I assume he couldn't take the abuse and disrespect, though I suppose he could have been let go. Once he left, I didn't have to attend any longer and was back at the ranch, floating between Jesus Grove, the office, and everywhere in between, all the while earning school credit.

Now, Sheela and her gang devised a program called "School Without Walls." It provided a legal framework for us teenagers to earn high school credit by working. The notion was, and had always been, that we could get a better education if we learned from experience. Nothing really changed—we all just worked, but now we earned high school credit while doing so.

CHAPTER FORTY-FIVE

AIDS

I N THE beginning of March 1984, everyone was summoned to Rajneesh Mandir for a meeting. Commune-wide meetings were unheard of. The only other times we all assembled were for Satsangs during the world festivals.

People streamed in from every corner of the ranch, taking their places on the floor as speculative whispers echoed through the hall. What could possibly be happening? What new demand would Sheela impose upon us this time?

When Sheela finally made her entrance, she stepped up to the microphone at the front of the hall. Everyone became silent with anticipation.

"Bhagwan predicts that within the next decade, AIDS will kill two-thirds of the world's population," she said. I think we all collectively held our breath. It sounded like the end of the world was coming. Just weeks earlier, all of us kids were instructed to watch the movie *The Day After*. I went to Antelope one afternoon to watch it with the others. It haunted me. After the movie, I walked the empty streets, seeing the desolation through an apocalyptic lens. It took me a couple of days to shake it off.

Sheela continued, saying Bhagwan's prophecy aligned with the prediction made by Nostradamus, the renowned sixteenth century French physician and astrologer. I remembered Bhagwan mentioning him during his discourses in India, but I never really listened or took any of it too seriously. I wasn't sure that I believed in prophecy. This time, it sounded like more than some woeful speculation—there was an actual disease spreading, and it was deadly.

To protect ourselves, Sheela went on to explain, we would all have to adhere to new precautionary measures, effective immediately. The new rules were:

If you feel ready to move to your next level of spiritual develop-
ment without repression, drop sex altogether. If not that, consider being with just one partner.

Kissing, oral sex, and anal sex were forbidden, even in monogamous relationships.

Condoms and rubber gloves were to be used when having sex.
There was to be no exchange of bodily fluids. Gloves and condoms would be stocked in all housing facilities.

Everyone would be tested for HIV.

A silent panic befell the hall. Questions flooded my mind. I wondered
how the new rules would work given all the partner-swapping going on.
Sex had always been so central to Bhagwan's teachings—the epitome of
freedom. How would individuals like Milarepa, known for their indul-
gence in multiple partners, navigate this new way of life? Would he choose
to be with only one woman? Who would it be?

How could so many people who were accustomed to a libidinous lifestyle adapt? Would anyone choose to be monogamous, or would things
just continue as usual, only now with rubber gloves and condoms as armor?

Over the subsequent weeks, I think everyone was tested for HIV. I don't
remember being tested. What I remember vividly is that eleven people
were told they tested positive. I couldn't imagine a worse plight. Those
unfortunate ones were quickly sequestered to Desiderata Grove, isolated
from the rest of the commune. They weren't allowed to mingle with everyone else. If they came to Magdalena, they could only sit together. If they
came to Rajneesh Mandir for Satsang, they had to sit in the back, isolated
from anyone else.

Around this time, a color-coded bead system was implemented. The
beads served two purposes: the first was to indicate your residency status; the second, your STD status. Permanent residents each received a dis-
tinguished brass bead to augment our malas. They were inscribed with
Bhagwan's signature on the front and a number on the back. Short-term
visitors who were participating in various work and meditation programs
were given different colored wooden beads denoting which program they
were in.

All new arrivals were tested for HIV and other STDs. During the time they were waiting for their test results, they wore an orange bead, indicating they were off bounds for sexual intimacy. Those who wanted to be exclusive with one person during the waiting period would each wear two beads, indicating they were in sexual quarantine with one partner. Occasionally, I'd see somebody wearing three orange beads, indicating they were in an exclusive group comprised of three people. When I ran into one of my adult male friends at dinner and noticed his three beads, he seemed embarrassed. He said people teased him about it. On the other hand, maybe some of the men were jealous of his mojo.

In the circles that I moved, specifically the group of men who slept with us teens, I only heard the men scoffing at the new rules, some even admitting they were still kissing and weren't wearing condoms or rubber gloves. As far as the community at large, I think some people took the guidelines very seriously. I do believe most people started using condoms. Moms were watching and enforcing the guidelines. If they found out you weren't following the rules, you would be scolded. I even heard rumors that the house cleaners were told to check the trash for condoms and make sure they had actually been used, and then report their findings to the Moms.

CHAPTER FORTY-SIX

JESUS GROVE 2.0

B Y THE fall of 1984, the ranch's official population had swelled to twelve hundred, though I believe the true number was closer to three thousand, especially with many people participating in the various RIMU programs. The ambitious city-building projects continued unabated by the legal troubles, with crews working around the clock.

The latest additions included a chic hotel near downtown Rajneeshpuram, offering lavish accommodations for the press and visitors. Each room featured round beds with plush bedspreads and private bathrooms. Meanwhile, Jesus Grove expanded significantly—the humble trailer now connected two new wings.

The public area boasted a spacious reception with a kiosk-style desk and a Zen-inspired mural of mountains. A large glass dining table stood near the kiosk, offering a clear view into the industrial kitchen through two service windows. The Moms often gathered at the dining table. Cooks prepared à la carte meals for them at any hour. When I worked in the kitchen, I helped with food prep, sometimes peeling grapes for Sheela or making chai or barley water for the Moms. Several of us took turns staffing the kiosk, answering phones, greeting visitors, and keeping the jar of freshly baked chocolate chip cookies stocked—a popular treat.

The new expansion also included a large meeting room near the front entry. Sheela, Vidya, and other Moms lived in one wing, while key figures occupied the five new rooms behind the kitchen. In total, the expansion housed about fifteen bedrooms and ten bathrooms.

* * *

One morning, I was sitting at my desk in Rajneesh Legal Services when I caught sight of Sheela meandering through the office, chit-chatting and laughing as she went. She rarely visited the office, so it was odd to see her, especially in such a good mood. It was a nice respite from her usual stern demeanor. The lightheartedness in the room reminded me of how things used to be in India—a time of community and celebration before our lives became consumed with work and battles with the government.

Sheela slowly made her way towards me and stopped at my desk. She smiled widely. "How are you, Sarito?" she asked. She rarely asked me how I was.

"I'm good," I replied, smiling back at her shyly.

"I'm moving you into Jesus Grove," she said matter-of-factly. I looked at her, perplexed.

"I want you to share a room with my niece, Anjali. You can look out for her," she explained.

"Oh, okay, I like Anjali," I replied, eager to please. Then she walked away. I took it as an honor that she trusted me to look out for her niece, but I also felt uncomfortable. I was scared of getting a big head. Sheela and Vidya always emphasized that getting a big head was terrible and a sign of someone not surrendering.

On top of that, I feared that living under the same roof as the Moms would mean I would have to be well-behaved amidst only adults. I would be even more separated from my peers.

Two days later, my clothes were relocated to one of the newly constructed rooms behind the kitchen. My new room had two fancy round beds, like those in the hotel, and an attached bathroom. It was so quiet. I felt like an imposter tucked away in a forgotten hallway far from the hub of activity. I felt too out of place to join the others in the dining area, now as a resident, not just a worker. I stayed in my room and unpacked my clothing into neat piles in the closet and waited for Anjali. There was no sign of her, so I took a shower. She never showed up that night or any night after that. I felt a little rejected, like she didn't like me or that I had somehow failed. Then it dawned on me that she might have feared I was part of a scheme to keep her away from her mother. She was only eight.

I assumed that since Anjali wasn't moving in with me, I would be sent back to live with the other teens. Weeks passed, however, and nothing happened. I had a room of my own for the first time since before I went to India, but that didn't last long.

One night I was roused from sleep by an unfamiliar man entering the room. I sat up in bed, startled.

"Who's that?" I asked.

"Sorry to wake you, I'm Ravi," he said. "Weren't you told I would be coming?" He was dressed in blue jeans and a white T-shirt, rather than the customary red attire.

"No, nobody told me." I didn't know him, and I don't think I had ever seen him before. Why was he staying in my room, and why was he dressed as a civilian?

"It's okay, I'm just going to take a shower and go to bed. Go back to sleep," he said. Once he had showered and was asleep, I finally nodded off again.

In the morning, he explained that he was engaged in some investigative work off the ranch that required him to dress as a civilian. As such, he said, he was away a lot. I sensed he was some sort of spy. I had long since known that several sannyasins were involved in covert operations, as I had seen several others report to Jesus Grove wearing civilian clothes. They would meet with Sheela and others and talk in hushed tones. I knew better than to probe further. All I could glean was that they were spying on people Sheela and her gang thought were in our way. I heard a few names, like Margaret Hill, the mayor of Antelope, and John Frohnmayer, Oregon's attorney general, but that was about it. Over the next couple of months, my roommate would periodically return, usually late at night. He would stay a day or two and then disappear once again into the shadows.

★   ★   ★

Jesus Grove became even more of a hub for the Moms. Most of them now lived and ate all their meals there, coming and going throughout the day. The collective vibe grew increasingly heavy, as if an ominous draft had entered. Sheela and her inner circle were always stressed and focused, often not even smiling or saying hello if I sat down at the table. There were more closed-door meetings in Sheela's room, sometimes lasting for hours. Occasionally, I or someone else in the kitchen would bring them food and drink. There was also a lot of whispering in the hallways or into each other's ears.

Concurrently, a shift in the dynamics among those closest to Sheela was underway. Some were rising in favor while others were being knocked down a notch or two, depending, I suppose, on how dedicated they were to her. Those who followed her direction, or whom she liked best, were in her favor. Those in her inner circle gradually appeared more devoted to Sheela than to Bhagwan. If they defied her, they would also be defying Bhagwan since she was his right-hand woman. I imagine if they dared to challenge her, they would be demoted, shamed, humiliated, or even ousted from the commune.

In the Moms' hierarchy, a couple of women in particular seemed to have quickly risen in status. Most notably, Shanti B, an Australian woman, and Puja, an American nurse of Filipino descent. They were constantly by Sheela's side. I don't know what Shanti B's actual position was, only that she was often delivering messages or carrying out tasks per Sheela's directions. Puja oversaw everything medical, including Pythagoras, our medical facility. When she wasn't with Sheela, she was often in her room working, though I was never sure on what.

What I did know is that people would come to the kiosk at least a couple of times a day, sometimes more, asking for her. They would say, "Puja wants to see me to give me a vitamin B shot." I think the Moms got them too. They were supposed to boost your energy. I would let Puja know when someone arrived and then escort the person to her room. She would greet them warmly, saying, "Have you been feeling exhausted? These shots are amazing, and you should have better energy right away." It seemed like a special treat, a kind of thank you to those who had worked themselves ragged.

When she was done injecting them, I would sometimes linger. "Can I have a shot too?" I would ask. I didn't work in the fields, and I didn't really work very hard during the twelve- to sixteen-hour workdays, but I had become chronically tired. I wasn't sleeping well. I often lay awake at night feeling revved up, and when I did sleep, I felt half-awake. My startle response that I'd had as long as I could remember, had only gotten worse. But Puja didn't know all that, and her answer was always, "No, you don't need one."

I drifted around Jesus Grove like a ghost, cautious to stay out of the way and not intrude on all the hushed conversations. It was unpleasant when the Moms went silent when they saw or heard me approaching, only to resume the conversation when I was far enough away. I didn't know why, but I had the eerie sense that whatever I did or said was being monitored. Even when I was cleaning toilets with one of the women, I no longer felt comfortable goofing off, gossiping, or complaining.

I did my best to read the cues, yet on several occasions, as I was heading from the kitchen to Vidya's or Sheela's room at the other side of the house, someone in the hallway would stop me and tell me to come back later. They would then promptly shut the door. On one such occasion, I entered the sometimes-forbidden hallway before anyone stopped me. The door to a room that was always locked and off-limits for cleaning stood open. All I saw was a bunch of electronic equipment and wires. I didn't think much of it. I didn't know what the wires were for. Nonetheless, it seemed I wasn't supposed to know about them. It made me curious, though, and it also made me wonder about what was in the bedroom next door to mine, since it too was locked and off-limits.

CHAPTER FORTY-SEVEN

SHARE A HOME

I WAS WALKING in front of the shops at Devateerth Mall when I saw a group of unkempt men huddled together, wearing non-sannyas clothes. They were bopping and seemingly singing in a talking, rhyming kind of way, taking turns as if riffing off each other. I stood a few paces away, trying to make sense of it. It was a sound wholly unfamiliar to me—a blend of hard-edged beats and spoken word. Little did I know, it was my introduction to rap music, and the men who brought this sound to the ranch had just arrived from the streets of major US cities.

The men I saw that day were just the first to arrive. Over the following weeks, a total of four thousand homeless men from different parts of the country were bussed in as part of the new "Share-a-Home" project. I had never heard of the project before their arrival. Weeks earlier, also unbeknownst to me, the Moms had dispatched sannyasins to walk the inner-city streets of several major cities, enticing them with an opportunity for a fresh start. They were offered free bus tickets, and the promise of clothing, shelter, and medical care. The only requirements were sobriety and non-violence. Surprisingly, they weren't even obligated to work or become sannyasins.

I felt unsettled. There were as many of them as there were of us. They were tough and street smart, and some seemed a little unhinged and rowdy. Our culture appeared gentle and affectionate on the surface, while theirs was hardened by living on the streets. The official word was that the homeless were welcomed to Rajneeshpuram as an act of generosity and charity—an opportunity for a segment of humanity who'd had a rough go at it to have a life-changing opportunity. Something about it seemed amiss, however. It contradicted our usual "me, me, me" or "us, us, us" mentality. So now not only were we a religion, but also a charity?

The newcomers were housed in the A-frames and tents that had been vacant since the conclusion of the Third World Festival. A new cafeteria was constructed near the airport, not far from their living area. They were to live and dine separately from the rest of us, although some of us opted to eat at the new cafeteria due to its proximity to our workplaces.

One afternoon, I accompanied Vidya, Puja, and Sheela to a meeting they held with the Share-a-Home participants. It was an outdoor event where beer and snacks were served. I don't recall the specifics of what Sheela and Vidya said, but I remember the unruly nature of the attendees. I also remember Sheela thanking them, boosting them up. They responded with exuberance and loud cheers. At the end of the meeting, she exclaimed, "Grab another beer and enjoy!" That sounded like a good idea, I thought. I wasn't a regular beer drinker at this point, but it was a sunny autumn day and a beer sounded good. I walked to the table where several plastic cups of beer, just dispensed from the keg, sat. I reached out for one of the cups, but before I could pick it up, Puja, who was dispensing the beer from the keg, stopped me.

"No, Sarito, you can't drink that." I figured it was because I wasn't old enough, and they were now enforcing that rule. I walked back to sit next to Vidya in a huff. A couple of minutes later, Puja joined us. "Sorry about the beer—we put something in it to relax them—that's why you couldn't have one," she said. My eyes widened with surprise, but I quickly neutralized my expression and nodded, indicating I heard her. I didn't really think about it again or wondered what they added. Though I thought it was a strange thing to do, I just accepted her authority and figured it was necessary if they thought it was.

Since the arrival of the Share-a-Home people, it had become commonplace for announcements to be made over the loudspeakers during meals. "Beloveds, if you are of voting age, please remember to vote." What were people voting for? I didn't know anything about governments, elections, or politics. I didn't know how any of that worked. All I knew was that I couldn't vote until I was eighteen, and since I was only fifteen, it didn't concern me. Since the announcements went on and on, I thought it must be really important. Why was voting suddenly such a big deal?

I soon learned that Sheela was trying to get a sannyasin or multiple sannyasins elected to the Wasco County government. On voting day, the Share-a-Home participants were bussed to The Dalles where they were to register to vote, and then cast their votes on the same day. But upon their arrival, the County Clerk decided to block same-day voter registration, saying, "Because I have reason to believe there are organized efforts to fraudulently register people in Wasco County to vote in the November general election, I have decided to do a blanket rejection of all new voter registrations in Wasco County as of now." The Share-a-Home men returned to the ranch. Sheela's plan to take over the Wasco County government failed miserably.

In the meeting Sheela held with the Share-a-Home participants and numerous sannyasins after the election, she denounced the Wasco County officials as bigots. She said the newcomers weren't being treated like human beings who had the right to vote. Her words rallied the crowd, and the angrier she sounded, the louder the crowd cheered. Others in the inner circle, such as Krishna Deva, Rajneeshpuram's mayor, followed suit, spewing similar vitriol when speaking to the media, resembling a rehearsed pundit. Since the real reason the homeless were bussed in failed, they were no longer needed. Just as they were bussed in, they were bussed out to the nearest towns—without money or return tickets to their places of origin. By the end of 1984, almost all of them had departed.

CHAPTER FORTY-EIGHT

BREAKING HIS SILENCE

W E WERE all summoned to Rajneesh Mandir for another communal meeting. This time, Vidya stood at the front of the hall, microphone in hand. She announced that Bhagwan would start speaking again. The overjoyed crowd clapped, some even cried. Vidya went on to say Bhagwan would commence speaking exactly 1,315 days after his silence began. Apparently, the number 1,315 was auspicious, as it was the same number of days he was in silence when he attained enlightenment at age twenty-one. The fact that Bhagwan would now speak for himself again, instead of through Sheela, came as a great relief for many. After all, Bhagwan and his teachings were why most were at the ranch in the first place. Maybe spirituality would once again take center stage.

On October 30, 1984, Bhagwan began speaking to a select group of disciples in his living room in Lao Tzu House. Videos of the lectures were then replayed in Rajneesh Mandir the following evening. Similarly, the videos were sent to the Rajneesh Meditation Centers in Europe, presumably as a means of being more inclusive.

In fact, Sheela had started traveling to Europe to visit many of the meditation centers. She checked up on them and made efforts to help them feel like part of the bigger family. She helped structure the centers much like the setup at the ranch. Each center had a "mom" who ran the place and a number of subjugates under them. The centers were now akin to franchises tied to the ranch, instead of independent enterprises. The European communes ran a number of profitable Zorba the Buddha Discos, bistros, and restaurants. They were required to send a percentage of their earnings to the ranch to keep it running. As a bonus, the members of the European communes, who worked for food and lodging like us, were each given a trip to Rajneeshpuram for the world festivals as a highlight of their year.

It wasn't until seven months later that Bhagwan would speak in Rajneesh

Mandir to the community at large. It was promoted as a major event, set to take place at the Fourth World Festival in July 1985. The festival brochure included a letter from Sheela, announcing that Bhagwan would be speaking again, with her goal surely to draw as many people as possible. She presented it as a blessing that any devotee wouldn't want to miss. It read:

> "We have so much to be grateful for this year. Our beloved master Bhagwan Shree Rajneesh has given us another beautiful gift by starting to speak to us again. He is speaking on His religion as a discourse series entitled the Rajneesh Bible and will give His first discourse in Rajneesh Mandir during the Fourth Annual World Celebration."

CHAPTER FORTY-NINE

THE EXCHANGE PROGRAM

I RECEIVED AN unexpected message that Sheela wanted to see me in her room. The request caught me off guard; I had never been called in to see her before. As I made my way through the maze of halls, my mind raced as I tried to recall anything I might have done to warrant a scolding. I couldn't think of a single thing. When I arrived at her room, I didn't see her or anyone else.

"Hello?" I called out.

"Come in, Sarito, come in," Sheela called from the bathroom. I plastered a smile on my face, did my best to look composed, and entered the bathroom. She was sitting on the closed toilet seat, and a couple of other Moms stood around her. It seemed odd that she was in her bathroom with others, but it wasn't the first time I'd seen it.

"Hi, Sarito," she said, smiling. "We want to send you to Europe. What do you think?" I was puzzled. Did I really have a choice?

"Why? For how long?" I asked.

"We want to give some of the sannyasins from the European centers a chance to come here for six months, so we are starting an exchange program," she said. I suddenly felt tense. My mind went blank. Why me? Was she trying to get rid of me? She went on to explain that twenty others would go too and that we would fly there in our Conveyor. "You and Kaya will be the air hostesses," she added.

"Um, okay," I said tentatively. "I'm glad Kaya is going too." At least I would have a friend my age, I thought.

"Kaya won't be staying. She'll fly there with you and then return," Sheela said. "You'll come back just before the Fourth World Festival." My heart sank, even though I thought I was supposed to be happy—I was being given a unique and special opportunity, or was it a form of punishment? I didn't have the courage to ask why Kaya didn't have to stay in Europe. She was always Sheela's favorite, even though she wasn't the little goody two-shoes that I was. And yet, I was the one being sent away.

"Okay," I said.

"You will leave in about two weeks."

I walked to my room on the other side of the house, feeling like I had been hit by a train. "Keep your chin up, you're okay, you're okay," I repeated to myself. Collapsing was not an option, but I wondered how I would hold myself together without Vidya and the others who always looked out for me and on whom I was so dependent.

A few days later, all of us who had been selected for the exchange program were told which communes we were going to. I was being sent to Munich. We would fly to Cologne, stay at the commune there for a couple of days, and then be dispersed to our respective cities.

As our departure day approached, I felt a blend of dread and numbness. I worried that nobody would even notice I was gone if I wasn't around. I tried to console myself by thinking six months would fly by and that I would come back with chic new European clothes and lots of chocolate to share.

* * *

Kaya and I prepared the Conveyor for departure. The plane once belonged to Howard Hughes. It didn't have rows of seats; it had two couch-like contraptions on either side, leaving us unsure where the nineteen passengers would sit. Why Sheela decided we would fly our own plane instead of flying commercial was a mystery. As I shuffled in and out with supplies, I overheard the pilots discussing fuel concerns. Apparently, due to the plane's tank size, we'd have to stop to refuel five times: twice in Canada, then Greenland, Iceland, and Ireland, before reaching Cologne, Germany. It would take forty-two hours.

The day of departure arrived. The passengers sat on couches or the floor, using blankets as pillows. The engines powered up, louder than the DC3s we flew to Portland, and we took off, the plane feeling like deadweight fighting gravity. Once at altitude, the engine noise remained unrelenting. We served drinks and tried to converse, but the noise made it impossible. The hours passed slowly in a monotonous routine. We left Canada as the sun set, and people made makeshift beds on the floor.

When we finally landed in Cologne, I had been up for almost three days with only a couple of hours of sleep. I don't remember arriving at Uta Rajneesh Meditation Center. The next thing I remember is waking up the next day and being told I was late for a meeting with everyone who was on the flight. Why hadn't anyone woken me earlier? When I arrived in the large room where everyone sat in a circle on the floor, it seemed the meeting was almost over. From the questions being asked, it quickly became clear that the pilots had revealed how close we had come to disaster, having lost radio communication and misestimated fuel usage. I felt a mix of relief and anger. Why was I the last to know, given that I was the one who stayed up for the entire flight? But at least we were alive.

CHAPTER FIFTY

EUROPE

Aꜰᴛᴇʀ ꜱᴘᴇɴᴅɪɴɢ a couple of days in Cologne, a Ma came looking for me at dinner. "Here's your ticket to Munich," she said, handing it to me. "Your train leaves early tomorrow morning." I wasn't surprised by the travel plans, as I knew I would be heading to Munich soon, but such short notice left me scrambling. I wanted to at least say goodbye to Kaya and the pilots before I left, but I hadn't seen them at dinner. They were probably preparing the plane for their return. A wave of sadness washed over me as I realized I wouldn't get the chance to see them before I left.

At dawn, a chipper Ma, with a singsong voice that cut through my sleepy haze, woke me up. "Sarito, time to get up, time to catch a train." I got up in an instant, dressed, grabbed my bag, and met her in the kitchen. She beamed a smile at me, making me feel welcome. "Here, I've made you a travel package," she said, handing me two bags. One held an assortment of juice and water, the other a pile of sandwiches—enough to feed at least three people. On top of the sandwiches were two bars of chocolate. Either Germans ate heartily when traveling, or I was in for a long journey.

"All of these?" I asked.

"Yes, definitely," she said, patting me on the shoulder. "You'll be hungry." Her warmth reassured me. Maybe things were going to be okay. I hoped the sannyasins in Munich would be as nice as she was.

At dawn, a swami drove me in a little minibus to the train station. After he dropped me off, I paused, feeling oddly untethered. I boarded the train, found an empty compartment, and took a seat by the window, reflecting on the whirlwind of the past few days. As others took the empty seats, I avoided eye contact. I felt like an eyesore with my orange clothes and mala. Everyone else wore black.

As the train chugged out of the city, rays of sunlight beamed through the breaks in the clouds. I gazed out the window at the changing landscape, soothed by the thrumming rhythm of the train.

About four hours into the journey, the others in my cabin disembarked. Minutes later, a petite woman with dirty blonde hair, wrestling with a cello, joined me in my cabin. Once she got situated and gently placed her cello next to her like a beloved friend, she smiled warmly.

"Hello," she said. She had a kind face and didn't look like the others who wore stiff business clothes. She dressed like an artist—black clothes with an edgy flair. I envied her confidence and ease—and her clothes. She must be so talented to play the cello, I thought.

"Hello," I replied, feeling tongue-tied and embarrassed at how unhip I looked compared to her.

"Are you headed to Munich?" she asked.

"Yes," I said.

"Me too, I'm playing with an orchestra tonight," she said.

"That's cool," I replied. I wanted to continue our conversation, but I froze up. I didn't know how to engage in normal society. Me and the woman smiled at each other for a moment, and then I resumed gazing out the window and munching on my sandwiches.

Four hours later, we arrived in Munich. The young woman said goodbye and wished me well. We both got off the train and headed in different directions. I made my way out to the Platz in front of the station, where I was told there would be someone to pick me up. I stood there eagerly scanning the crowd for someone dressed in red, as others scurried around me. Nobody was there. For the next half hour, I walked back and forth across the Platz looking for any pop of orange or red. Nobody had come for me. I didn't even have a phone number to call the center, nor did I have any money. Moreover, I didn't speak German.

Just as panic began to set in, I spotted the young woman from the train standing by the curb. She waved, seemingly sensing my bewilderment. As I walked toward her, she asked, "Are you supposed to be picked up?"

"Yes," I responded, a tinge of fear seeping into my voice. "I was told someone would be here, but they're not."

"Where are you going?"

"To the Rajneesh Meditation Center here. I don't know what it's called. I don't have a phone number," I said. She looked concerned.

"I'll help you. I think I can find their number and call them for you," she said.

"Okay, thank you," I felt undeserving of her generosity and blessed once again by the kindness of strangers. With determination, she strode towards a nearby phone booth, somehow procured the commune's phone number, and called them. She spoke to them in German. After a couple of minutes, she returned to me.

"They are on their way. They thought you were arriving tomorrow," she informed me.

"Okay," I murmured. I wanted to cry. "Thank you so much!" She looked at me and gave me a warm hug.

"You're welcome! I'm glad I could help," she said and then walked off to get her ride. For a split second, I wanted to go wherever she was going—I wanted to slip into her world—a world that seemed freer and more independent than mine.

Ten minutes later, a van pulled up to the curb, and a red-clad swami got out and waved his hands in the air to get my attention. I walked to the van and got in.

"Welcome to Munich," he said in a nonchalant tone. Inwardly, I rolled my eyes, thinking, "whatever," as relief mingled with my agitation.

*   *   *

When we arrived at the commune headquarters, the driver grabbed my bag and led me up the stairs to a large office. The setup was similar to the office at the ranch—a sea of desks and a couch for the woman in charge. In this case, the mom in charge was a sturdy German woman who didn't beat around the bush. I didn't even sit down before she said someone would show me where I would be living. Then she announced: "Your job will be to manage the hair salon. You will start tomorrow."

"I don't know how to manage a hair salon," I said.

"You can learn," she said. "Breakfast is from 7:00 till 8:00 and after that someone will tell you how to get there." I was so stunned that I didn't say much at all.

The next morning, I went to the dining hall where I found a buffet with pastries, soft-boiled eggs, cheese, and an array of cereal. It was far more lavish than what was on offer at the ranch. I loaded up my plate and awkwardly found a place to sit alone. I didn't know a single person. I knew I needed to learn to interact but froze even at the thought of it. Admittedly, I was used to people knowing who I was and being nice to me merely because I was associated with the Moms. Now I was on my own. I had no status and scant social skills.

After breakfast, I got directions and walked to the salon a few blocks away. As I made my way through the streets, I peered into the shop windows. Mannequins dressed in beautiful clothes stood elegantly posed, while a patisserie showcased artful sweets, and a chocolatier displayed its decadent creations. Everything seemed so la-di-da.

Arriving at the salon, I introduced myself to an Italian man and a German woman who sat in the salon chairs waiting for walk-ins. He was the hairdresser; she was an esthetician.

"It's pretty quiet here. What will you be doing?" the woman asked.

"I'm going to be your manager," I said. Their eyes widened in disbelief.

"We don't need a manager," the Italian said haughtily. "How old are you anyway?"

"I just turned sixteen," I said. He looked irritated. But the esthetician smiled.

"Always a lesson to go with the flow," she said.

The salon wasn't thriving—only a few customers came each day. But I returned each morning. With little to do, I started barking out orders to clean or organize, just like I had seen the Moms do back at the ranch. They had instilled in me that we must always be working, not slacking off. The Italian, annoyed to have a sixteen-year-old telling him what to do, retaliated. He was an artist, after all. When he couldn't take it anymore, he started ranting.

"How can they send a child to be my boss? I refuse to work here if you're in charge," he spewed. I contracted. Clearly, he was not surrendered, I thought. But his comments hurt. I wanted to be liked.

In the evenings, I stayed in the salon after the others left. I think I was avoiding the dining hall teeming with people I didn't know. So far, people weren't going out of their way to include me, and I wasn't making much effort either.

I turned on the radio and began to clean. Familiar songs like Wham's "Careless Whispers" and Tina Turner's "Private Dancer" played, providing melancholic companionship. As I listened, I thought about Milarepa and how he had screwed me over. I thought about the other men who didn't care enough about me either. Rage welled up inside me, then bored inward, morphing into self-hatred.

After a couple of weeks, the hairstylist left and went to another commune. I wondered if it was because of me. I was called into the office and told that the salon was closing and that I was being transferred to the commune in Berlin.

★   ★   ★

For the next six months, I found myself constantly moving, never staying in one commune for more than a few weeks. In Berlin, Rosie, a jolly British woman who ran the place, took me under her wing, instantly making me feel welcome. In fact, something about her reminded me of Vidya in the days before she was so bogged down with work. In the Berlin office, I was assigned menial tasks that left me feeling utterly bored. I mostly waited for the tea breaks where an assortment of freshly baked fruit breads were served. Sometimes we even had scones with jam and clotted cream. Plus, there was always chocolate. I indulged. I think I was trying to eat away my loneliness.

By far the highlight of my time in Berlin was visiting the disco most nights. I would sip on Sekt and dance to the latest hits. The dance floor was packed mostly with non-sannyasins, but when the DJ played one of our favorite songs, like "Life is Life" by Opus or "Lady Marmalade" by Patti Labelle, the sannyasins working at the bar would abandon their posts and flood the dance floor. We belted out the lyrics and danced with abandon. These songs perfectly embodied the commune culture. "Life is Life" captured the essence of our celebratory, live-life-to-the-fullest attitude, while "Lady Marmalade," with its "voulez-vous coucher avec moi" (do you want to sleep with me) lyric mirrored our casual approach to relationships. However, nobody asked me to go to bed with them. I slept alone, and I liked it.

After a month in Berlin, Rosie called me over to her desk. "Sarito, you're being transferred to Zurich," she said. "You leave tomorrow."

"Why? I am just getting to know people here. I don't want to go."

"Well, you are needed in Zurich. Word came from Sheela." How could I possibly be needed in Zurich? I stood there reflecting on how absurd it was. I knew if the order came from Sheela, then there was no use questioning it. Sitting in the Berlin office that afternoon, a sense of despair washed over me. Was I a burden that nobody wanted?

Another very long train ride later, I arrived in Zurich. The people were very pleasant and especially well dressed. Everything was clean and efficient. I was put to work in the bookkeeping department. I was given a desk amid a large open workspace. Someone put a huge green and white striped accounting ledger and a pile of invoices in front of me.

"Here, you can input these into the ledger and then make sure it balances," they said.

"I don't know how to do accounting," I said.

"It's easy, just put the items in the correct columns." I sifted through the papers, struggling to distinguish debits from credits, feeling increasingly anxious about my ineptitude. I anticipated that I would be found out and reprimanded for doing a bad job. Clearly, the sannyasins in Zurich hadn't been informed about my lack of skills. But nobody ever said anything about my bookkeeping.

In Zurich, I kept to myself. In fact, I hardly remember a single person from my time there. I could feel myself withdraw more into myself, my will to try to engage decreased by the day. All I wanted was to return to the ranch, the place that felt most like home.

The one person I do remember is my friend Rani from the office at the ranch. Sheela sent her to Europe to help set up administrative systems. During her week in Zurich, I asked her to please ask Sheela if I could return to the ranch early. The next day, she found me. "I'm sorry, Sarito, Sheela said you can't go back to the ranch yet. She said to tell you to try harder to join in and surrender to this opportunity." I can't say I was surprised; nonetheless, I felt hurt, and it only hammered home the fact that I had no say in the situation. I would just have to hold on for another four or so months. At the time, it seemed like an eternity.

A few days later, I received news of yet another transfer—this time to Freiburg to work at the Zorba the Buddha disco. The next day, I was off.

Unlike the other communes I had been to, there was no Rajneesh center in Freiburg; all the sannyasins who were there worked in the disco. I was given a job in the cocktail bar. I was shown all the different glasses for the different cocktails, given a tutorial about the various liquors, and most importantly, a recipe book.

First, we would prep all the garnishes for the night; then, when the disco opened, the fun began. I made tequila sunrises with fancy orange garnishes that emulated the sun. I made martinis with an olive, and many other concoctions whose names I don't remember. I mixed each drink following the recipe in the little recipe book, always making a little extra so I could taste-test. As the night drew on and the crowd grew, I became more and more intoxicated. The time flew by. My fellow bartenders and I bopped to the music. At 3:00 a.m., once the disco closed and we cleaned, we all piled into a couple of vans and headed to our crash pad—a large room with numerous beds on the floor.

I enjoyed Freiburg. It was a party every night, and because we were creating a celebratory environment, the other sannyasins were interactive and inclusive. I'm sure drinking cocktails all night also helped bring me out of my shell.

After about three weeks, I got word I was being sent to Amsterdam. No reason was given. I didn't even protest—there was no use. Maybe it was because it didn't look good to have a sixteen-year-old working in a bar, but who knows.

The Amsterdam commune was a lot larger than the small clan in Freiburg. When I arrived at the commune headquarters, a sense of doom set in again. The commune was housed in an old jail, and the cells were now used as accommodations.

The woman who picked me up from the train station showed me to my cell. It was a tiny room with a bunk bed. The bottom bed was occupied.

"Your bed is up top," she pointed. My stomach dropped. The upper bed was very close to the ceiling. I climbed up the ladder and lay down to check it out. I couldn't even sit up without hitting my head on the ceiling. I hated it. I felt claustrophobic. When I met the commune mom, I asked if I could have a different room. She wasn't amused. "That's where you have been assigned," she said. There was no charming her. The rules were the rules.

That night, I lay awake in my bunk, ruminating and tossing from side to side. A bit later, my roommate arrived. He was surprised to find me there.

"Oh, I didn't know someone moved in," he said. "I've been enjoying having my own room. I could bring women when I wanted." I could feel his disappointment.

"I'm sorry," I said. But I wasn't actually sorry. I was thrown by how rude and unwelcoming the people in Amsterdam seemed so far. They were blunt, and I was sensitive. Not a good combination.

I was put to work doing construction. I was even tasked to help break up a concrete floor with a jackhammer, but when I hurt my back, I was assigned to painting. I hated it there. I counted the days till I could go back to the ranch. I had made it five months; I could manage a few more weeks.

CHAPTER FIFTY-ONE

BACK AT THE RANCH

AT THE END of June 1985, I arrived back in Portland along with the members of the Amsterdam commune who were headed to the Fourth Annual World Celebration. As our bus reached the high plains where the sky stretched open, I exhaled with a profound sense of relief. The past six months were finally in the rearview mirror.

When we passed through Antelope and began our descent to the ranch, the familiar rock outcroppings and panoramic vistas evoked a bittersweet nostalgia. I recalled sitting in the back of Glenda Harvey's Ford Bronco three and a half years earlier, when I still believed in fairy tales with happy endings. Back then, I had imagined an idyllic homestead or the Marlboro man astride his horse. Now, though the landscape looked the same, nothing felt the same. I worried that things had changed even more during the time I was away.

When we all got off the bus in the middle of the ranch yard, I looked around, hoping somebody, maybe even Vidya, would be there to welcome me. But I didn't see anyone I knew, only festivalgoers moving in every direction. I felt lonely and forgotten.

I assumed I would still be living in Jesus Grove, but a Ma with a clipboard approached me and asked for my name. She looked at the list and then told me I would be living in one of twenty or so new townhouses in Lao Tzu Grove. Not Lao Tzu House where Bhagwan lived, but at the mouth of the valley to his compound, about halfway between the ranch yard and Magdalena. I was too jet lagged to say anything, so I just grabbed my bag, got on one of the yellow school buses, and was dropped off near the new site. Where there used to just be a few mobile homes, there were now several rows of beige, boxy townhouses.

I found my way to my new room. There were two beds on the floor. One was clearly occupied, but I didn't know by whom. I opened the closet to find my belongings arranged on the shelf that someone had moved from Jesus Grove. Besides my clothes, I didn't have much else. But when I saw my miniature teddy bear, Melinda, the only stuffed animal I still had since before we went to India, I smiled to myself. As I looked through my clothes, I was reminded of the letter Milarepa had written me that I had put in the folds of one of my sweaters for safekeeping. As pathetic as it was, I occasionally still pined and read it. Part of me still took what he wrote as a compliment, though I really wasn't that dumb.

I pulled the sweater from the pile. The letter wasn't there. I was puzzled. It had to be there somewhere—I had been so careful to place it where it would be safe. Agitated, I pulled everything off the shelves into a pile on the floor. I then shook out every single piece of clothing. The letter was gone. I grew tense with anger, the adrenaline piercing through my jet-lagged haze. How dare anybody go through my stuff and take what was mine, I fumed. And anyway, why would anybody take my letter? Did whomever moved my stuff just decide to throw it away? Then it struck me, there really was no privacy, though this seemed downright invasive. I put my clothes back in the closet and lay down on my bed.

Hours later, I woke up when my roommate arrived. It was Prema, an Indian girl my age. Her mother was one of Bhagwan's first disciples, and as such, ranked high on the spiritual hierarchy. Despite Sheela's pervasive power, Bhagwan still had a group of special devotees, to whom he gave special attention, like stopping his car and talking to them for a few moments at drive-by. As such Sheela didn't have total power over them.

Prema and I barely knew each other. She had always seemed quiet, serious, and aloof—a lot like me. She was part of the spiritual clan, while I was part of the administrative clan. I thought I was beneath her since I wasn't very spiritual and didn't mingle with the women in Lao Tzu House like she did.

She said hello, and we spoke for a few minutes. She was friendly enough. I could tell she was sensible and respectful, and I wouldn't have to worry about her borrowing my clothes. I also sensed we wouldn't become best friends.

★　★　★

I didn't know where I was supposed to work, so the next morning I headed to Jesus Grove. As I approached, I noticed an ugly barbed wire fence had been installed around the compound. It struck me as odd. When I entered, everything was humming along as usual. Sheela and several other Moms sat at the large table by the kiosk, deep in conversation.

When Sheela saw me from across the room, she called out to me. "Hi, Sarito." The others looked up, half-smiled, and then resumed their conversation. I timidly moved closer. "You doing fine?" Sheela asked.

"Yes," I responded.

"Good!" she said. "You can come back to work here."

"Okay," I said, conscious that staying longer would be taking up too much of her time. I wanted to ask her where Vidya was. I thought I would have seen her by now. I wondered why she hadn't come looking for me yet. A knot was forming in my stomach—didn't she care about me anymore?

I entered the kitchen. The same people I used to work with stopped what they were doing to give me hugs, cheerfully saying, "Welcome back! Good to see you." I felt so relieved to be back with people I knew and who cared about me that I was moved to tears.

I got right to work chopping veggies with Shara, an American woman with voluminous curly black hair and no filter when it came to speaking her mind. We had worked a lot together in the past, mostly cleaning bathrooms, which was much more fun to do together than alone. After a few minutes of silence, she looked me right in the eye.

"Are you okay?" she asked. I was on the verge of tears again. She must have sensed my unease and how disorienting reentry was for me.

"Where's Vidya?" I asked. She paused for a long moment, her smile replaced with a grave look of concern.

"Vidya's been very ill. She's been in isolation for months," she said. The words hit me in the heart.

"What's wrong with her? Will she be okay?" I asked.

"I don't know. I haven't seen her. Nobody talks about it. We just make her meals that Puja and others bring to her. Nobody else is allowed to see her," she said. An eerie fear coursed through me. What was going on? She had always been my anchor, even if she was often too busy to give me the attention I longed for. So many questions raced through my head. I wanted to do something but knew I had to keep my mouth shut. I probably already knew more than I was supposed to.

Soon after that, I learned that Ira, as well as a few other notable people, had left the ranch while I was in Europe. I didn't understand why. Nobody talked about it except to imply they must not have been real sannyasins. It took immense courage to leave, I thought, since they would be blacklisted by Sheela and her gang. Mostly, I was sad they were gone. I would miss Ira, the steadiest person I knew. I hoped she would decide to come back.

★   ★   ★

The Fourth Annual Festival commenced in Rajneesh Mandir. We all sat on the floor, waiting with anticipation—after three and a half years of silence, Bhagwan was about to speak publicly again. His Rolls-Royce limousine pulled up behind the podium at the front of the hall. He came into sight dressed in his full regalia: an opulent robe with a matching hat and a glistening diamond watch. He slowly made his way to his throne. What struck me most was how frail he appeared, as if he was only partially inhabiting his body. He sat down, closed his eyes, and delicately placed his hands in an esoteric position in his lap.

A few minutes later, he opened his eyes, and a woman read the first question, just as she did in Pune. Then he spoke. I don't remember the question nor what he said. I was fixated on his speaking pattern. His uniquely slow cadence, punctuated by long pauses, which I remembered from Pune, was now certifiably languid. His intonation lacked the passion and animation I remembered. The twinkle in his eye was dimmed by his droopy eyelids. It appeared as though his health had waned, as if inhabiting his physical form had become arduous. He had previously said that as an enlightened being, he had no need to remain in his body, and that he was only staying for the sake of his disciples.

Despite his frailty, Bhagwan spoke each morning of the festival and continued even after the festival was over. We all now went to discourse each morning before we started our workdays. I usually sat in the back of the hall, where it was spacious and where I didn't feel guilty for spacing out. The soothing rhythm of Bhagwan's voice lulled me in and out of consciousness. I only took in fragments of what he said.

However, on one particular morning, I was abruptly jolted out of my stupor by the mention of a name—Milarepa.

The woman who posed the questions to Bhagwan read aloud, "Beloved Bhagwan, the other day I fell in love with Milarepa. It was so beautiful, but after ten minutes it was gone. Bhagwan, is that the way things really go?" After a long silence, he responded.

> "Lolita, I wonder that the love affair continued for as long as ten minutes. With Milarepa, things are more speedy. Of course, this is the way things really go. But with Milarepa they go with express speed. His love affairs are just hit and runs." Laughter erupted throughout the hall. He continued. "He is really a great guy—my musician. Only the music seems to be his really permanent love affair."

I tightly gripped my knees to my chest as if to curl into a ball and hide. I felt humiliated. I felt so stupid for innocently walking into the arms of the person who everybody, even Bhagwan, knew to be the most notorious womanizer. Everyone else was laughing. I just couldn't accept or laugh off his behavior as if it was normal. I had been drawn into his web under the pretense of genuine care, adoration, and love. I had been played.

Bhagwan continued speaking, telling jokes, and assuring the woman she would fall in love again, saying there were many "Milarepas." Yes, there were many aspiring to seduce women, and some admired and envied Milarepa's womanizing. One man even asked Bhagwan what he was doing wrong, and what did Milarepa have that he didn't.

During yet another morning discourse, Bhagwan spoke of Milarepa again, saying "He is certainly a personality like Lord Byron, in that even though he goes with so many ladies, no lady feels offended. They all accept that he is such a person that you cannot possess him."

Accept it? I didn't accept it. But clearly, I was supposed to. I was supposed to see my time with Milarepa as a beautiful fleeting experience and nothing more. Couldn't somebody have warned me?

CHAPTER FIFTY-TWO

LONELINESS

WITHOUT VIDYA, my sense of being valued and important had evaporated. I now had to navigate my own path. When I was immersed in work, I managed well enough. But in the evenings, as others mingled and socialized, I felt adrift. Sometimes, I would sit on one of the benches in front of the shops at the Devateerth Mall, observing the ebb and flow of people. Occasionally, I would attempt to interact with acquaintances at Magdalena at dinnertime. Yet, I felt a pervasive sense of disconnection, as if an oppressive fog followed me everywhere. It was the same melancholy that had clung to me in Europe, which I had hoped would dissipate once I returned to the ranch. It stubbornly lingered. I didn't have the tools to deal with it. I suppose having a more supportive environment during my developmental years would have helped.

On the nights of the teen discos, I forced myself to attend and try to reconnect with my old friends. We'd exchange greetings, but then they quickly clustered into their tight-knit groups. Their bonds had strengthened in my absence, both during my time in Europe and over the years I spent isolated in the office, perched on my high horse. I yearned to belong again, but it felt like an impossible feat. I convinced myself they no longer liked me, and my heavy-hearted demeanor certainly didn't help matters. Nevertheless, I kept pushing myself to go, at least to dance and try to be a part of their world again.

It was at the disco that a teen, I can't remember who, walked up to me with a sense of urgency.

"Do you know why Kaya and Gita left?" they asked. I was stunned.

"What? They left? When?"

"Last night. All I heard is that they were going to California," they said.

"I didn't know they left. I'm in shock."

"I know, it's crazy. We're all in shock," they said.

"Why did they leave?" I asked.

"I don't know. I hoped you'd know," they said. I really didn't understand. I couldn't make sense of it. They hadn't even said goodbye. Nobody seemed to know any of the details. That was that. They were gone, and nobody talked about it, at least not to me. I was too intimidated to ask Sheela if she knew why they left. Meanwhile, Ira was also gone, and Vidya was somewhere in isolation, so I couldn't ask them either.

★ ★ ★

I was walking away from the mall when I was startled by a man's voice calling after me. The voice wasn't wholly unfamiliar. "Hey, Sarito," he called again. I turned around. It was Mutribo, the tall, dark-haired British man who was part of the "cool guys" that included Milarepa and Vish—the group of men who were chummy with many of the teenagers. He was the one who had gone to Eton and infused their conversations with off-color jokes and quick banter. He'd barely given me the time of day before. The only time I remembered talking to him was when he sat with me and Milarepa at breakfast many months earlier. He looked at my breakfast of two fried eggs and a piece of toast and told me a joke. "Sarito, what's the difference between an egg and eating a woman out?" he asked.

"What?" I replied.

"An egg only gets laid and eaten once." I just rolled my eyes. I had long since learned to go along with things, no matter how off-color. It wasn't dissimilar to calling Milarepa "the rapist," as if it was a loving pet name. Now, Mutribo was standing in front of me, and I didn't know what he wanted. He had never sought me out.

"Hi, Mutribo," I replied.

"What are you doing tonight? Do you want to get together?" he asked. I was taken aback. I had always figured I was way below his level. Not to mention, I knew he had been in a relationship with another girl who was a couple of years younger than me, on and off for years. It seemed serious.

"I don't know. I think I may go dance at the kids' disco," I said. I wasn't quite sure what to make of his invitation. Why was he suddenly interested in me? Was he just being friendly, or did he want to get into my pants? The same old question.

"I'd like to get to know you. I don't know why I've never spent more time with you. You are such a beautiful girl. Please meet me at the disco tonight," he said. I admit, I was intrigued. I felt a surge of exhilaration. I could feel the chemistry between us that I had never noticed before. As far as grown men went, he was handsome and charming, but I was still determined to stay away from all men who chased me, and I had been succeeding. In fact, since my return, I hadn't received any attention from men. As much as I despised being sexualized, feeling invisible was even worse. I attributed the lack of interest to my ornery mood and the ten pounds I had gained in Europe from indulging in too much bread and chocolate. While I still didn't want to sleep with anyone, my loneliness gnawed at me.

"I'll think about it," I said and walked away.

"See you later," he called after me in a playful tone.

I spent the rest of the afternoon ruminating. I considered that maybe he really liked me; maybe he saw something genuine in me. Or he could just be another player. By day's end, I decided it was wiser to stay away. I went home early and was in bed before 9:00 p.m.

I don't know what time it was, but I woke up to the sound of a knock on my door. Half asleep, I muttered, "Yes, who is it?" The door swung open, and there stood Mutribo.

"What are you doing here?" I asked.

"I looked for you at the disco. I waited for you. Why didn't you come?" he asked.

"I said I wasn't sure. I just didn't feel like it," I said.

"I went there to be with you. I really wanted to connect with you," he said. I felt both flattered and uncomfortable. "Can I stay with you tonight? We don't have to have sex." I was silent. Would I be walking into another tragedy? I wondered what happened with the other girl he was involved with—was he seeking me out to get over his feelings for her?

"I don't know," I said. He came and sat at the end of my bed. He reached out and held my hand.

"I think you're amazing. I don't know why I didn't notice you before," he said, his voice so warm and caring. Yearning swelled in my heart.

"I'm staying away from men. I don't want to fall for you, so it's probably best that you leave," I said.

"I know you were in love with Milarepa," he said.

"Yes, and I don't want to go through that again," I said.

"So don't fall for me, just enjoy my company," he said with levity. We sat there for a long while as I pondered. Living in the moment was what we were all encouraged to do. It was supposed to free us from suffering. It hadn't worked for me before. Maybe I needed to embrace the moment and try again. I was torn. If I said no, he would see me as uptight and wouldn't want to hang out again; if I said yes, I was risking being duped and misled again.

"Okay," I said, finally.

He took off his clothes and got into bed beside me. He held me, and then we went to sleep. Even though he had already said we wouldn't have sex, he apologized that he didn't have enough energy for it, as if I would be offended. I was relieved. I was off the hook for the moment. I thought he must really like me if he was willing to spend a whole night with me without having sex. I had never done that before.

The next morning, we got up, showered, and caught the bus to Magdalena for breakfast. Were we an item? I was already somewhat smitten. But I remained on guard. One thing I learned was not to seem too eager or attached. I was determined to play it cool and not let my heart get crushed. The only problem was, vulnerability was just beneath the surface, and my heart didn't listen to logic.

Over the next couple of months, I saw Mutribo regularly. The first time we had sex, I was nervous. But after a few times, I let go and even found it pleasurable. I was falling for him, but the more vulnerable I became, the more he retreated. So I hid my affection the best I could. If I played it cool, he pursued me with vigor. He'd even come find me in the middle of the day, and we would sneak off. He got a thrill by having sex in the strangest places, like at Bhagwan's father's grave site off of one of the side roads. I liked the thrill of being with him. He would passionately remove my clothes and then have his way with me in whatever position best suited the location. When he was done, he would often look at me standing or lying there naked. "You know, we could make a fortune if we made porno movies together," he would say.

"No way, that's crazy," I would retort. I didn't think he was serious.

"Really, if we ever find ourselves not here at the ranch, we would make great movies," he said. That was ludicrous—I didn't think we would ever leave the ranch.

CHAPTER FIFTY-THREE

PRESS MEETINGS

Now that Bhagwan was speaking, he agreed to be interviewed by various prominent journalists from around the world. The site for these meetings was the Jesus Grove conference room, which could seat about fifty people.

Because of Bhagwan's health issues, everything had to be immaculate. In the afternoons before his arrival, the Jesus Grove staff and I thoroughly cleaned the room, right down to dusting every slat of the mini blinds. I was also given the special task of preparing a fruit bowl that sat on the table beside the journalist's chair. I thought it an honor to have my creations on display for Bhagwan to see, even if it was just fruit artistically arranged in a silver bowl.

When Bhagwan arrived in front of Jesus Grove most afternoons, he was greeted with the customary enthusiasm. Musicians played, our camera-man maneuvered in front of him, and a horde of invited devotees stood along his path, beaming, dancing, or jumping up and down. As he walked, he would stop in front of someone, raise his arms, and thrust them in the person's direction, as if showering them with his rarified essence. It was the closest thing to the energy darshans he gave in Pune, though now he didn't touch anyone, and the time he spent on any individual was brief. Nonetheless, those who received his undivided attention were ecstatic.

Much to my surprise, one day, as I stood in the hallway clapping to the music, Bhagwan stopped in front of me. He smiled and thrust his arms toward me. I jumped up and down, as I had seen others do. As the music got faster, I jumped faster. I remember thinking, Put your all into it. I thought I was so lucky to get that direct attention, that I better not ruin the moment. I didn't think Bhagwan even knew who I was, and maybe he didn't, but nonetheless, he picked me out of the crowd that day—which was a great honor. I think it was more of an ego boost for me than actually feeling blissed out by his energy. Everyone around me looked at me with awe when it was over.

* * *

The first time I saw Vidya was as the crowd dispersed after Bhagwan had entered Jesus Grove. She stood two hundred feet away next to Bhagwan's car. She appeared gaunt, to the point of resembling a different person. Yet, I recognized her from her blond curly hair and posture. I called out to her, "It's me, Sarito," and headed straight toward her. She didn't seem to recognize me. She looked at me, appearing bewildered.

I stood before her, anticipating a warm welcome-back hug, but she continued to look at me blankly, as if I were a ghost. Or perhaps she was the ghost. "It's me, Sarito. Do you remember me?" I asked. She gazed at me intently, scrutinizing every nuance and freckle of my face. Finally, a faint smile crept onto her lips, as if summoning whatever soul remained within her.

"Oh, yes, Sarito. I do remember you," she said meekly. A profound sorrow gripped my heart. The woman whose strength and vivacity had given me a sense of safety was now only a wisp of her former self. It was like 80 percent of her was gone. With all my might, I held back the tears that were on the verge of erupting. I didn't want to add to her burden. She looked at me again. "Ok, I'll see you soon," and then walked feebly towards the house.

After that, I didn't see her much. She was no longer in isolation, but rarely left her room. When I did see her, I was careful to be contained. Her demeanor seemed so fragile, like she got no pleasure out of being alive. Though I had no idea what had happened to her, it clearly had a profound effect on her.

Something felt off—I could sense it deep in my bones. Initially, I dismissed it as my imagination, attributing it to the shift in perspective from being away. However, as the weeks unfolded, I couldn't shake the eerie feeling that gripped me. And now seeing Vidya in her current state only amplified my unease. It wasn't just her; other peculiarities stood out—the ominous barbed wire fence encircling Jesus Grove, the sudden departure of my friends, and the Moms' solemn and almost robotic demeanor. They moved with an urgency and secrecy reminiscent of undercover spies. What were they hiding? And where was the joy that once permeated the halls, at least some of the time.

CHAPTER FIFTY-FOUR

IN THE DEAD OF NIGHT

I WAS WORKING in the Jesus Grove kitchen when I suddenly became so dizzy and nauseated that I had to sit down. The symptoms came on rapidly and almost violently. It was not like any other sickness I recalled ever having. Someone hurried off to fetch Puja, who arrived moments later and asked what I was feeling.

"Everything is blurry, and I feel wobbly," I said, trying to keep my voice steady despite the concern in her eyes.

"You need to go to the sick ward where you can be taken care of," she said firmly. "I'll take you now." Ten minutes later, I was at the sick ward, whisked into a bed, hooked up to an IV, and told to rest. I lay there staring at the ceiling, as chills and nausea came in waves. "The IV should kick in soon, and you'll start feeling better," Puja assured me.

Hours later, I awoke from a long nap, feeling strange. My arms ached, and my legs felt heavy, as if everything was moving in slow motion. Whatever was wrong with me was unlike anything I had ever experienced. I sat up, placed my feet on the floor, and attempted to stand. It felt like my legs were too weak to hold me. The nurse came to my side and helped me to the bathroom and back.

"Can I go outside for a minute?" I asked her, needing a change of scenery.

"No, Puja says you have to stay in bed," she replied, leaving no room for negotiation. Puja was way at the top of the Moms' hierarchy, so there was no challenging her.

I lay there for several days, barely eating or drinking, sustained only by whatever was in the IV. Each afternoon, Puja visited me, treating me like a VIP patient, checking on my condition, and personally tending to my IV. Just when I thought I was starting to feel better, the haziness and nausea would descend upon me again.

After several days, I opened my eyes to see Vidya standing by my bed, looking like an apparition from a dream. I sat up, surprised, and touched by her presence. "Hi," I said softly.

"I just wanted to check up on you and see how you were feeling," she said, her voice filled with genuine concern.

"I feel weak," I admitted, my voice barely a whisper.

"My darling, you are going to be okay. You are strong and capable," she said, her words soothing me. I wondered if my illness had been severe enough to prompt her visit. What was wrong with me? I looked at her, my heart swelling with emotion. I was so relieved to see her more vibrant and spirited. She seemed like herself again. She reached out and squeezed my hand. "Remember, you are very dear to me. You are going to be okay."

The next morning, I awoke feeling almost normal. The haziness, nausea, and heaviness had vanished as quickly as they had appeared. The nurse removed my IV and told me I could leave. Just as I was getting dressed, someone burst into the trailer, looking stunned.

"Sheela and her gang are gone," she exclaimed. The nurses and I gathered around her, the air thick with tension.

"Left for where?" one of the nurses asked, her voice laced with disbelief.

"They left in the middle of the night on a private plane," she said.

"Was Vidya with them?" I asked, my voice trembling.

"Yes, all the top Moms from Jesus Grove left," she replied. The news didn't compute. They must have just been taking a trip together, I reasoned, though that seemed odd. Whatever the reason, I believed they would surely return. As my mind raced with possible explanations, my body tensed with dread. If they were leaving, surely, they would have told me. Then it dawned on me—Vidya's visit must have been her way of saying goodbye, just not in so many words.

As the others continued to discuss the scant information they had, I slipped out of the trailer and made my way to the ranch yard. The vibe was noticeably different. People walked hurriedly, and as they passed me, they repeated the news, "They're gone. The Moms are gone." A few people were standing together, talking about it. When I approached them, again the same news. "Sarito, Sheela, Vidya, and thirteen other Moms are gone," one of them said. A knot formed in my solar plexus, my breathing growing shallow.

"When are they coming back?" I asked, desperation creeping into my voice.

"They aren't," she said. I quickened my pace and made a beeline to Jesus Grove, dread mounting with each step.

I entered the reception area, a place where I was once an insider, to find a flurry of people gathered around a woman who now sat where Sheela used to sit. Her name was Hasya. She was known mostly for being very wealthy and part of a group of other wealthy sannyasins we called the "Hollywood crowd." Sheela had never seemed to like them, yet Bhagwan did. The "Hollywood crowd" had generously gifted him Rolls-Royces and some of his diamond watches. In turn, Bhagwan knew who they were and gave them special attention, including private meetings with him. I imagine Sheela felt threatened and saw them as competition for Bhagwan's favor.

I made my way over to a woman I knew from the kitchen. "What's going on?" I whispered, my voice barely audible over the murmur of the crowd.

"Hasya's Bhagwan's new secretary. Sheela is out," she said. The knot in my solar plexus tightened. It began to sink in—the Moms were actually gone. So much of my life had been ripped away from me in just one night.

I looked around for something or someone familiar. I had spent thousands of hours in the very room where I stood, but I felt like a stranger amid the new regime. I didn't know what to do or where to go. I needed to occupy myself with something lest I implode. I don't know where I went, but I must have gone to my room, and I must have talked to numerous people. I have no recollection.

*   *   *

The next thing I remember is being told to go to Jesus Grove for a kids' meeting. I made my way to the large deck just outside the kitchen and sat among the others who were gathering. I stared into the sky, barely aware of the conversations around me.

"Hi everyone," I heard a familiar voice say. I looked up to see Ma Arup standing before us, squinting in the sun. She must have been asked to step in since the Moms left. She had been one of Laxmi's assistants in Pune but was not part of Sheela's posse.

"As you probably know, Sheela and her inner circle have left," she said. I pulled my legs tightly to my chest, trying to hold myself together.

Every time I heard the news again, I found it hard to breathe. I braced myself for what she would say next. She spoke for at least fifteen minutes. I missed many of the details, but I did hear her main message clearly: she assured us that things would be much better with new people running the show.

When the meeting was over, the others dissipated. I could hear them chatting with each other. I sat a bit longer, in a daze. Then I felt a hand on my shoulder. It was Arup. I stood up, and she looked at me. Tears welled in my eyes as I fell into her arms. I barely knew her, but she was still familiar and had known Vidya well. I felt comforted by her warm hug. After a few seconds, I pulled myself away from her chest. She looked at me again, her eyes filled with empathy.

"Vidya wanted me to tell you goodbye and that she hasn't forgotten about you," she said. She gave me another reassuring squeeze on the shoulder and walked away. Tears streamed down my face. My heart hurt, as if it had been physically crushed. The pain felt unbearable.

CHAPTER FIFTY-FIVE

CRIMES REVEALED

IN THE AFTERMATH of Sheela and her inner circle's sudden and secretive departure, a tidal wave of rumors circulated through the commune, revealing a litany of alleged criminal activities. Conversations fixated on their misdeeds, each passing remark more shocking than the last. "They embezzled millions of dollars," one voice claimed. Another chimed in, "They poisoned Devaraj, Bhagwan's doctor." And yet another revelation was of a massive wiretapping operation, allegedly set up, in part at least, to spy on the "Hollywood crowd." It turned out Sheela didn't just dislike them—she loathed them. Now they were running the show.

As I absorbed the shocking and bewildering insinuations, my grief over the Moms' sudden absence intensified. The realization that the women who had served as my role models for the past seven years could be involved in such heinous acts left me feeling bereft and disoriented. I grappled with the reality that I had unknowingly borne witness to some aspects of their crimes. I had placed my trust in them, obediently following their guidance without question, suppressing any inkling of doubt or suspicion that dared to arise. Based on all the secret meetings, the guns, the sannyasins coming to Jesus Grove in civilian clothes, and the wires I saw, the accusations rang true.

On September 16, 1985, just two days after Sheela and her inner circle departed, Bhagwan called a press conference. Bearing visible signs of exhaustion and weariness, he appeared before all of us and the eager reporters in Rajneesh Mandir. His eyes carried the weight of hurt and betrayal, challenging my assumption that an enlightened being was above such emotions. I thought he was supposed to have transcended the Maya, the illusion of life.

He began by stating, "This is a moment of great rejoicing for my commune. I have been silent for three and a half years. The people who were in power took advantage of my silence." I found it peculiar that he claimed no knowledge of the actions implemented during his silence and was using it as an alibi. Sheela had visited him every evening, consistently asserting that her every move had been directed or approved by him. While I could imagine that Sheela could twist facts and actions to suit her own agenda, the idea that Bhagwan knew nothing was inconceivable.

He continued, saying, "The moment their airplane left, immediately people started coming, saying so many things that they have done while I was in silence, that it seemed, listening to them, that instead of being a meditation commune they had turned it into a fascist concentration camp." He referred to them as the "Fascist Gang" and said he himself had requested that the authorities be called in to investigate.

Bhagwan confirmed every allegation: the wiretapping, the alleged embezzlement of an astonishing $55 million, and the poisoning of his own doctor. The attempted murder of Bhagwan's doctor had taken place after discourse one morning. Shanti B, one of Sheela's closest allies had stabbed him with a syringe of poison. He was rushed to the hospital and survived, but just barely. The revelations didn't stop there. The scope of the poisonings expanded, shocking me to my core. Bhagwan revealed that his dentist, his confidant Vivek, and even a Jefferson County district attorney named Mike Sullivan had also been poisoned. Nobody died.

I soon learned that the incident involving Mike Sullivan had taken place two and a half years earlier, in February 1983. The realization that this darkness had plagued the commune long before its recent exposure was unsettling. I pondered whether Sheela and her cohorts actually intended to murder Mike Sullivan, or if their aim was simply to incapacitate him, as a means of asserting their power and instilling fear.

The authorities also revealed that the wiretapping schemes were more elaborate and extensive than initially thought. Sheela's gang had bugged not only the "Hollywood Crowd," they had also bugged all the phones at the ranch and even planted bugs in Lao Tzu, Bhagwan's own house. As such, Bhagwan claimed that he himself had fallen victim to their manipulation, revealing that they had bugged his own room.

When questioned about Sheela's whereabouts, Bhagwan suggested she was likely in Switzerland. She had recently married Swami Dipo, a Swiss man. When I first found out about their marriage, I found it peculiar since Dipo was gay. Now Bhagwan explained that the marriage was a strategic move on Sheela's part in order to secure Swiss citizenship. Switzerland didn't have an extradition treaty with the US at the time. Sheela must have expected what would come after her departure and carefully planned her escape.

Bhagwan delved deeper into Sheela's motives, claiming that she had become addicted to her power while he was in silence. He said, "absolute power corrupts absolutely," a saying he often used over the years in other contexts. Furthermore, he asserted that Sheela aimed to eliminate those closest to him, desperate to silence anyone who might expose the true nature of her operations.

Bhagwan reassured the press, "I have called you media people here especially to inform you of glad news, that this commune is free from a fascist regime. Adolf Hitler has died again. And now we would like in every possible way to be an intrinsic part of Oregon, to contribute whatsoever we can contribute, and expect your friendship, your love, your hospitality."

As the press conference concluded, a wave of relief and jubilation washed over the community. People rejoiced, embracing everything Bhagwan said, aligning with his assertion that Sheela and her cohorts were solely responsible for all the problems that had plagued the commune—the crimes, the authoritarian management style, and the divergence from the spiritual precepts at the heart of Bhagwan's teachings. Sheela and her gang were labeled criminals and dictators, while Bhagwan emerged, as ever, the beacon of light. For most, Bhagwan's every utterance was sacred, unquestionable, and beyond scrutiny.

★   ★   ★

A couple of days later, I pulled myself together and headed to Jesus Grove to return to work, though I wasn't sure if I still worked there. As I approached the compound, I spied several government vehicles parked out front. They must have come to investigate the crimes. When I entered, I could feel the tension in the air. Non-sannyasins, I assume FBI agents, sat at the dining table questioning various individuals, while others passed through, guided by Twinkies.

I walked into the kitchen, where everyone worked in silence. "What's going on," I whispered.

"The police and the FBI are questioning people and searching the premises. They found the wiretapping equipment, a secret bunker, and an arsenal of guns," Shara said. My eyes widened.

"What bunker?" I asked.

"There's a secret bunker with a hidden door right off the hallway towards Sheela's room," she said.

"What?" I said, astonished.

"I didn't know either, it's crazy," she said. More weirdness was the last thing I needed, but I had to go see the bunker for myself.

I walked to the hallway off the reception area, the very same hallway where, on numerous occasions, I had been told to "come back later." As I entered, I looked to my right. The door to the room where I was forbidden, where I had once inadvertently peered in and saw wires, now stood open. A man sat at the desk taking notes. I hesitantly approached to get a closer look. I saw shelves of books, wires, and audio equipment. The man sitting at the desk looked up at me sympathetically. "All this was part of their wiretapping operation," he said.

"Oh," was all I could manage to say. I slowly proceeded down the hall no more than thirty feet, where the secret door to the bunker stood open. When closed, it masterly blended with the grooves of the fake wood paneling that lined the walls of the original Jesus Grove trailer. I had walked and skipped down that hall too many times to count. I wondered if I had just been blind since I didn't suspect anything, or maybe they were that good at hiding their operation. I stepped in to find a large underground room with bookshelves and a Jacuzzi. I just stood there, bewildered.

Next, I made my way to the other side of the house, to the wing where I once lived. I wanted to know what was in the room next door to my former bedroom, since it was always locked. When I entered, it was empty—no beds, just remnants of a storage room. I soon learned it was the room where the Uzis and other weapons had been stored. I imagined all those nights I lay in my bed, an arsenal of weapons on the other side of the wall.

* * *

The following day, Bhagwan called yet another press conference. He welcomed everyone to what he deemed a "historical event." With an air of conviction, he proclaimed:

"For the first time in the whole history of mankind, a religion has died. I have never wanted it to be born in the first place. But because I was in silence and isolation, a gang of fascists managed to create it. It is absolutely necessary that it should be completely destroyed. I am against all religions, because they have done only harm to humanity."

And so it was, the religion of Rajneeshism, which Sheela had worked so eagerly to promote, was declared dead. Bhagwan emphasized his aversion to the term "ism" and denounced the book, *Rajneeshism,* as not his own. In the following days, in a symbolic act, thousands of copies of the book, along with all other religious memorabilia, including Sheela's high priestess outfits, were piled onto stretchers and incinerated in our crematorium.

Bhagwan continued asserting:

"I am going to destroy everything, so history never repeats again. I will not always be with you—one day I will have to go. Before that, I want to destroy every possibility. I don't want any popes behind me, any high priestess, any Ayatollah Khomeini . . . no, I want to leave you alone, so content and fulfilled that you don't need anybody between you and the truth of existence."

Then he went on to say we no longer had to wear red or a mala with his picture. It was a relief. I had never been fond of standing out like a sore thumb during my visits to Portland. Where I would get other clothes was a whole other thing. I could only hope that the powers that be would soon provide us with blue jeans and T-shirts.

Bhagwan condemned everything Sheela's gang did, from the Share-a-Home project to taking over Antelope. As part of the effort to undo the wrongs they committed, Bhagwan assured the press that the city of Rajneesh would be changed back to its original name, Antelope, and that we would eventually move out of the small town and leave the Antelope residents alone. In regard to Attorney General Frohnmayer's legal case against us, claiming that Rajneeshpuram's incorporation was invalid due to violations of church versus state laws, Bhagwan passionately exclaimed, "There is no religion. If the religion is not there, the city becomes immediately legal."

* * *

As the days unfolded, the government revealed even more details of Sheela and the gang's crimes and conspiracies. One of the most shocking revelations for me was learning that 750 residents of The Dalles, the Wasco County seat, had been poisoned during the elections one year earlier, in September 1984. Sheela and Puja had sent sannyasins dressed as civilians to taint various salad bars with salmonella. The objective was to make voting citizens too ill to go to the polls to cast their votes. It was another ploy to swing the vote in favor of the Rajneeshee candidates, just like bussing in thousands of homeless people was. As it turned out, it was the largest bioterrorism plot ever carried out in the US. Many became extremely ill, but thankfully nobody died.

The Rajneeshee candidates still didn't get elected. Since that plot didn't play out as Sheela hoped, she and her gang were apparently planning something bigger. As another audacious ploy to seize control of the Wasco County government, they were planning to dive-bomb and poison The Dalles water supply.

So many of the criminal plots involved poison. And much of it, if not all of it, was overseen by Puja, the trusty nurse who was ever at Sheela's side. When I reflected on my interactions with her, a chill went down my spine. She was always nice enough to me, but there was most certainly something a little sinister about her. I had ignored it, just as I did so many other hints of the crimes now being revealed. I could never have imagined the depths of the darkness.

As it turned out, Puja had set up a laboratory in the old laundry building between Jesus Grove and the ranch yard, a building I walked past several times a day, without a clue what it was being used for.

It was in her lab that she allegedly cultured the salmonella that was used to contaminate the salad bars in The Dalles. It was also in this lab that she must have prepared the poison used on Bhagwan's doctor, dentist, Vivek, and the list grew.

Then there was the Haldol. It was uncovered that Haldol was what the Moms added to the Share-A-Home people's beer to calm them and keep them under control. That explained why I was not allowed to drink their beer that autumn afternoon.

It got even worse. Puja was apparently trying to culture the HIV virus with the aim of infecting people they didn't like or who stood in their way. As it turned out, only two of the eleven people who were told they had HIV, actually had it. They had spent months in isolation, seemingly as a means of punishment and humiliation.

It made me wonder if using drugs and poison to control people went beyond what had been uncovered. I remembered the vitamin B shots that Puja administered to select people. Were they mere vitamin B shots, or was she lacing them with uppers so people could work harder, or sedatives and poison to punish people? My thoughts were racing as I considered numerous possibilities.

All these dark agendas haunted me, making me wonder if I had been poisoned myself? Was that why I fell ill so suddenly just before Sheela and the gang left? Were they trying to get me out of the way while they plotted their departure so they wouldn't have to deal with my pleas to take me with them? I would never know.

I lay in bed at night thrashing and ruminating. One night I woke up to a nightmare in which Puja was trying to kill me. In my dream, she snuck into my room wielding a fountain pen filled with black poisonous ink. I woke up at the point where she was about to jab the pen nib into my carotid artery. Terrified, I reassured myself she was gone and that I was safe, but I was too riled up to go back to sleep.

*   *   *

Over the next weeks, I was in such shock that my body buzzed. I survived in a haze, barely remembering anything beyond the routine of daily life— eating, sleeping, and mustering a smile when someone said hello. I longed for a comforting embrace—for someone to reassure me that everything would be alright. All the people I would have normally turned to were gone. Everyone seemed to despise Sheela and her gang, and my previous association with them now felt shameful. A couple people even scowled at me saying things like "why are you still here, you're one of them." I was too proud to show how shattered I was, especially when everyone else was celebrating that the "fascist gang" was gone.

My mother hadn't checked on me. It wasn't surprising since we had barely spoken in four years, except for the several occasions when I mediated between her and her boyfriend when they had troubles. I wanted them to stay together—he seemed decent, even if a bit quirky. She knew nothing about my life, as far as I knew. Though she certainly knew I worked with the Moms who had just left. Yet, she hadn't made an effort to talk to me.

Occasionally, I crossed paths with Mutribo and spent the night with him, but our interludes were less frequent, and I could feel his withdrawal. I rationalized that he was just busy with all his video work. In my heart, though, I knew he was losing interest in me. I pined and counted all the reasons why I wasn't good enough, chief among them was my less than jubilant demeanor. If I wasn't fun and celebratory, what use was I?

Unfortunately, my effort to not fall for him failed miserably. I found myself experiencing the familiar ache of longing and heartbreak that I had once felt for Milarepa. Both men possessed a knack for charming and seducing, only to withdraw into indifference once they had captured my heart. I felt so stupid for once again attaching to someone who didn't care. But it felt like it was out of my control. I thought I was in love again. I basked in whatever attention Mutribo would give me. I was a beggar looking for every crumb, devoid of self-respect.

CHAPTER FIFTY-SIX

BHAGWAN FLEES

STERN, A German magazine, learned of Sheela and her gang's where-abouts. I wouldn't be surprised if Sheela herself tipped them off. They had taken refuge in a secluded town nestled in Germany's picturesque Black Forest. The next issue of *Stern* featured Sheela's face on the cover, with a striking headline translated as "To Hell with Bhagwan."

In the accompanying interview, Sheela leveled a series of stunning accusations against Bhagwan. She painted a picture of a man consumed with materialistic desires more than genuine spirituality. According to her, Bhagwan became petulant when she informed him that the commune couldn't afford the million-dollar diamond watch he wanted. After all, she said, he already had three million dollars' worth of watches, not to mention a fleet of ninety-six Rolls- Royces.

Sheela went on to insist that Bhagwan's three years of silence was a hoax, not something mystical. She said it was actually a calculated deci-sion—Bhagwan was to remain silent until the threat of deportation had dissipated. I wondered if that was because the lawyers worried he would stir the pot if he said something outrageous, as he was known to do. Sheela also asserted that if Bhagwan had been giving discourses during the com-mune's construction, we wouldn't have been able to accomplish the aston-ishing amount of building we did in such a short amount time.

The story of Sheela's departure and Bhagwan's reaction continued to play out in the press. After Sheela's whereabouts were revealed in the *Stern* article, a reporter from *60 Minutes Australia* seized the moment. He decided to visit Sheela and her gang to interview them, and then go to the ranch to play the footage for Bhagwan. He would then ask Bhagwan to respond. It all came across like a lover's quarrel captured on reality TV, though reality TV wasn't yet a thing back then. It was still unclear how the dust would settle. I think many hoped that Sheela and the gang would be locked up and the ranch would continue under the new regime.

⋆ ⋆ ⋆

Two weeks later, on the evening of October 27, 1985, Bhagwan left Rajneeshpuram on a chartered plane. We were all kept in the dark. When word spread of his departure, many thought it was fine, saying things like "He likes to keep us on our toes—it's great." It was not immediately clear where he was going, why he left, or when he would return.

Two days later, we learned where he was from the newspapers that some sannyasins had access to. The *New York Times* headline read "U.S. Indicts Oregon Guru and Says He Tried to Flee Country." The *Los Angeles Times* headline read "Guru, 8 Followers Jailed After Cross-Country Flight." The news disseminated quickly.

Bhagwan had been arrested in North Carolina. When his plane stopped to refuel, government officials were there waiting. They immediately swooped in, handcuffed him and those with him, and took them to jail. Bhagwan was charged with at least two counts of immigration fraud—two felonies. One charge was for being part of a scheme to arrange sham marriages so his disciples could stay in the US; the second charge was for lying about his own visa. He entered the country on a temporary medical visa, which the officials said was a lie. They said he had invented it all along, just using the medical visa to gain entry.

The official word coming from his new secretary, Hasya, and others in Bhagwan's new upper echelon, was that they were taking Bhagwan to Bermuda for a vacation. They insisted that the government had no grounds to assault their beloved master.

But, as it turned out, Bhagwan was under investigation and the government had been tracking him. His claim that his years of silence left him out of the criminal loop didn't fool the Feds. While they were at the ranch investigating the other crimes, they were also looking into Bhagwan's role in it all. Rather ironic since Bhagwan was the one who invited the Feds to investigate, thinking it would help him look innocent.

I later learned that the Rajneeshee attorneys had been tipped off that Bhagwan was going to be indicted in a couple of days. I assumed it was with that knowledge that the new inner circle planned Bhagwan's escape.

So the story that he was going on vacation sounded pretty bogus. It was clear to me that they were trying to get him out of the country before he would be arrested.

Meanwhile, Krishna Deva, who I thought left with Sheela, had actually turned state's evidence. The former mayor of Rajneeshpuram confirmed that Sheela and her inner circle had a list of people they planned to kill. He revealed that among the most prominent on the list were US Attorney John Turner and Oregon Attorney General John Frohnmayer. Turner had initially been appointed to investigate the four hundred or so sham marriages between foreign and American sannyasins. Later, he took charge of the federal prosecution concerning the 1984 Rajneeshee bio-terror attack in The Dalles, as well as other crimes. Similarly, John Frohnmayer, who worked alongside Turner, was also investigating various illegal activities at Rajneeshpuram. Krishna Diva informed the FBI that he was present in meetings where Sheela and the other top Moms meticulously devised a plot to assassinate Turner, hoping that getting him out of the way would thwart the INS investigation. She believed that if the investigation continued, it was likely that Bhagwan would be arrested and deported.

* * *

During Bhagwan's stint in jail, Sheela, Puja, and Shanti B were arrested in Germany for immigration fraud, and the far more serious charge of attempted murder. Similarly, many of the others in Sheela's circle were indicted on charges ranging from wiretapping and arson to immigration fraud and conspiracy to commit murder. It was soon reported that Vidya too was indicted for immigration fraud, but she had not been arrested. Given that she was the president of Rajneesh Neo-Sannyas International Commune, it was no surprise. Nonetheless, it was disturbing for me, especially given what I had just learned about how she was treated during those last months at the ranch.

Once the crimes came to light, someone told me that Vidya had reached the end of her rope and wanted to leave or speak out. This was just around the time I was sent to Europe. As the story went, Sheela would have none of it and feared Vidya knew too much. So, to keep her quiet, she essentially drugged her and locked her up in solitary confinement for several months. On top of that, Vidya was told that her boyfriend, the love of her life, whom she had joined the commune with, was dead. He was not, in fact, dead. He was sent to Europe at the same time I was. Learning of her alleged harrowing experience horrified me. She had been tortured, and when I saw her that day in front of Jesus Grove, she was a shell of her former self. The fact that she was still under Sheela's influence was tragic. I wondered what would happen to her now.

After seven days in jail in Charlotte, Bhagwan was moved briefly to an Oklahoma county jail, and then moved briefly to the El Reno Federal Correctional Institution. On November 7, Bhagwan arrived back in Portland. On November 8, he was released on $500,000 bond and returned to Rajneeshpuram. On July 14, Bhagwan returned to Portland to cut a deal. As part of an Alford plea, he pleaded guilty to two counts of immigration fraud, agreed to pay a $400,000 fine, and agreed to leave the US immediately, never to return without the express permission of the US Attorney General. Bhagwan never returned to the ranch to give a goodbye speech. He left the country. Destination unknown.

CHAPTER FIFTY-SEVEN

EXODUS

THE SHOCKING reality hit the community: Bhagwan was gone for good. The belief in his untouchable status shattered. The motto "celebrate everything" now rang hollow. Though there was talk of the commune continuing, I doubted it could survive without him. I felt the last remnants of my world crumbling.

Suddenly, there was no one to guide us or assure us we'd stay together. The thought of entering the real world, almost foreign to me, filled me with paralyzing panic. While others made hasty plans, I stood frozen, my mind blank, fearing I'd be left behind. The shame of having no close friends left to make plans with paralyzed me further. The only thought I clung to was going wherever Mutribo was going, though I knew he was indifferent to me. Yet, I desperately hoped I was wrong. I was clearly not thinking straight, nor able to face reality.

Since Mutribo and Milarepa were close friends, I assumed they would end up in the same place. At just sixteen, I knew I needed a legal guardian. I couldn't quite imagine leaving with my mother. So, in a bold and desperate move, I approached Milarepa, whom I spotted in the ranch yard, and asked about his plans. He vaguely mentioned visiting family in Virginia and said that he hoped "we" could all reunite. I had no idea what he meant by "we," but I hoped it included me. Despite him not asking me how I was or what my plans were, I impulsively blurted, "Can you be my legal guardian?"

"Sure, no problem," he replied casually. He didn't ask me any questions about it. It seemed he thought of it as a mere formality, as did I, for the most part. I thought myself grown up enough to fend for myself, though I would soon learn I was wrong.

I hurried to Rajneesh Legal Services and found a familiar lawyer. "Can you draft papers making Milarepa my legal guardian?" I asked.

"I can, but why do you want to do that?" he inquired.

"I'm only sixteen and need someone to be responsible for me if I leave."

"What about your mother?"

"We've barely spoken since the start of the ranch. We don't get along," I said.

"Are you sure you want to do this?"

"Yes, what's the next step?"

"I'll prepare the papers, and both your mother and Milarepa will need to sign them," he said.

"Okay, that won't be a problem," I assured him, though internally, I was anxious about asking my mother to sign over custody. Driven by my desperate and delusional resolve to attach myself to the men I thought I needed to survive, I set out on my mission.

I found my mother and explained about the papers I wanted her to sign. I don't remember her exact words, only that she didn't object. That afternoon, both Milarepa and my mother went to Rajneesh Legal Services and signed the document, making Milarepa my official legal guardian.

★ ★ ★

One of the other teens blindsided me with the news that Mutribo was leaving for England in two days. I was shocked but tried to hide it, realizing I was the last to know. The familiar knot in my stomach throbbed like an alarm, triggering my feelings of worthlessness, and reminding me that I was a desperate, needy mess. Despite this, I clung to the dregs of hope and resolved to find him and talk to him. I rationalized that maybe he hadn't told me because he didn't know I had feelings for him. Perhaps if I told him, it would change everything.

Later that day, I found him walking near his house, arm in arm with a woman. Our eyes met. "Hi, Sareets," he greeted me, using the nickname he had given me.

"Hi, can I talk to you for a minute?" I asked. He turned to the woman and said he would catch up with her.

"What's up?" he asked.

"I heard you're leaving the day after tomorrow."

"Yes, I am," he replied.

"Were you going to tell me or say goodbye?"

"I didn't think you cared."

"What do you mean? I've fallen for you," I confessed.

"I thought we agreed that you wouldn't."

"Well, I have," I replied.

"I didn't know," he said. "I don't know when we'll meet again, but since you have feelings for me, I'll spend my last night with you," he said matter-of-factly. I fought back tears.

"Okay." He walked away and caught up with the woman, who was now a little distance off. Was he offering to spend his last night with me out of pity? I felt even worse.

The next night, I went to his house, and we spent his last night at the ranch together. It was awkward. He was distant. Any warmth that he once expressed was absent. It was as if he was going through the motions devoid of feeling.

The next day, we said goodbye like acquaintances, not as lovers who had just spent the night together. He assured me that our paths would cross again, but he didn't fill me in on his plans. I just hoped we'd see each other again soon.

Milarepa left a couple of days later without a goodbye and without giving me his contact information. I thought that since he was now my legal guardian, he would've kept me informed. But I'm sure he didn't really take that new responsibility seriously. I just hoped I would end up where he and Mutribo did, and I thought I needed an adult as a guardian.

★ ★ ★

As people left the ranch in droves, full-blown panic set in. I had nowhere to go, no one offering me a helping hand, and no money—not a cent. Whatever faith I had in the universe taking care of me and all that gobbledygook was long gone.

I stood in the large, now-deserted office. The desks were empty, and people huddled in clusters of three or four, discussing their plans. Nearby, Heather, one of the other teens, was talking about going to Laguna Beach. I inched closer, eavesdropping. When the conversation ended, I pulled her aside.

"Are you going to Laguna Beach?" I asked.

"Yes, I think so," she replied. "The people I was talking to said I could get a ride with them."

"Can I come too?" I asked, desperation tinging my voice.

"Sure, I don't see why not," she said. While I felt a glimmer of relief at having a plan, my distress lingered. I barely knew Heather. She was always nice, but we had never spent time together. Now, I was planning to leave with her. I worried she might see me as a burden. My mind raced, my inner voice wielding a fierce whip, accusing me of being too needy and clingy. I couldn't shake the conviction that if someone truly cared about me, they would have already offered to take me with them.

A couple of days later, my mother came looking for me. She found me in the office. She approached me with the tentative air of a scared animal. On the rare occasions that she'd approached me over the past few years, she often looked deflated and afraid. She was probably fearful of my rage, but instead of probing as to why I was so angry, she seemed to cower. As she walked toward me, familiar feelings surged: grief, sorrow, rage, and heartache. I hated seeing her look so meek. She wasn't a meek woman; she was tough and capable but never seemed to embody that strength around me.

"Hi," I said.

"Hi," she replied. We stood there for a moment, the air thick with unspoken words. Then she continued, "Eric and I are going to Boston. You're welcome to come with us."

I hesitated. Being with her seemed like a bad idea, we'd never gotten along. I was convinced she didn't want me, and I didn't want to be a burden. "I'm going to Laguna Beach," I said.

"I'll respect whatever you want to do, but if you change your mind, you're welcome to come to Boston," she said softly.

"Okay," I muttered. She reached out and took my hand.

"Do you have any money?" she asked.

"No," I admitted. She pulled out a small wad of cash from her pocket.

"Here, this is half of what I have, and I want you to take it," she said, pressing it into my hand.

"No, no, I don't want your money," I protested, my pride getting the better of me. Truth was, I desperately needed it. Without it, I wouldn't even have money for gas to get to California.

"Really, it's okay. Please take it," she insisted. I felt grateful as I accepted it.

"Okay," I said. We hugged each other goodbye, and I could hardly breathe. My heart felt physically broken as the floodgates opened, and pain and love flowed over me.

PART FOUR
The Real World

CHAPTER FIFTY-EIGHT

LAGUNA BEACH

HEATHER AND I were dropped off at Utsava, a large Rajneesh Meditation center on the outskirts of Laguna Beach. With our meager luggage at our feet, we faced a new reality. We weren't entirely sure where we would stay that night. My mother had given me a phone number for Anthony, her boyfriend's brother, suggesting he might let us stay with him. I walked inside to use the phone, and after a couple of rings, Anthony answered. With a heavy dose of British reserve, he agreed to let Heather and me crash on his living room couch for a couple of days until we found another place. When he told me it would cost ten dollars a night, I tensed with fear. It struck me as ungenerous to charge us to crash on his floor. My $300 wasn't going to go far. I had barely arrived and was already worrying about how I would survive.

Clearly, I needed to get a job as soon as possible, but I had no idea how to go about it. I didn't even know what skills I had. I wondered if it was legal for a sixteen-year-old to work.

Heather and I slept on the fold-out sofa that night. The next day, one of Anthony's housemates gave us a ride downtown so we could look for jobs. I was apprehensive about interacting with the world. I feared how people would respond to me. Before beginning my mission, I sat on a bench for a while. The streets were clean, the shops fancy. Palm trees swayed in the breeze, and passersby with sun-kissed skin wore fashionable clothes and sunglasses. I didn't fit in.

I finally gathered the courage to approach my first shop to ask if they were hiring. The answer was no. The answer was also no in the subsequent shops I inquired in. Nobody was hiring, at least not the likes of me. Did people think I was weird or dim? Did my appearance play a part in not being hirable? I wore a black velour track suit with vertical white stripes. It was the only non-red outfit I owned. The girls working in the shops were not only fashionable but engaged customers in a carefree, bubbly manner unfamiliar to me. It seemed so phony, yet I envied them. They seemed unburdened, while I felt like a timid fawn.

After a few nights at Anthony's, Heather and I moved to a dorm in Utsava. It was also ten dollars a night, but I felt more comfortable among other ranch strays. As an epicenter for Sannyasins in the area, mostly others who had just left the ranch, a steady stream of people passed through. People were focused on figuring out what they were going to do. I had no plans; the only thing I could think about was trying to make money and what would happen to me if I couldn't.

Soon Heather's parents and two brothers showed up in Laguna Beach too. She and her brother moved into a camper her parents parked in the Utsava parking lot. Though we still saw each other and did things together, we weren't a duo tackling the real world anymore. I was essentially alone.

*　*　*

Each day I hitchhiked downtown to continue my job search. I soon learned that standing on the side of the road with my thumb out solicited more than just rides. Guys in shiny, fancy cars would stop and ask, "How would you like to make fifty bucks?" or "I'll give you a ride if you give me a blowjob."

"Absolutely not!" I always retorted, even though I desperately needed the money. I was beginning to see how necessity could push someone in that direction. I heard through the grapevine that Kaya and Gita, once my dearest friends, had slipped into that world. They were working as strippers in San Francisco. Worse, Kaya had also turned to prostitution and cocaine. It anguished me to hear what they were up to, but I understood how the need for survival could lead them down that path. I knew that was not my path, as the very thought of it infuriated me and made me feel slimy. I didn't want to be objectified. There had to be another way.

As the days passed, I felt wobblier and lonelier. So, when I caught sight of the charming Irishman at one of Utsava's dance nights, I was relieved to see a friendly face. Our eyes met from across the room, and we both smiled and made our way to each other. Though his past sexual pursuits of me had fizzled out, we had remained friendly.

"Sarito, my dear, lovely to see you," he said in his Irish lilt. He gave me a hug and then took my hand, guiding me outside where it was quieter. He said that he and his girlfriend had landed in a dump of a house with several other sannyasins and that he was picking up enough basic jobs to pay the rent.

As the night progressed, he cooed his romantic sentiments, just like in the past. I basked in his attention like sustenance for my loneliness, but I knew he had a girlfriend. I also knew that sannyasin men saying they were enamored with me didn't mean much—they just wanted to have sex. Yet, his words warmed my heart and sparked hope that love and romance did exist. I still dreamt of being swept off my feet, though I was pretty sure the Irishman wasn't the one to do it. Still, I appreciated his charm stirring my romantic heart, giving me hope.

When he invited me home, I agreed. I knew it was just for sex, but if that was the price for connection, so be it. I resolved not to get attached. Anyway, I was still pining for Mutribo.

Over the next couple of weeks, the Irishman would find me with some frequency. We'd talk a bit, have sex, and then he'd head home. He was free most nights because his girlfriend worked at a local strip club, but the sneaking around and participating in something illicit felt devaluing. I didn't like being so insignificant that I was his lover in the shadows. Yet, I feared that if I didn't sleep with him, he would want nothing to do with me.

Day after day, I continued my job search to no avail. I was getting desperate. I only had $120 left, and I hadn't yet paid for the three weeks I had stayed at Utsava. I asked the Irishman if he had any ideas of what I might do to make money. He thought about it for a few minutes.

"I can ask my girlfriend if the club where she works needs more strippers," he said.

Every cell in my body revolted at the idea. I couldn't imagine exposing my body like that. Plus, I wasn't lanky and attractive anymore, my body was curvy now. I was certain I wouldn't be sexy enough for the job. Plus, I had no idea how to flirt or be seductive.

"No, I would never do that," I said.

"You don't have to have sex with anyone. You'd be in charge," he said.

"I couldn't do it," I insisted.

"You could make good money," he persisted. I thought about it for a minute. I knew that many sannyasin women were stripping to make fast cash. Some said it wasn't hard because our sannyas culture was so sexually open. They claimed that being with Bhagwan for so many years had freed them from their inhibitions. Not true for me. I felt inhibited as fuck. There was no way I could do it.

★ ★ ★

Each new interaction with the outside world emphasized just how different I was. Physically, I blended in except for my mostly red, unfashionable clothes and unkempt hair. I spoke perfectly good English and knew of popular musicians like Madonna and Prince. Yet, beyond these surface similarities, I felt like an alien reintroduced to society as part of a social experiment.

I struggled to keep up with casual pop culture references sprinkled into every conversation. People would discuss shows, sports, or the latest news. I often found myself staring blankly, scrambling to find a response that wasn't a lie or an admission of my cluelessness. Usually, I managed a smile and come up with a generic reply like, "I haven't seen it (heard it, or read it)—do you recommend it?"

But it wasn't just pop culture that eluded me; basic cultural norms and common knowledge were also unfamiliar. I didn't know simple facts like that the sun set in the West. Most of my understanding of the real world came from movies or my sporadic outings to Portland. I wasn't completely isolated, but I had never truly engaged with mainstream society since leaving it at age nine, and even then, I lived on the fringes. Now, at sixteen, attempting to navigate this world as an almost-adult was daunting. Growing up in the commune left me unprepared.

My lack of formal education, which I once viewed as a safeguard against being brainwashed, now felt like a curse. Basic skills such as reading, writing, and arithmetic, all of which I struggled with, were essential qualifications I needed for any job beyond dishwashing or other basic service jobs.

★ ★ ★

I ran into Heather in the Utsava parking lot. "Did you see Milarepa?" she asked.

"No. Was he here?"

"Yeah, he just left. He told me Mutribo will be arriving in LA in a few days." I felt a pang of dejection. I was hurt that Milarepa seemed to have all but forgotten me. After all, he was my legal guardian. I was also hurt that Mutribo hadn't communicated with me since he left the ranch. Despite all signs pointing otherwise, I was living in a bubble of delusion, hoping Mutribo would be happy to see me again.

"We should go to LA to meet him at the airport," I said. Heather agreed to come with me.

A few days later, as we navigated through the bustling airport, my nerves buzzed with anticipation. We located the appropriate arrival gate and stood waiting behind the black rope barrier. Out of the corner of my eye, I caught a glimpse of a familiar face and turned reflexively. It was Milarepa, accompanied by two young women, one blonde and one brunette, strolling in my direction.

He smiled casually. "You've come to greet Mutribo too?" he asked. I hesitated, feeling a surge of shame and uncertainty. Clearly, Mutribo and Milarepa already had plans, and all my efforts now seemed foolish and meddlesome.

"Yes," I stammered, my voice barely masking my discomfort. "Heather and I thought we'd be here to welcome him." Milarepa's nod seemed to acknowledge my vulnerability while also conveying a tinge of pity. I wished I could disappear, to rewind the events that had led me here.

Then, amidst the throng of disembarking passengers, I saw Mutribo—tall, with dark brown hair and broad shoulders. He stood out in the crowd. With a bright smile and a relaxed swagger, he walked toward us. He seemed honored to be surrounded by five people eager to greet him with warm hugs and cheerful welcomes. When he saw me, all he said was "Hi Sarito," as he brushed past me. It was as if he barely acknowledged my existence. No hug, no "how are you." He then joined Milarepa and the young women, as if they were dear friends.

Milarepa and Mutribo walked arm in arm with the two women, laughing and chatting. Heather and I trailed behind. I wondered who these women were and how Milarepa and Mutribo had connected with them, especially since I didn't recall seeing them at the ranch. They still always found women.

Once outside the airport, the awkwardness continued. What next? The two women informed us that Milarepa and Mutribo would be staying with them in their studio apartment in Venice.

"You can stay too!" the brunette offered, perhaps out of politeness. Without hesitation, I accepted, not realizing the complexity of the situation.

Before long, we were all seated at a large booth in a noisy Mexican restaurant. Someone ordered a pitcher of margaritas for the table, but I abstained, counting my pennies. As the evening progressed, an unsettling scene unfolded. Mutribo snuggled up to the brunette, his arm draped around her; Milarepa's hand lingered on the blonde's shoulder. Though I sat at the same table, I felt like a mere spectator, taking up space. Watching the men I had idolized fawn over other women while ignoring me made me feel insignificant and worthless.

After dinner, we all headed to the women's apartment. It was smaller than I had imagined, more like a single room with a loft. We quickly set up makeshift beds. I clung to a faint hope that Mutribo might choose to sleep with me, given our history, but he was much more interested in the brunette.

"Okay, you and Heather can share that bed," the brunette said, pointing to one of the makeshift beds. "Mutribo and I will take this one." That left Milarepa and the blonde to sleep in the loft. Disappointed, I resigned myself to the arrangement, telling myself it was more like a slumber party.

We all got into bed, but I couldn't sleep. The events of the day churned in my mind. Soon, the sound of heavy breathing and moaning from the loft kept me awake. Milarepa and the blonde were having sex. I tried to ignore it, relieved that it wasn't Mutribo—yet. He seemed asleep, just a few feet away from me.

I was finally drifting off when the rustling of sheets and the sound of kissing jolted me awake. Mutribo was on top of the brunette, humping. I heard every sound, every moan, and every breath.

Rage, humiliation, and hurt coursed through me, threatening to explode. It took all my self-control not to scream and make a scene. I hated him and hated myself for falling for him. I tossed and turned in bed, my distress waking Heather.

"Are you okay?" she asked.

"No. Mutribo was having sex right here. I can't believe he could be so cruel."

"I'm sorry. What do you want to do?"

"I don't know, but I can't bear this!"

"Try to sleep. Maybe you can talk to him in the morning."

"Okay." But I knew I wouldn't sleep, and I certainly wouldn't talk to him. I was too mired with self-doubt and fear. I lay there, adrenalin pumping until the sun rose.

At the first light of dawn, I quietly got out of bed, dressed, and tiptoed across the room. The bright morning light flooded the room as I opened the door.

"Where are you going?" Milarepa whispered from the loft.

"For a walk," I replied flatly.

"I'll come with you." He quickly dressed and joined me outside. My foul mood was palpable; even an imbecile couldn't miss it.

We walked to the beach in silence. How ironic that the man who had caused me so much grief was now walking beside me as I lamented over another man. I wanted to confront him, to tell him how his cruelty had tainted my heart with pain and mistrust. I wanted him to know that I wasn't just another pretty face or a plaything.

My anger made me feel powerful, but I didn't confront him. Instead, I had an epiphany. I finally saw the truth about these men. They didn't care about me, and the last twelve hours had made that crystal clear. My delusions about them had burst, and my raw emotions throbbed like an open wound. I had to get away from them.

I decided to go to Boston to join my mother and her partner. Back at Utsava, I gathered my things and reticently went to enquire about my bill. The woman in charge said, "Thanks for helping out around here. You don't owe us anything." It was a blessing. There was no way I could have paid what I owed, which by then must have been several hundred dollars. With just over $100 to my name, I bought a $99 ticket to Boston on People's Express.

CHAPTER FIFTY-NINE

THE AFTERMATH

M Y MOTHER and her partner, Eric, came to pick me up at the Boston airport. Despite the mutual awkwardness and clumsy hugs, I was grateful for their presence. However, the last time Shreya had truly been my mother was seven years earlier. Now, approaching my seventeenth birthday, us being together felt like foreign territory. A complex mix of hurt, rage, and love simmered beneath the surface. At the ranch, I was always with the Moms, and I thought I was self-sufficient, believing I didn't need my mother. But now, despite my resistance, I realized I did need her— at least until I could find my own way in the world.

From Boston, the three of us traveled to Europe, eventually landing in Torquay, a small coastal town in the south of England. Why they chose that location, in the middle of winter no less, was beyond me. It was dreary and devoid of work opportunities. I spent my days feeding fifty pence pieces into the electric meter to keep the power on, allowing me to watch endless hours of TV. I sank into a deep, listless depression, not knowing what to do, only that I had to get out of there.

I borrowed $500 from Ira, who was living in Beverly Hills, and whom I had visited for a couple of days when I was in LA. She had always looked out for me, especially in Pune, but asking to borrow money was humiliating. However, she was happy to lend me the money and wired it to me almost immediately.

I returned to Boston. I found a place to stay in a sannyasin group house, signed up with a temp agency, and began doing clerical work around the city. It wasn't long before people at my temp jobs started asking about my background. They wanted to know where I grew up, why I wore so much orange, and why I had a strange accent. I was horrified. I guarded my past like a dark secret, fearing I'd be judged as weird and stupid. I hadn't even realized I had a strange accent, but I suppose I picked up a certain speaking style, or cadence, by living in a community with people of multiple nationalities.

After a few months, a new friend, Margaret, suggested I clean houses instead and even gave me a couple of clients to get started. Though my existence was still wobbly, I managed to pay my bills and get by.

Within six months, Surya and Eric returned to Boston. Both Margaret and I moved into the house they rented in Newton, a nearby suburb. Though I paid my own rent, having my mother nearby acted as a kind of security blanket, but also an aggravation. Our relationship was volatile, picking up where it had left off years earlier before we went to India. I would explode into fits of rage and collapse into despair. I thought she didn't care, as she would shut down whenever I was upset. Just like before, I was the "terror," unfairly acting out in her view, while she was the mother who, as she claimed, always tried to do what was best for me. In this scenario, my rage was seen as unwarranted, and she was the victim. And so the cycle continued.

In time, I got to know my grandparents, who lived nearby. Although they were initially cool and unwelcoming, my grandfather, Saul, started inviting me to have lunch with him. Both he and my grandmother, Flip, were still furious with my mother and were particularly appalled by my lack of education. Saul slowly challenged my steadfast belief that education was brainwashing, and I agreed to take my GED and, if I passed, to enroll in junior college. I felt ashamed of how academically deficient I was. I had a notion that if I were truly intelligent, I should have learned everything on my own without formal schooling. I really wanted to prove to my grandparents, and myself, that I was smart and capable.

A few months later, I took my GED. By some stroke of grace, I passed. I seriously believed there was an error. I hadn't learned math beyond multiplication, making the probability of passing the math section nearly impossible. Nonetheless, the fact that I did pass was a blessing. That fall, I began classes at Mount Ida Junior College. I did fine—actually, I did really well.

The completion of my first year at Mount Ida marked three years since Rajneeshpuram had collapsed. Though I was forging my way into mainstream society, I didn't really feel at home in Boston. I wasn't planning to move, but when I came across a photo of the Colorado mountains in a magazine, I decided to visit during my summer break. As soon as I stepped onto the University of Colorado campus in Boulder, with its meticulously manicured lawns and Neo-Gothic buildings set against the majestic foot-hills, I impulsively declared that I wanted to move to Colorado and attend the university. My grandfather was dismayed, saying that the university wasn't on par with Boston University, Tufts, or other prestigious institutions in the Boston area. That didn't bother me; in fact, I was relieved. I needed less pressure, and I also hoped moving would put a buffer between me and my mother.

I arrived in Boulder, moved into a dorm, and started classes. Though there was less pressure than if I attended an East Coast school, attending a full-fledged university, instead of a junior college, was intimidating, none-theless. I had a severe case of imposter syndrome and was wracked with anxiety that someone would discover I was an imbecile. I was so ashamed of myself that I hid in plain sight, slipping in and out of classes like a ghost. I never dared speak up, and on the rare occasion that I was called on, I froze, fearing anything I said would reveal my ineptitude.

Fueled by fear and the need to prove I wasn't a failure, I pushed myself to persevere. After a rocky first semester, I found my way. Aside from spending time with my first real boyfriend, Dave, who was my age and whom I met on a blind date, I devoted most of my time to studying. Dave was the only person I told about my past. When I did, he looked shocked.

"Wasn't that the sex cult where the guru had all the Rolls-Royces?" he asked.

"Yes," I said, ashamed. The word cult made my guts churn, but I was starting to question if the commune was actually a cult or not. The next day he went to the library to read anything he could about the Rajneesh movement. Thankfully he didn't judge me or dump me.

*   *   *

It wasn't long after the ranch ended that Sheela and many in her inner circle served jail time. Despite the evidence and convictions that emerged during the court cases, most devotees absolved Bhagwan of any responsibility for the events at Rajneeshpuram. Even when two different Moms testified that Bhagwan himself had authorized violent actions, among other crimes, most devotees squarely blamed Sheela and her cohorts, keeping Bhagwan elevated on a pedestal.

Meanwhile, Bhagwan returned to the ashram in India for a phase of his movement, which people called Pune 2. Soon after, I learned that Bhagwan changed his name to Osho, which in Japanese means "highest ranking virtuous monk." He also gave new names to most of those in his inner circle, like Vivek, his close confidant, whose new name was Nirvano. It was curious, but I didn't think much of it. I assumed it was related to a legal issue.

A couple of years later, I heard that Vivek committed suicide. However, rumors swirled amongst the sannyasins I knew in Boulder, suggesting she hadn't taken her own life, but that she'd been intentionally overdosed by one or two people in Osho's current inner circle. It didn't surprise me, and I believed the rumors. It made me intensely sad. I imagined her being psychologically tortured like Vidya had supposedly been as well. What struck me the most is that even under a new regime, dark agendas were seemingly still at play.

Not long after that, Dave and I ran into one of his friends on campus, who looked at me with a grave expression. "Did you hear that Rajneesh, um, I mean Osho, died."

"No, I didn't know," I said. I just stood there. I didn't feel anything. It was strange.

"Is that hard for you?" he asked.

"No, I'm fine," I said. "I just wonder what all the sannyasins will do now that he's gone." I assumed that with Osho's death, the Rajneesh movement would end, especially since he had instructed his disciples not to idolize him after his passing.

*   *   *

Quite a few sannyasins had settled in Boulder after the ranch. Some even opened a Rajneesh Meditation Center. I didn't participate in group gatherings. In fact, I became increasingly wary of anything related to Osho. I diverged from the collective perspective that he could do no wrong, that everything he said or did was sacred. To many, even the absurd or tasteless aspects of his teachings were considered part of his spiritual message. I became aggravated when I heard people say, "Osho said this" or "Osho said that." I was also turned off when I saw large photos of him hanging on the walls of the Rajneesh Meditation Center. I was convinced that Osho was aware of most of what happened at the ranch, and to me, he seemed manipulative and cunning. However, the facts didn't seem to matter—devotion to Osho seemed to drown out any conflicting evidence. The glaring hypocrisy of it all disgusted me.

Yet, I kept my feelings concealed from the sannyasins I knew. I didn't yet feel confident enough in myself to trust my own feelings. The need to belong, even loosely, still had a pull on me. I lived with one foot in the Osho community and the other in mainstream society.

★　★　★

Though I was doing well in school and outwardly seemed to have adjusted to life outside the commune, a torrent of buried emotions simmered within me. Ever since the ranch ended, I had been in survival mode, determined to prove my strength and that I could overcome my shortcomings. But now, those suppressed feelings refused to stay dormant. I felt tense and restless, often struggling to sleep or waking up with night terrors. A relentless voice in my head berated me, insisting that people saw me as a weird loser.

While I knew I had issues with my mom, I hadn't stopped to consider any other sources of my feelings, or why I thought so poorly of myself. I didn't really reflect on my past, particularly my time in the commune. Looking back, I think I avoided it because, on some level, I knew it would be an emotional minefield.

Admitting that I wasn't fine, or that I needed help, made me feel like even more of a failure. Many sannyasins looked down on traditional therapy as if it was beneath them. It seemed to be for those who weren't spiritually evolved. However, I was beginning to reject the commune stance on things. I especially despised the holier than thou, elitist stance that many sannyasins possessed, seeing everyone else as below them. I had now met many non-sannyasins who were nice. I wasn't sure what to do or who to talk to. And things were getting worse.

Shortly after I moved to Boulder, my mother and Eric decided to follow me there. So much for my buffer. Though I didn't live with them, my relationship with my mother was as contentious as ever. Sometimes I felt like I would explode with rage. Whenever I confronted her about some of her actions during my childhood, she would usually respond by saying, "Here we go again, what did I do wrong now?" I didn't get the answers I wanted; instead, she looked hurt and exasperated, as if my inquiries were unwarranted. She would insist she did the best she could. I would then feel pangs of guilt and self-doubt for confronting her, all the while my rage about to blow a fuse.

Then, during one of our standoffs, the conversation went differently than it usually did. Out of left field, my mom said, "I don't think your anger is about me—I think it's displaced anger about your father."

"What do you mean? I don't even remember him," I protested.

"Do you remember that last afternoon you spent with him in New York when you were three?" she continued.

"I have a couple of vague memories," I said, "like standing on the sidewalk while you argued." Beyond that, I remembered Tom's dank apartment, and that he had laid down on the single bed in the corner. I remember wanting him to get up and that he told me to be quiet. That was it.

"You changed that day," she said.

"What do you mean, I changed?" I asked, my anger simmering. Why was this the first time I was hearing about that fateful day?

"You started hating me," she replied. "You wouldn't even let me touch you, and you'd wake up every night with screaming nightmares." Learning of my nightmares was new information. She was right that I didn't want her to touch me, and I never understood why. I always felt guilty and ashamed about it, especially when she pointed it out to other people.

"What happened that day?"

"I don't know what happened when you were alone with Tom. What I know is that he didn't bring you back when he was supposed to. After he was a couple of hours late, I started roaming the streets looking for you."

"Didn't you know where he lived?"

"I knew the neighborhood he lived in, but not his address. I'd told him not to take you to his apartment. I insisted he take you to the park," she recounted.

"Why did you let me go with him? You knew he was unstable."

"I didn't really want to, but he insisted. He said he was clean and sober," she said.

"How did you eventually find me?"

"I kept walking the streets, and eventually I saw you and him walking towards me," she said. "Your face was streaked in tears, and you had lost your voice from screaming."

"What did you do then?" I prodded further.

"I didn't know what to do. Tom and I argued, and I could see he wasn't sober. After a few days, I decided we should leave New York. I thought getting away from what had happened might help you."

"But didn't my nightmares and pushing you away indicate that I needed professional help?" I asked stridently.

"At that time, people didn't approach these things like that. I thought that by taking you away from New York, you'd calm down," she replied.

"Did I?"

"No, but I always tried to do things that I thought would help you. That's why we went to India when you were nine," she explained.

"What! What do you mean?" More new information.

"When we were living in Hawaii, I wrote a letter to the Rajneesh Ashram, explaining the difficulties I was having with you. They wrote back, suggesting we come," she revealed. I was speechless. I couldn't fathom that the major life decisions she'd made, decisions that had taken us thousands of miles away from any semblance of home, had somehow become my responsibility. What about therapy or a stable living environment, I wondered. Had those options never crossed her mind? Now at the age of twenty, and through my studies of psychology, I had come to understand that children needed stability.

"I thought I was doing better in Hawaii. I even had friends," I protested.

"Yes, you did, but you never wanted to be around me. You spent most of your time with Roland and Akala," she reminded me. It was true. I did spend a significant amount of time with them. They felt like a family, and I liked being part of it. I cherished looking after their son Jora. It made me happy.

"I can't believe you're suggesting we went to India because of me. That's unfair," I said, exasperated.

"The past is the past, and I hope we can start fresh now." Her words irked me further. I had no idea how I could just let go of all my bad feelings, especially if I was the scapegoat. I could see that whatever happened with my father deeply affected me, which at least helped me understand some of the relentless tension and caution I felt most of my life. But that didn't change my understanding of my mother—my bad feelings about her were still about her.

I would never learn what really happened with my father that day in New York. What was clear is that I was terrified. I wondered if he had sexually abused me, but that seemed unlikely. All I could think was that he must have taken some pills or shot up, and then passed out for a while. I must have screamed and screamed trying to wake him up. Maybe I thought he was dead.

Despite knowing very little about my father, I had always wanted to find him. When I lived in Boston, I watched The Oprah Winfrey Show most afternoons. I saw her instigate reunions with estranged family members, which stirred a newfound desire to find my father. I thought he might still live in New York, which was not that far away. I started asking my mom to help me find him, but she always said it would be difficult since there were so many Tom Carrolls.

Then, in the winter of my junior year in college, my mom called me out of the blue. She was in New York for work, and I was visiting my grandparents in Boston. When I picked up the phone, she announced that she had found Tom in the phone book, under TC Carroll, his nickname that I had never heard of before. She said that she met with him the day before and that he wanted to meet me. The next day, I flew to New York and met with him and my mother for a couple of hours. He was warm to me and expressed a genuine desire to get to know me. We planned for me to visit him in the summer. However, that was the last time I saw him. Ten days before my planned visit, he passed away from liver cancer, complicated by hepatitis C.

★ ★ ★

It was my mother who suggested I see a therapist, primarily to work on my issues with her, and to "start fresh." I was reluctant, but I needed to talk to somebody who would listen to me and not just tell me I needed to let go of my bad feelings. If the sannyasins I knew thought I wasn't spiritual, or looked down on me for needing help, so be it.

I approached my first therapy session with skepticism, but meeting Jennifer changed that. She was slight, with delicate features and thin, wispy blond hair. She spoke softly and lacked the authoritative and directive traits of the group leaders in Pune and the ranch. Nothing about her was intimidating.

Sitting on her couch, I began to unravel the complexities of my existence—my tumultuous relationship with my mother, my fear of failing in college and not fitting in, and my general self-loathing. She asked about my past. I talked about the commune and my relationships with Vidya, Milarepa, and others.

Jennifer listened intently, and then she shared her thoughts. Though she may have said many things, one statement pierced through loud and clear: "You've been sexually abused." She said it as though it were an obvious truth. I was taken aback; I hadn't endured overt violence or threats like a scene from a crime drama. The men seemed loving, at least when they were trying to get into my pants. How could it possibly be abuse?

"I never said 'no,'" I retorted, rejecting her perspective.

Jennifer looked at me with an intense, knowing look. "I can discern that you've been sexually abused just by observing your body language." I suddenly felt intensely vulnerable, as if my innermost secrets were laid bare for all to see. Did everyone I encountered see what she saw? I had chalked up my bodily tension to anxieties about fitting in and finding my place in a world where I didn't feel I quite belonged.

She continued, "Moreover, the exploitation started when you were twelve, or maybe even when you were younger. That, by any definition, is child abuse." Her words hung in the air, my mind grappling with the weight of their meaning.

In subsequent sessions, I staunchly defended my belief that I hadn't been abused, demanding that "Milarepa and everyone else just followed their energy—that it was just normal. I was just heartbroken when he didn't choose me." Or "No one ever said anything. If it was abuse, somebody would have done something." It struck me that even if I would have seen it as abuse, nobody else would have. After all, when I told Vidya of my heartbreak, she encouraged me to move on and be with someone else.

"It's not your fault. The men who abused you should be ashamed," Jennifer reassured me repeatedly. My whole world view was being turned upside down. As what Jennifer was saying started to sink in, I was relieved there was finally an explanation for my feelings of being used and worthless.

As it sunk in more, an inferno of rage surged within me. Not only was I furious with Milarepa and Mutribo and the other men who had tarnished my body and heart, I was enraged that it all happened under the guise of spirituality. I wanted to somehow reclaim myself and return to my virginal innocence, but that couldn't happen. I wondered how I would ever feel okay.

Next, Jennifer dropped another bomb: she called the commune a cult. That ugly word again. Just hearing the commune referred to as a cult made my skin crawl. My understanding of cults was that they were dark and scary. While I tried to rationalize that our community was about love, my body clashed with my racing mind. There I sat, with my arms across my chest gripping my elbows. It was as if I was trying to block out what she said, lest I would collapse. Yet, though I didn't want to hear it, I knew what she was saying was true.

★ ★ ★

In 1992, I graduated from the University of Colorado, Phi Beta Kappa, with a degree in humanities and comparative literature. I now had to figure out what to do with my life. I briefly panicked but soon landed a good job as a technical writer, even though that was not the kind of work I envisioned myself doing. Nonetheless, it provided security and safety—the two things I needed most.

By all outward appearances, I was succeeding. I had a good job, I owned a house, and I had friends. Yet, even with my basic needs taken care of, my emotional wounds, and the coping patterns I had subconsciously devised as a result of those wounds, continued to rise to the surface. Now, they played out most readily in my romantic relationships. Trust didn't come easy for me. I was ever on the lookout for someone to deceive me, use me, or lie to me. I swept the land for minefields that often didn't exist. My endless doubt, need for reassurance, and general unease would eventually push most partners away. And once they were gone, I'd become engulfed in a profound sense of self-loathing, regret, and desperation. I did love my partners, but I later came to see that I sabotaged my relationships as a means of keeping people from getting too close. But this act of protection only hurt me.

After years of playing it relatively safe, I plunged headfirst into a relationship that, for many reasons, shattered the barriers around my heart. The love I felt was exhilarating but also entwined with intense fear. In that vulnerable state, I was terrified of being obliterated, as if my fate rested entirely in my partner's hands, leaving me with no sense of autonomy. The relationship became a catalyst, unearthing and triggering even more long-buried traumas. These wounds, stretching far back into my past, were torn open once again. Tragically, the very things I longed for—connection and love—were being sabotaged by my unresolved pain. I spiraled into deep despair, a reckoning that upended my life for a while. It was during this time that I was diagnosed with severe PTSD. And now that my trauma had been unearthed, I could no longer run from it or suppress it. It demanded I pay attention. Little did I know that the years ahead would be spent grappling with the aftermath of my upbringing.

*   *   *

As I continued therapy, I became clear that I was no longer a sannyasin. I no longer bought into the groupthink or accepted many of the precepts. I distanced myself from the sannyas scene, maintaining contact with only a few friends. Eventually, I confided in them that I now viewed my relationship with Milarepa and others as abusive. While I hoped for support, deep down, I knew I wouldn't receive the empathy I sought. Most responses were lukewarm apologies, followed by spiritual platitudes like, "Stop identifying with your pain, it's just your ego," or "Let go already, it's been years." Others deflected, focusing on their own experiences: "I had a great time at the ranch; it's just how you choose to see it," or "Whatever happened, we were still so blessed to be in the Buddhafield; Bhagwan changed my life."

The irony was that the sannyasins I confided in genuinely believed they were being supportive. Their worldviews were so deeply entrenched in Osho's teachings, and the culture that emerged around him, that normal societal codes of conduct didn't seem to register—at least not to the degree I expected and hoped for.

On one particular occasion, a friend asked me point-blank, "Why do you hate Osho?" I didn't want to talk about it, especially to her. I had recently come across a few pictures she had posted on Facebook of her and Milarepa that were taken during a recent trip she had taken back East. Just seeing those photos triggered me. She kept probing. I finally told her about how Milarepa and others exploited me. As I spoke, I felt the familiar and telltale signs of trauma that I had come to recognize. I could literally feel the adrenaline course through my arms, my jaw tighten, my heart pound, and my blood course through my veins. My friend looked at me perplexed.

"Why are you so worked up? You seem as upset as if it happened yesterday," she said.

"That's how trauma goes. When I'm triggered, it takes over," I said. Whenever anyone insinuated that my feelings weren't appropriate, I would seethe.

"Why not just sort this whole thing out?" she said. "I have Milarepa's number. Just give him a call now and put this thing to rest."

"No! That won't help. He's a perpetrator! He should go to prison. He should make proper amends," I said, flustered.

"Okay, your choice," she said. "I just can't understand why you could be this upset after all these years. I want you to be happy." I didn't know what to say. I wanted to be happy too, but when I was triggered, I barely had control over what I was feeling—it was a powerful force that I couldn't will away.

"I don't think you get how much this has affected me," I said sharply.

"I'm totally against the abuse. I support you. This can be sorted out," she said. I didn't believe her. I knew that she cared about me, and I also knew she would never see the abuse as a serious offense.

I often left my conversation with sannyasins feeling overexposed, shamed, and enraged. On top of that, just hearing some of the familiar commune speak stirred self-doubt. The last remnants of that denigrating voice of commune dogma that said, "It was no big deal, you're too sensitive," or "You shouldn't feel what you feel, you're the problem," reared its head. But I was learning not to let that voice overpower me. I was learning to believe myself rather than collapse under the shame and dismissal.

Even when I told my mom and Eric about the abuse and that I wished they had looked out for me, they seemed unfazed. "I didn't know it was happening," my mom said. Eric took it even a step further, saying "You didn't have it that bad, maybe you seduced the men," or "Let me play my little violin for you," as he outstretched his little finger and played an imaginary bow with his other hand. My rage would well up. It felt impossible. Over the years, whenever I mentioned the abuse or anything from my past that troubled me, my mom responded, "I'm sorry it was hard for you." She seemed unable to admit to her parental failings.

As I found my own strength, the more I wanted to scream at the denial coming from the sannyasins I knew, including from my mother and Eric.

All the excuses, bypassing, and using Osho's quotes to back them up were bullshit and only fortified my bitterness. The more I spoke out, the more my remaining sannyasin friends distanced themselves from me. Some simply disappeared or stopped calling me back. No explanation needed.

PART FIVE
The Fight to be Heard

CHAPTER SIXTY

WILD WILD COUNTRY

IN THE SPRING of 2018, I opened Netflix to find a new documentary called *Wild Wild Country* featured prominently on the banner. A throng of people dressed in red caught my eye, and I did a double take. It was only then that I realized it was about Rajneeshpuram. I never imagined that this story, with all its divisive twists—from the legal battles with the government to the attempted murders, the immigration fraud, and the sheer craziness of it all—would resurface and gain notoriety again, especially not decades later.

I binge-watched all six episodes in two days. I was mesmerized. It was as though I was peering into a time capsule, transported back to a reality that now felt like a surreal dream. Through the lens of time, the world that once seemed normal now appeared more bizarre than any fictional tale. Back then, I believed we were a clan of kind, loving people dedicated to truth and authentic living. Now, it seemed like we had all been under a spell.

The scenes of red-clad sannyasins in the middle of the ranch's desolate landscape stirred a mix of outrage, nostalgia, and sorrow. While I remembered many events from that time and had learned more over the years through the rumor mill, much of it had become jumbled in my mind. Being in the middle of the chaos while it was happening didn't allow for perspective, especially in relation to the outside world. Now, as I watched the footage—much of which I had never seen before—the whole saga came into sharper focus.

There were moments, like watching Sheela's heated exchange on *Nightline* where Ted Koppel had to cut her microphone, that left me cringing. Sheela, with her fearless bravado and blatant dismissal of anyone who didn't give her what she wanted, was just as I remembered her. She was entitled and gutsy back then, and decades later, she didn't seem to have any remorse or regret about her actions. She still held to her conviction that everything she did was necessary and in service to Osho and his vision. I was surprised to see that her unwavering love for Osho endured, even after the public betrayal he hurled at her, branding her a traitor and a fascist. She still didn't seem to recognize that she was a criminal.

It was similarly perplexing to see Niren, the lawyer, still a devotee enraptured by Bhagwan, presenting the legal proceedings of the past in a measured way, as if nothing had changed. He was of the belief that Bhagwan remained the pillar of spiritual truth while Sheela and her cohort were responsible for the downfall. He went on and on about how wonderful it all was. His confidence was persuasive, reminding me that part of being a good lawyer is having total conviction in the argument you're making; wavering in any way is a tell that one cannot afford if they want to win. He was a masterful attorney, and he didn't budge from his well-honed perspective.

Yet, despite how dark things had turned, there was no denying we accomplished amazing things. I was reminded of all the good, kind people I knew—many had become disciples with a yearning to make themselves and the world a better place. Seeing everyone celebrate stirred a longing to feel that kind of joy again. I recalled the sense of connection we all had with each other, a feeling I had not found in the outside world. Even now, after so many years, I recognized that there was nothing more compelling than community and the sense of belonging. That was the one aspect of the commune I missed. I could see how Bhagwan's charisma and the promise of a life of celebration drew people to follow him. We were to live our lives to the fullest. That sounded pretty good. But that's not how it actually was.

Everything portrayed in the series was accurate, but the footage was limited to the political struggles and whatever else the media had captured over the years. It didn't address what it was like to live there as a disciple. More importantly, it didn't examine the abuses that happened, especially to the children, nor the aftermath we faced when we were thrust into the world, ill-prepared.

CHAPTER SIXTY-ONE

DOWN THE RABBIT HOLE

JUST A COUPLE months after I watched *Wild Wild Country*, I was browsing Facebook when a photo of fifty or so sannyasins dressed in red and strewn on a side of a hill in Rajneeshpuram appeared on my screen. Smack bang in the middle of the picture was me at age fourteen, holding a bottle of beer in the air. We were celebrating something, though I don't remember what. We all looked joyful—as if high on the Buddhafield energy.

What is this? I thought as I clicked on the photo. As it turned out, it was the cover image for the "Rajneeshpuram Residents" group. I didn't want to join the group and be drawn into a web of New Age shapeshifting and denial about what happened at the ranch. But damn it, I wanted that photo. I had so few pictures of myself from that time. When I tried to save it, a pop-up message informed me that I couldn't without first joining the group.

Fine, I concluded, I'll join the group, copy the photo, and then leave. The next day, I was notified that I'd been accepted into the group. So, down the rabbit hole I went. Surprisingly, one of the first posts I saw was from a woman asking about the abuse and neglect of the commune kids. Accompanying the post was a picture of us kids gathered in front of the school building in Antelope. There we stood, our smiling faces a stark contrast to the barren landscape in the background.

I began reading. The woman posting spelled out the neglect and inappropriate physical advances that she witnessed in both Pune and Rajneeshpuram. She went on to say that some of the men who were inappropriate with tween and teen girls were praised within the commune for being lovely people. Besides my own story, I had heard of an instance of another commune girl who posted in a different group about being raped in Pune when she was thirteen. Apparently, it turned into a battle where she was belittled and eventually silenced. I was told that many, if not most who heard her story sided with the man she was accusing. It seemed they were unable to deal with a subject that clashed with their steadfast belief that everything that happened in the commune was beautiful or fodder for spiritual growth—that it was all love and light. They didn't want these negative revelations to see the light of day. Similarly, I'd heard many people suggest that one of the teachers, the man who looked like Jesus, had molested many of the young girls, some as young as six years old. Were those stories quashed too?

Now, this woman's post was inquiring about the kids in general, calling for perpetrators and those who saw what was happening but never did anything, to make reparations to us, the then children. She was asking for the truth to be brought out of the shadows. I was relieved. Finally, a subject that had been too taboo for discussion was being acknowledged. Maybe now, after thirty-five years, the community could face the issue of our abuse and neglect. Maybe now, I and others could speak out and be heard.

I voraciously began reading the comments. Many echoed the familiar justifications that I had heard over the years: "It was an experiment, so there was bound to be some duplicitous behavior," and "It was the '70s, what do you expect?" Another wrote that he joined the commune because everyone was welcome including misfits and social deviants. I grew angrier with each new excuse or justification I read. The deflection and cognitive dissonance astounded me, especially from people who thought they were so evolved.

Next, I read comments from two girls my age, whom I knew pretty well back in the day. They said they appreciated their experiences in the commune, including their sexual freedom, more than anything in their lives. They said they felt empowered, not abused. Were they in denial? Was it just me who was traumatized by the experience? Self-doubt reared its head again—was I just exaggerating? I refocused. In my bones, in the marrow never touched by harm or manipulation, I knew I was not inventing tales, and I knew that others were affected too. And now, I was ready to throw down flames and walk into the fire roaring. I impulsively typed a response to the post:

> "I was in Pune 1 and the ranch (Rajneeshpuram) from the very beginning. I don't want to go into much detail since it still disturbs me, but there was rampant sexual abuse. It started when I

was 9 and became more intense when I was 12. This would not have been accepted in the outside society. However, at the ranch it was not stopped, and many people knew about it. Yes, I seemed mature, but frankly it was a survival mechanism. For those who say let the past be the past, you don't understand trauma. The nature of trauma is that it can feel like it's living in you in the present. Those of you who think this was just part of the whole Buddhafield experience are dead wrong in my opinion. I can see why you may not want to see the shadow of the whole thing, but the shadow was dark and very creepy."

I knew my testimony would soon reach sannyasins around the world. I suspected at least some of them would shame me, or at least minimize what I was saying. I contemplated deleting my comment, but I just couldn't. I was strong enough and had enough self-respect to handle it—I was determined that I was not going to be intimidated, which felt like a little triumph.

*   *   *

Responses to my comment started coming in. Initially they were supportive, with people telling me that they had my back, and that this time I was being heard loud and clear. I was relieved that what I was saying wasn't being shot down.

However, by the next morning, a debate was emerging. No one questioned the veracity of my claims, but instead questioned whether adults having sex with twelve-, thirteen-, fourteen-year-olds was actually sexual abuse, as if it was a debatable topic. There were also those who claimed they never had any idea it was happening—even though it was happening in plain sight.

As the thread unfolded, some acknowledged that they knew the "kids" were being sexualized and abused. One person admitted: "After the ranch I knew a Swami who boasted about his sleeping with kids. It never seemed to occur to him that there was anything wrong with his behavior. I now regret not talking about it." Another said: "I actually talked to several male peers at the time about the underage girls they were sleeping with. I was told that I was missing out on spiritual realizations." So, sleeping with underage girls and boys was spiritual? I felt sick. It was certainly a culture where traditional mores were thrown out.

Then Dickon, one of the boys I knew at the ranch, shared that he had been abused too. "I was fourteen—it happened to me, and I knew all those in my age group. None of us were mature enough to understand what that all meant," he said. I was so relieved he spoke up. I was not alone after all. I wondered how many of us there were, and I was beginning to think far more than I had even known.

The next day I received a message from a woman named Chiara. I didn't recognize her name, only that she was one of the people who responded to my post the day before, commending me for my courage to tell the truth. I wasn't sure I knew her. I opened the message:

> "Sarito, dearest, I am a witness to some nights you spent with Milarepa since I was living in the adjoining bedroom in the double wide across the road from Magdalena. You were sometimes spending nights with him, and I saw you. I was shocked to my core but said nothing. I apologize to you for my cowardice, I was every bit as manipulated as you and many others were in those years."

Her words landed in my chest before my brain could fully take in what she was saying. *She was a witness to my abuse.* I hadn't named who had abused me and she knew him, at least one "him," and said his name. Her message touched me, and for a few moments I let down my guard and felt the grief that was underneath my tough exterior. Tears streamed down my face.

★　★　★

Over the ensuing days, some encouraged me and others to "name them, name the perpetrators!" At the same time, others chimed in saying they were against naming them, arguing it was careless to potentially destroy their lives given that the alleged abuse happened within a culture that encouraged experimentation. "It's not like all the kids who had sex felt abused; there's lots of gray area," one said.

I was too scared to name anyone. I worried if I did, I would be shunned, denigrated for being "negative," be sued, or even threatened. None of my peers named anyone either.

After a few weeks, as the discussion about the abuse of the children continued, the group's admins announced that they wanted to restore the group to a place for discussing their love and joy for Osho, not the dark side. At the same time, several people who were advocating for us "then kids," wanted us to have a safe and supportive place to share and feel heard. They created a new secret group just for us. Soon those who wanted the topic to go away shooed us to the new group with comments like: "If anyone truly wants healing, maybe go to the secret group. It sounds like it's rooted in healing, not hysteria."

While I appreciated that those who created the secret group did so out of care and good intentions, I didn't want my story to be relegated into the hidden belly of Facebook. What I really wanted was for me and my peers to go public about the abuse and neglect. I spoke to several others, asking them if they would speak out with me. Nobody wanted to. In fact, many were still loyal to the community and didn't want to rock the boat. Before long, the new secret group was all but inert. Was that the end of the discussion? It felt like the Osho community at large had managed to quash the topic once again. This only fueled my need to speak out.

I didn't know how to do it. I was intimidated, even terrified. The Osho community was a strong force to reckon with, and I imagined if I did speak out, the backlash would be enormous. I didn't know if I could handle doing it on my own. Nonetheless, I thought of writing an article to publish somewhere. I even tried to contact key people who I thought may be interested in the story, like Ronan Farrow who had uncovered the Harvey Weinstein story, the Duplass brothers who produced *Wild Wild Country*, as well as other media. My attempts were in vain. Nobody responded. For the moment, I put the whole thing on the back burner and did my best to get on with my life.

★   ★   ★

A year later, in the summer of 2019, I visited Hawaii. While there, I met up with a woman I knew from the ranch whom I hadn't seen in a long time. Unexpectedly, she brought up Milarepa, telling me she knew I was with him and that she didn't ever say anything because she didn't want to be told to leave the ranch. Then she introduced me to her houseguest, who told me that his wife had left him to be with Milarepa, and that they now lived in his old house in Connecticut. I was appalled. That's when I got the idea to write Milarepa a letter since I now had someone sitting before me who knew his address.

Back in Boulder, I sat in front of my computer for days, unable to find the words. I kept reminding myself to just tell the truth, and to be honest. Then, one night as I lay restless in bed, I got my computer, and the words I needed to express flowed out of me in fits and starts. As I wrote, I cried, remembering how I felt back then. I was finally able to express myself. I had enough perspective to look back at my younger self and understand her feelings. Now, I didn't care if Milarepa didn't like me, I didn't care if what I said wasn't "evolved." I no longer cared about this man to whom I had given all my power so many years earlier. He didn't have a hold on me anymore, but the way he treated me had left an indelible mark on my heart and psyche that had affected me ever since. Being with him was my first experience of romantic love, and I projected all my fairytale notions onto him. But he was a grown man, and the fairytale was torn to shreds.

When the letter was written and ready to post, I sent it by certified mail. I tracked it daily over the next couple of weeks. There was no receipt for delivery. Did he refuse to sign for it? I double-checked the address and sent another copy by regular mail. Then I waited.

After a couple of months, I gave up on Milarepa responding to me or even acknowledging he got my letter. His silence made me feel like he was trying to deny my existence and any accusations I was making. I imagined he thought me beneath him, unworthy of a response. He was now an "old sannyasin," and people called him "Osho's musician." He apparently traveled around the world playing music at Osho Meditation centers and Osho festivals. That was all I knew about him. I thought it hypocritical and cowardly for him to claim to be a spiritual man searching for truth while refusing to face the truth I confronted him with.

Being ignored only rekindled my desire to tell my story publicly. I would find a way to do it. I was gathering my courage.

CHAPTER SIXTY-TWO

THE OSHO BRAND

Two years later, in the fall of 2021, I received a call from one of my peers who was also abused in the commune. When we'd spoken before, she had been clear that she didn't want to take the story public with me. Now, she was telling me that she had a connection with the *Osho Times*, and that her friend suggested she and others could write open letters to the commune about our abuse. But, she added, they didn't want us to name the perpetrators. They didn't want anyone to feel uncomfortable.

"Sarito, I'm going to do it, and you should too," she urged.

Hesitant, I responded, "I don't know. I kind of wanted to go bigger. I want nothing to do with anything Osho."

"Well, it would be something," she said. I agreed to think about it.

When I called her the next morning to say I would write an open letter, she promptly informed me that *Osho News* had changed its stance. They wouldn't publish our letters at all, fearing legal repercussions. Apparently, they had consulted an attorney or advisor, who outlined their reasons for changing their mind. They essentially wanted every identifying factor removed, including names, setting, and descriptions. Also, and I think more importantly, they said publishing the story threatened to put the Osho name in disrepute. They were worried the story could fall into the hands of hawkish media.

This made me wonder what reputation the *Osho Times* was trying to preserve. I hadn't paid attention over the years, but I assumed that most sannyasins had taken initiation while Osho was still alive. I thought he said not to follow him when he was gone. However, when I did a few Google searches, I discovered that there were Osho centers around the world, a new generation of sannyasins, and that Osho was revered like a god.

I was shocked to discover how huge a brand Osho had become. At the helm of this vast domain stood Osho International Foundation (OIF), a legal entity orchestrating everything. It held dominion over the Pune ashram, all of Osho's intellectual properties—spanning over two hundred books in multiple languages—and the Osho name itself. I discovered that Osho International Foundation's YouTube channel boasted a staggering million-strong following. Some snippets of Osho's discourses had garnered more than 1.5 million views, each accompanied by advertisements, signaling a strong and well-established financial enterprise.

Besides all the content put forth by the Osho International Foundation, I found numerous websites and memes related to Osho, including the *Osho News*, another online periodical run by sannyasins. They not only posted articles about Osho's teachings, but the website was also chock-full of ads for various therapy groups and esoteric readings being offered by Osho devotees.

What struck me further was how sannyasins, especially those fondly dubbed the "old sannyasins," who were seen as wise since they had been in Osho's presence the longest, had now evolved into self-styled experts across various facets of Osho's teachings. From bodywork techniques to trauma therapy, tantra to tarot, they were proselytizing Osho's teachings for their own financial and social gain. The extent of this propagation was astounding—some devotees crisscrossed the globe, leading groups and workshops they had either devised or adopted from other self-help movements.

One key example was the "Path of Love," a week-long intensive that promised deep shedding of personal patterns to connect with one's genuine self. Led by seasoned Osho therapists, the program apparently borrowed its structure from Kalindi, another guru. The Osho group leaders incorporated Osho elements such as dynamic meditation, snippets of his discourses, and adorned the walls with large photos of Osho, rebranding the group as their own. The Path of Love groups, offered worldwide, became a financially lucrative enterprise with a rapidly growing following over the years.

In essence, the Osho brand had burgeoned into a full-fledged enterprise, transcending mere spirituality to become a thriving business venture—Osho's notion of Zorba the Buddha in action.

CHAPTER SIXTY-THREE

OUT OF THE SHADOWS

A FEW WEEKS later, my peer called again. "I'm going to do it. I'm going to confront the Osho community. I've had it!" she said. She told me she planned to post her story on the Rajneeshpuram Residents Facebook group, as well as another group called "Pune Sannyasins," and she was going to name names. She explained that her sudden change of heart came after she heard of a recent rape at the hands of a sannyasin musician who was not being held accountable.

"I'm glad that you are. But aren't you scared of the repercussions, like having a lot of hate coming in your direction, or getting sued?" I asked.

"They can't get away with this. If we are telling the truth, naming names won't hurt us," she said.

"You're probably right," I said. Maybe all my fears about being sued were unwarranted. Plus, now I had several people who said they witnessed my abuse, so it was no longer a case of "she said, he said."

"You should post too. We are more likely to be heard if we both do."

"When are you going to do this?" I asked.

"Soon. Please, Sarito, post your story too. Post that letter you wrote to Milarepa." I was silent for a minute, thinking it all through.

"Okay, I will!" I said.

"Good," she said.

⋆   ⋆   ⋆

The next day, my peer posted her story to the two Facebook groups. She spelled out in graphic detail the many abuses she endured, beginning when she was six years old, when one of the key members of the Pune ashram molested her. She went on to reveal that she lost her virginity when she was twelve, to a man she worked with at the ranch who lured her with sweet talk.

I read and wept. Then I sat down at my computer and wrote my message and posted it to the same two Facebook groups. I included my letter, pointing out that I sent it to Milarepa two years earlier and that he hadn't responded. The moment I clicked "Post," I felt shaky. Apprehension replaced the clarity and strength I felt moments before. I laid it all out there. There was nowhere to hide now.

Sept 22, 2021

Dear Osho Rajneesh community:

In the name of truth and to stand in solidarity with all of us "kids" who were sexually and emotionally abused in the commune, I feel compelled to step forward about my abuse. I have grappled with going public for many years, and repeatedly ended up feeling too shaky and unsupported to speak out. When I have shared my story with commune members in the past, the general response was, for the most part, to minimize the gravity of it, and whitewash my experience. In fact, a couple of years ago there was a post in the Rajneeshpuram Residents Facebook group inquiring about the abuse and neglect of the children. I did speak honestly about the fact that I was abused and felt traumatized by it, though at that time I did not name names. I received some support which was invaluable, but sadly, many of the responses only left me feeling angry and silenced. Dismissive comments like "The children seemed so mature," "It was an experiment, so there was bound to be some duplicitous behavior," "It was the '70s, what do you expect?" just left me thinking the cloak of spiritual denial could never be penetrated. There were people worrying about ruining the lives of the abusers, suggesting not to mention names. What about my life? Does the suffering I endured not matter? Doesn't truth matter? Isn't that what we were all seeking after all? One woman even privately messaged me trying to talk me out of my experience, saying that she would have loved to have men pursue her when she was the age I was when the abuse started. So I just walked away from the Facebook conversation feeling deflated, hopeless, and worthless.

The social mores of the commune normalized poor sexual boundaries, and idealized sexual promiscuity all in the name of freedom, non-attachment, and spirituality. In this context, I became a great actress, and dared not speak of my internal angst, confusion and torture. I thought I couldn't. The predatory behavior of the pedophiles in our midst was just accepted and normalized. I believe that some of you didn't know about what was going on. But I also know that many of you did, and simply chose to look the other way. As a child I was vulnerable and needed protection and guidance. The fact is that adults having sex with anyone under eighteen is abuse and rape. Plain and simple. It is not a debatable fact and cannot be justified or pushed aside simply because it's an inconvenient truth that muddies your spiritual delusion.

My first sexual encounter where I lost my virginity was with Milarepa, also fittingly known as the "Rapist" to his friends, at the age of twelve. He continued to have sex with me on a regular basis for most of the time we were at the ranch—in between numerous other conquests. I was also abused by Mutribo, one of Milarepa's close friends. There were also lesser offenses, such as fondling my breasts on several occasions by Swiss Raja, and fondling my breasts by another very prominent man in the commune whose name I don't feel comfortable revealing at this time. I know for a fact that Milarepa and Mutribo had sexual relationships with other kids at the ranch, but it is not my place to tell their stories. However, it's important to understand that Milarepa in particular was a serial offender.

The "relationship" with Milarepa has haunted me all these years, and I am sickened that he is still at large and revered within this community. It's humiliating and belittling to say the least. After walking away from the Facebook group discussion in 2018, I decided that I would write Milarepa a letter in hopes of being heard and in hopes that he would reflect, apologize, and own up to his offenses. I sent the letter by mail and also by certified mail. I never received any kind of response. I am disgusted that he touts himself as a spiritual man who travels around playing music and teaching meditation. Does he have no conscience? I suppose responding to me would amount to him admitting guilt to what happened. I have not been in touch with him since shortly after the ranch when I saw him in Los Angeles along with Mutribo. The last night I saw them I was hoping to see Mutribo who was passing through town. Mutribo ignored me, had sex with another woman in the bed next to me. Milarepa was in the loft in the same room having sex with somebody else. About twenty years ago I wrote a message to Milarepa because I wanted to confront him when he came through Boulder. He responded saying I could come to the Osho center to hear him play. I didn't go and have never heard from him again.

Below is the letter I sent to Milarepa that details what happened and how his actions affected and still do affect me. It is my hope that sharing it here will help you understand the facts of this matter and the great impact it has had on my life. There is really nothing that can reverse what happened, but there can be some healing by hearing me, standing with me against abuse, and demanding that Milarepa and other abusers come out of the shadows and take responsibility. Even better would be if they would stop being slippery and stop trying to justify or minimize their actions. I hope the community as a whole will have the good sense to knock these people down from their revered positions within the community and see them for who they really are. To those who have reached out to me with your love and support, I thank you from the bottom of my heart. I would not have had the courage to share all this without you. For those of you who are hearing of my experience for the first time, I ask that you take it in and believe me. I am telling the truth.

Oct 1, 2019
Dear Milarepa,

For many years, over 35 years in fact, I have held inside of me a pain that eats at my core. This is the result of the sexual and emotional abuse I experienced at Rajneeshpuram. What happened to me then has affected every day of my life since. Along with the incessant negative feelings, shame, and collapse, there is another part of me that is self-respecting and strong. It's time to set the record straight. It's time for the truth to be told and for you to take responsibility for your actions. There is no kind of sugar coating or spiritual justification that excuses exploiting a minor.

When I was twelve years old, shortly to become thirteen, you began having sex with me. This continued for two to three years. This should have never happened! Not only was it morally wrong, and legally "rape of a minor," and "statutory rape," it was also just despicable human behavior. It was emotionally deceptive, a misuse of power, and cruel. Ironically this happened in the midst of a community that touted love, deep personal inquiry, honesty and the pursuit of enlightenment. Your actions were the opposite of these precepts. Instead, your actions were self- centered hedonism with no consideration for me, or for the hurt and damage you would leave in your wake.

When I arrived at the ranch, I was a lonely young girl who had a strained and complicated relationship with my mother. In fact, I arrived alone. I was a daydreaming tween, who despite some wounding, believed in romance and love. I engaged in magical thinking and imagined scenarios in which I'd be rescued. I, in fact, believed whole-heartedly that romance was inextricably tied to love, and as an extension, sex was an expression of that love. My heart was not yet hardened, and my mind was not yet disillusioned. I was innocent and vulnerable. I was not aware of the complex emotional games adults played with each other. I had no reference point. I was a virgin. I had never even had a date with anyone. I didn't know anything about romance. I didn't know anything about sex. This is when you inserted yourself into my life.

We both arrived during the early days. I was the 32nd person to arrive, and I believe you arrived a couple of weeks later. Those were the days when I lived in Howdy Doody with 14 men, and one of them was you. You played music with Sam after dinner outside the ranch house, singing many Eagles songs that I still remember well. You started talking to me and seeking me out. I thought your interest meant you must really like me, and in my naiveté, I hoped your love would make my trouble go away, help me feel safe and appreciated. It was all very innocent in my eyes, but you had different plans.

One night a poker game formed with some of the men. You invited me to the game, where you offered me beer, and I obliged. Soon after, I was sitting next to you while you had one hand down my shirt, fondling my breast, and the other holding your hand of cards. I felt uncomfortable, frozen, but I didn't react. Nobody else was reacting, so it must have been fine, I thought. Many people witnessed what you were doing, but just watched and didn't show any signs that it was inappropriate. That didn't mean it was okay, but means they were in fact complicit. As it turns out, many of the men at the game also had sex with young girls as time went on. I believe you set an example that your friends then followed. At that time, I didn't know what your attention and fondling meant. Did this make me special, I wondered? I also thought that if I wanted you to like me I should go along with it.

A couple weeks later, there was a party at one of the build sites, Desiderata, I think. Many of us rode there in the backs of pickup trucks, with beer and music in hand. We were there at the party, and as it was getting dark, you pulled me aside, sweet talking me, and guided me away from the others and into the bushes. Foreigner's song "I've been waiting for a girl like you to come into my life" blared out of the boom box. I felt shy and embarrassed because as you sang along with the song, I thought you were serenading me. It was exhilarating to be wooed, but scary because it was happening so fast I didn't know how to react or what I felt. You nudged me toward the ground where you kissed me, felt me up and began to take off my clothes. But, before it went any further, someone yelled at us from the distance, saying it was time to go. So we got up and piled into the pickup truck. I remember sitting in the back of the truck feeling embarrassed and like I had something to hide, like I had a dirty, yet special secret. You sat next to me casually as if nothing was going on between us. When the truck stopped where you lived, you took my hand to help me up and then guided me home with you.

This was when you broke my virginity, or as you and your friends put it "popped my cherry. " I remember lying there stiffly. I had no real interest in the sex, and in fact it was never pleasurable, I just took it. I took it because I thought it would make you love me. I thought sex was supposed to be an expression of love. But after it was done, I just stared at the ceiling all night. As you slept, I wondered what was so special about sex. Where was the ecstasy and joy of which people spoke? Nonetheless, I formed an attachment, and I believed that the sex proved I was special to you, that it "sealed our bond." After that first night you continued having sex with me either regularly or periodically for the following three years, until I was fifteen.

When things first started with us, I thought we were "together." Although we were living in a community where everyone was sleeping with everyone else, it didn't cross my mind that was the case with you and me. I made romantic assumptions, as young girls do. We never had real conversations. You spoke very little besides to say "Wanna come home with me tonight?" You didn't really know me, and I certainly didn't know you. Finally, I realized that I was not special at all, that you had not chosen me, and that I was in fact just one notch on your very notched belt. First, I found out about your relationship with Chetna. Then, soon after that, I saw you seducing and taking home, dozens and dozens of women, maybe one or two each day. I was so hurt and confused. I felt used and devalued. I wondered how one day you would lavish me with compliments that made me feel special, and use me sexually, only to treat me like I was invisible the very next day. I felt so much shame for even existing, and from that place of shame I had no courage to stand up to you.

I thought it was my fault because I was not attractive, accepting, or agreeable enough. Even though things felt so bad, I swallowed my pain and hoped things would change. At that point I felt emotionally trapped. I would feel some relief when you would come back around to me in your rotation of many women. For those few hours I thought I must be worthy, and then during the remaining time I would pine in torment. You lured me back in over and over again. You said the right things to make me feel attractive and special. I wanted to believe the things you said, and at first, I did. I formed an unhealthy bond with you, thinking I needed you to survive or to feel okay. This bond should never have been given the opportunity to form. Young emotions and hearts are fragile. That is why there are laws about age of consent and sexual abuse. At that young age, I was not psychologically or emotionally mature enough to make such decisions or handle the emotions of being treated like a disposable object. I wonder if you ever even stopped to think about how your fleeting whims, those of a horny Lothario who wants his girls as young as possible, would mess with my psyche?

While your interactions with me may not have been memorable to you, perhaps just small blips in your long list of sexual conquests, the impact for me was monumental and traumatizing. You had no shame, and somehow you got away with it. What was worse was that you and your similarly inclined pedophilic friends, would joke around about whose "cherry" you popped, or whom you took home the night before. It was like a sport. Your friends called you the "Rapist," which was indeed an accurate description, and a term that never made me laugh. There I was caught in the fray of your sick drama, a pawn in the game of corrosive conquest. I was just a piece of meat that you would chew up and spit out.

As time went on, you began sleeping with other girls my age. I remember throwing a party and inviting you, only to be entirely ignored. Instead, you seduced one of my friends right in front of my eyes. Later you were sleeping with one of my roommates. I just swallowed it and carried on keeping up appearances. But then it got to be too much. I needed to know why I was being discarded and why you were torturing me by sleeping with my peers. I tried to hide from facts, act tough, and tried my best to not see how sick it was. I expressed my distress in a letter, which I remember was very scary for me to do at the time. In the letter, I asked you why you no longer showed me attention. I came up with some stupid simile like "what we have is so beautiful that we should not dissect it like a rose, petal by petal." A couple weeks later you wrote back explaining that there were so many other men out there, and that there were in fact "hundreds of men who would give up enlightenment to be with you." That line was so absurd and dismissive that I could never forget it. That was clearly your modus operandi: going with the flow, following your energy, not attaching, and not considering anybody but yourself.

Now, putting all the details aside and the emotional damage aside, the facts remain: sexual relations with a young girl is a crime. While the details fade in my memory, what fades less readily is the psychological and emotional impact I've had to carry. I know that there is no way to undo what happened or for justice to be served. Even if you were in jail, the emotional wounds will always be with me.

Over the past couple of years, several people have reached out to me to tell me they knew about, or even witnessed, the sexual relationship you had with me. They have offered support, and have strongly urged me to expose you and the others who also abused underage girls. I appreciate their support immensely, and it has helped me find courage to speak up on this matter. Since you are well known in the Osho community, and since you teach meditation and are a "seeker," I hope you will take a good look at your actions and confront the hypocrisy that is so blatantly clear. I now place the responsibility in your hands to expose this ugliness to the community. Your shame is yours, not mine, and I ask you to take ownership of it. This is not a time for cowardice, but rather a time for you to shine light on this ugly truth so that there can be healing—healing for me, for the others you have used, and for the community. I also hope that the other men who were in your "posse" will come forth with the truth. This would be the most mature thing you could do to honor me, as well as any others who have similarly suffered.

Sincerely, Sarito

★　★　★

A deluge of comments flowed in. Initially they were all supportive, caring, and adorned with a colorful array of heart and prayer emojis. Some people were shaken, saying things like, "This shatters everything I once knew. We were blinded by our selfish desires, failing to protect our most vulnerable." Several even admitted to their lack of awareness, even owning their complicity for not recognizing the abuse.

I was most touched by the comments from some of my peers from the ranch. Jutta, my once roommate said:

> "My dear dear friend, words cannot express the gratitude for you coming forward again after what you've been through before. I am a witness to what you describe - every single word of it is true. I hope you finally get the apologies and healing you deserve. Thank you for articulating so clearly the emotional entanglement that we felt with our abusers. I love you, I'm so sorry for your sorrow...if only I could take it away."

Some saw the crimes for what they were and wanted to help. One woman said, "There is nothing to forgive. These actions are criminal and should be pursued as such. More importantly, how can those of you who have been so wronged find real healing?"

It was a good question, and I didn't know the full answer. What I did know is that being heard and believed was a good first step. I hoped in time the discussion would go deeper—that people would take a firm stand and demand accountability and reparations not only from the perpetrators, but also from Osho International Foundation since the commune culture played a large part in making the abuse of children permissible.

*   *   *

Over the next couple of weeks many other "then kids" came forward and posted their own stories of abuse and neglect. For some, it started back in Pune. The rumors that circulated for years about the teacher—the one who looked like Jesus—molesting young girls, were true. Several women named him, saying it started when they were as young as six years old. And it wasn't just in India. He continued when he was a teacher at Medina, the Rajneesh school in England. Seemingly all the kids in that cohort knew about it. I felt queasy and enraged. All I could think was why in the hell didn't anyone pay attention back then. Was it the sexualized culture that made people so blind?

Another testimony came from a woman who was just a couple years older than me. I remembered her from Pune as soft spoken, sweet, and innocent. She wrote of how one of the commune's most revered group leaders, a man whom many thought was close to being enlightened, took her virginity when she was fourteen. He was known for taking many women to bed, including anyone he fancied in the groups he led. When he approached her, she relayed, he asked if she was a virgin and if she had started menstruating yet. When she told him she hadn't started menstruating yet, he was relieved—that way he didn't have to worry she would get pregnant. That day he took her virginity. That was it. He was done with her. After that, she said, other men were always after her. They would get her into bed, have sex with her, and then just get up and leave. She said she learned to just let them because that's what the culture mandated. She explained how she felt used and learned to numb her feelings.

Dickon posted about how an adult woman seduced him when he was fourteen. He said he was on cloud nine—he thought he was in love. But just a couple days later, he saw the same woman dancing with his best friend, whom she took home and seduced that night. He was crushed.

Then, one of the girls who I always envied because she was the sexiest, wrote about how much shame she carried. She learned her sexuality helped her feel better about herself, at least momentarily. She too thought being chosen by a man meant she was special. That theme of feeling used, objectified, and sexualized was pervasive in all our stories. Many also felt that giving up their bodies for sex was mandated by the culture. Saying no meant you would be judged as negative and uptight, so they dared not say no. Some of the girls revealed that they had sex with seventy to over a hundred men during the ranch days. I had no words.

Each new testimony was painful to read. I learned so much about what others went through and felt a new kind of solidarity with my peers. I hadn't known the half of it, and many hadn't spoken out yet.

CHAPTER SIXTY-FOUR

MY PEERS

MANY OF my peers from the ranch and Medina stayed in touch over the years. They had even gotten together for several reunions. They communicated with each other via a WhatsApp group. I was not a member, nor had I attended any of the reunions. I had never felt compelled to join, especially since my three closest friends from that time—whom I would have liked to stay in touch with—weren't members of the group either.

I hadn't seen or heard from Kaya or Gita since they abruptly left the ranch. However, I had heard of them. Kaya continued working as a prostitute for many years before she severed all contact with her family and the other teens. I didn't know why. Her sister, whom I saw around 2003, told me stories of how Kaya visited the ashram in the early '90s and was overly seductive, even trying to seduce her good friend's boyfriend. That came as a shock. I couldn't even imagine her that way.

As for Gita, I heard that she parted ways with Kaya and moved back to the UK. At some point, she had an emotional crisis and ended up in a mental health institution. I was told that while she was there, she tried to commit suicide by jumping out of a second-story window. Later, I heard that she married and had two children who adored her. Tragically, her mental health remained fragile, and she wasn't able to raise them herself or even fully function in society. She had become a ward of the state, or the UK equivalent.

As for Devi, she remained a devoted member of the Osho community. She was beloved, and many sannyasins saw her as an embodiment of the freedom and openheartedness that Osho espoused. When she was passing through Boulder to assist in leading a Path of Love group, we met up. It was so good to see her. Despite how different we had become, we still had a strong and sweet connection. Over the next year, we stayed in touch. Our most recent correspondences had been to plan my visit to Australia to see her. I was back in school, this time studying Chinese medicine, and I hoped to visit her over my summer break.

It was while I was in class that I received a text from a sannyasin friend saying, "Call me. It's urgent." I left class and called him.

"Sarito, it's about Devi," he said.

"What happened?"

"She's in the hospital. She had to be helicoptered out from her house in the jungle. She had an ectopic pregnancy and was bleeding out."

"Oh, but she's going to be okay, right?" I asked.

"I don't think so." I simply could not take it in. "She's lost a lot of blood; she's in a coma," he said.

"No, I can't believe it." I was pacing in the hallway.

"Sarito, it's almost certain she's not going to make it," he said again. I was collapsing on the inside; I couldn't take it. But I was not in a place where I could fall apart. I found my teacher and told him what was happening. He told me to go home.

I curled up on my couch and cried. She died sometime later that day.

In her late teens or early twenties, she had been sterilized while back in India. In her thirties, she decided she wanted to have kids, so she returned to India to have the sterilization reversed, something I didn't even know was possible. She was told that she was at high risk for ectopic pregnancies. Yet, when she went to the ER in Australia with extreme abdominal pain, the doctor sent her home. The next day the pain intensified, and she started bleeding heavily. By the time the helicopter got there, it was too late. She had already lost too much blood.

⋆ ⋆ ⋆

The tragic fates of my friends shook me. The trails of destruction left in the wake of the commune was profound and pervasive for all of us. Even for Devi, who had become a kind of poster child for the movement, ultimately died due to complications as the result of her decision to get sterilized, like many sannyasin women did, and having it reversed. With Devi gone, my primary link to the other commune kids was severed. I rarely, if ever spoke to or heard of my commune peers. But now, with the recent upheaval created by so many of us finally speaking out about our abuse,

I apprehensively joined the WhatsApp group. I hoped I wouldn't feel too out of place.

It was clear everyone was stirred by the recent revelations. Some were coming to see that what they experienced was sexual abuse and neglect, and were now ready to name it as such, rather than minimize it. A staggering number of them had or were still struggling with financial challenges, drug abuse, and mental health issues.

I returned day after day to read the new threads, get totally wound up, and then return for more of the same.

CHAPTER SIXTY-FIVE

APOLOGIES

A COUPLE OF DAYS after I posted my story, I received a WhatsApp message from one of my peers saying, "Milarepa just posted an apology video on his One Sky Music Facebook page." It hit me like a shockwave. Someone must have forwarded my post to him, and maybe people were contacting him to ask if my claims were true. It struck me as odd that now, two years after I sent him a letter, he was responding, and via a public video message to boot. Buzzing with adrenalin, I opened Facebook.

I typed "One Sky Music" into the search box. His page loaded. There it was, his most recent post, titled "Apology to Sarito and the Osho Sangha." Accompanying his video was the following message:

> "If anyone would like to take this up further, please contact me personally by email. Once again, I am so deeply sorry for the wounds some of you still carry from my actions of the past, Rajneeshpuram in particular. Please accept my sincere apology, Sarito, and others who have been impacted by my behavior."

His image frozen on the screen conjured a familiarity but no pulls on my heartstrings. He was no longer a demigod in my eyes. He was just a normal looking man with a shaved head, wearing a baseball cap and a pair of ill-fitting, red-framed glasses that didn't look like his own. I took a deep breath and played the video.

> "Hello, friends. As some of you know, there have been a lot of things going on on the internet, circulating about me—Things that happened at Rajneeshpuram.

I don't deny any of it, I take full responsibility for all of it. I wish I could dial back the clock to those times and do things differently from the perspective from where I sit today, but I can't. I can't change the past. What I can do, and what I want to take the time here to share, is that I can apologize, and I want to apologize very deeply for anyone who has been hurt during our time at Rajneeshpuram by my actions, by my insensitivity, by my lack of awareness. If I've hurt you, if I've caused a wound in your heart that you've been unable to address and set aside, I really want to say I'm sorry.

I hope this small sharing will help move the needle, even just a little bit, towards coming to a better understanding, better connection… I hope that we can be friends after all of this.

It's been a long time since the ranch, but it doesn't diminish the feelings anyone has from that time. I feel it's great that it's coming out, that it's being shared. I would like, if it's possible, for there to be a way to connect by email. I'm also open to having a Zoom online sharing—just the two of us, or if you'd like a therapist to be there, that's fine. So we can hopefully move this thing forward and get beyond all the pain and the trauma it has caused and is still causing."

I was struck by the fact he didn't mention my letter or the allegations to which he was responding. Most people watching the video wouldn't know what he was apologizing for. He looked anxious, like he had been cornered and was scrambling to save his reputation. Every sentence seemed deliberate and obtuse, as if guided by a lawyer to admit to nothing and name nobody. He wasn't truly "standing in the fire," as sannyasins would say. He ended by pleading for the community's forgiveness, saying:

"It's affected the community—the worldwide international community of Osho lovers. I know people are hurt, people are disturbed, freaked out, not understanding. Again, all I can say to you as a community is I am sorry. I really am deeply, deeply sorry. I don't feel good about this. It's definitely something I need to look at moving forward in myself. And I will be . . . I really hope

you can accept my apology with the sincerity and open heart that
I am giving it. That would make me really happy. Thank you."

I sat for a few minutes trying to process what I had just watched. I felt
like he was appealing to the community more than he was to me. He was
speaking their language. Saying he was "openhearted" and needed to look
at some things within himself aligned with the sannyas ethos. It felt so shallow. I couldn't and wouldn't trust his apology.

Resolved to not let him get away with omitting my letter, I decided to
post it to his page myself. At least that way people would know what he
was talking about. But his page didn't allow posts, so I pasted my letter into
the comments below the video. That too was futile. Soon my letter was
buried amidst a barrage of other comments that were coming in.

Meanwhile, word of the video had spread, and people were talking
about it in the Facebook groups. Most thought that his apology wasn't
sincere. Some went to his page and posted comments to say as much. One
of my peers wrote, "You can't do more? Really? Find something you can
do!" Another wrote, "I can't help feeling your video is more of a PR stunt
to minimize the negative impact on you and your business than an authentic apology. The least you could have done in the video is address Sarito
specifically and offer to make it up to her somehow. I know for a fact that
she's spent tens of thousands of dollars in therapy, trying to deal with this
damage."

However, there were just as many messages from his supporters saying
things like, "I stand with Milarepa—he didn't do anything wrong. Sarito is
just throwing a tantrum. It seems her mental age is still twelve years old."
Or "Milarepa is such a great guy, a spiritual man."

As I continued to read the comments that were amassing, they suddenly
started disappearing. It seemed that Milarepa, or someone managing his
page, was deleting them. A little while later, commenting was turned off
entirely. He had essentially erected an electronic moat around him; the
only way to reach him was by email.

* * *

Next, Mutribo had someone post a letter addressed to me and the Osho community to both of the Facebook groups. Like Milarepa, he wasn't a member of either group, so he wouldn't be able to see any of the responses.

I was surprised to see his letter. Yes, I had named him in my post, but I had never written to him privately. Yet, he was writing me an open letter. It seemed he took it upon himself to address the issue. It made me wonder if he was writing to save face, as it seemed Milarepa was attempting to do, or if he had taken what I had written to heart. I braced myself and read his message. He started out saying:

> "I want to acknowledge the courage and risk you took in sharing all that you did with the clarity and feeling that you expressed. Thank you for taking that risk in naming me and giving me the opportunity to go back once more inside myself to that time on the ranch when all of these events took place. It has been intense and confronting to delve into those memories again and to feel all the feelings that arise in that looking and let them be.
>
> You have been bearing the pain and suffering you describe for an intolerably long period of time. I am so, so sorry for what-ever part I played in causing or intensifying all that hurt and con-fusion. My own lack of emotional maturity and sensitivity, and my total absence of awareness around the imbalance of power between us at that time, meant that I failed completely in meet-ing and caring for your delicacy and vulnerability. I understand why you felt so used.
>
> I want to apologize to you now for that lack of love and respect towards you. My behavior was arrogant and very hurtful. I have no excuses to offer. It was abuse. I am to blame. I am so sorry to have ever treated you in this way."

He went on to apologize to anyone else he may have hurt. He also shared about the other girl he was with, with whom he said he had the deepest connection. He said he had reflected about that relationship and how it affected her. He said that he and the girl met some time back and that it was healing for them both.

As I read, tears of relief and grief welled up. He validated my suffering with what felt like empathy. It was clear that he actually read my letter and responded to my specific points. He came straight out and said his relationship with me was abuse. He didn't blame me or avoid the topic.

Yet, it stung to hear him admit that he used me. It was a harsh reality check, a confirmation that love was not part of it.

As far as an apology could go, he said all the right things. I believe he was being genuine for the most part, though I didn't fully trust him. I was well aware of his charm and knack with words, and at the same time, I was starting to have a shift in perspective. I didn't want to continue raking through my past to make my point over and over again. He clearly heard me; the secret was out. There was not much else he could do. The thing I wanted most—that the abuse never happened—was impossible. This was a hard truth that made me mad as hell. Ultimately it was on me to process my sorrow, grief, and shame. That felt existentially unfair.

Overall, I was thankful for his letter. I could feel his regret and sorrow, and that wasn't nothing. Even if every word he said was a well-executed facade, even if he didn't remember how dismissive and cruel he was to me that night in LA, I needed to let go. There would never be a perfect ending.

★   ★   ★

The following morning, Milarepa had someone post a letter addressed to me and the Osho Rajneesh Sangha to the two Facebook groups. It seemed that the collective voice of disapproval about his video had reached him, so he was trying again. I didn't have high expectations.

> To Sarito & the Osho Rajneesh Community:
>
> I want to follow up my initial video sharing which I feel did not go far enough. It comes across as insincere and disingenuous. I understand this. Over the last days, I have been digging deeper to better understand my actions, patterns, and responsibility.
>
> There is no way to justify my behavior. I feel ashamed how irresponsible I was. That I chose to be with you, Sarito, in such a reckless, selfish, and insensitive way is an understatement. I was the adult in the room. You were a young, vulnerable, and innocent child. I used my power as an older man to engage in what was a gross violation of your trust, the Commune's trust, and

a betrayal of Osho's vision. Over the years since, I am growing in my understanding that the freedom Osho speaks of is not a licentious freedom. It is freedom that comes with tremendous responsibility and includes honesty, love, sincerity, and awareness. I had no sense of this at the ranch. I take full responsibility for the tremendous pain and confusion I have caused you and other girls who were teenagers I exploited. My heart burns knowing you have carried this wound for so many years. It took a lot of courage for you to confront and expose me. Much more courage than I have.

You sent your letters by certified mail several years ago. The fact I didn't take time to honor you with a reply is inexcusable. It was arrogant, dismissive, and cowardly. I am sure this only added to the pain and anger you were already feeling. I have been spinning in my mind trying to rationalize my actions, but I see this as just a clever way to deflect and distract from reality and what I need to take responsibility for. I know this is not Osho's way nor the path forward; nor is it the way to begin healing. I can understand the anger, shock, and resentment many of you feel.

There is a big, big lesson in all of this for me. I will continue looking inside and peeling through the layers. It's a painful process, a work in progress. Saying sorry is an empty gesture. It needs to go much deeper. I lay my heart at yours and Osho's feet, Sarito.

His words repelled me. He evoked Osho's name four times, which seemed like an appeal to readers' perceptions of him—to show that, by his devotion, he was not quite as bad an actor as he seemed. Saying "I bow to your and Osho's feet," was beyond off-putting. He assumed I was still an Osho follower and that he could appeal to me using Osho's name. He clearly knew nothing about me.

Both he and Mutribo said their actions were due to their lack of awareness. How ironic given they had spent decades in a community that touted self-awareness.

The next day I received two different direct emails and a text from Milarepa. He said he got my contact information from somebody with whom I spoken to the day before, who thought I wouldn't them sharing my contact information. I did mind. All of Milarepa's messages pleaded with me to sort this whole thing out, seemingly so he could feel better. He said:

> "I feel, and I think you might agree, that love and only love is going to heal this thing....Let's initiate the healing process and the love which will surely flow from this will bring transformation -- to you, to me, and for our whole Osho Sangha. I want this with all my heart. And I think you do, too."

He was clearly scrambling; I could feel the desperation behind his flowery words. I was not willing to meet with him nor negotiate with him. There was nothing to negotiate. If he wanted to show respect and remorse, he could respond to my letter in detail and hold himself accountable. I doubted any of that would happen. Somehow, I would need to accept this. I didn't know how I would.

Roughly ten days after Milarepa posted his video on his One Sky Music page, he took it down. There were no new posts and commenting had been disabled. His page was essentially inert.

★   ★   ★

Over the next several days, I received a flurry of messages via Messenger, WhatsApp, and email. Many were from people I didn't know, at least not well, who wrote to tell me how sorry they were. Some wrote to share their own stories of abuse, or to tell me about other girls that were abused, but who didn't recognize it as such, or were being silenced through some kind of spiritual sweet talk. Two different people wrote to tell me that Milarepa had been in a relationship with another twelve-year-old girl in Pune 2. One even relayed that the girl's mother was thrilled that a man as special as Milarepa had taken her daughter's virginity. As it turned out, the girl was still friends with Milarepa and despite several people asking her to come forth, she refused. She didn't see her relationship with him as abuse. She still loved him. Some begged with me to reach out to her, hoping I could somehow influence her perspective, or provide some support. She was apparently in the middle of a mental health crisis, though she said it had nothing to do with abuse.

Then, shockingly, she was found dead. Her mother said she died alone in her apartment from a seizure. The mother announced on Facebook that she was honored that Milarepa had agreed to travel thousands of miles to play music at her memorial. I was disturbed. He was still being treated as a revered member of the community. I tuned into the Zoom ceremony to see it for myself. After about five minutes, I couldn't stand it and left.

★ ★ ★

Next, a message from Vidya landed in my inbox. A strange mixture of anticipation and apprehension gripped me. What would she say, I wondered? Perhaps she was angry with me for bringing to light something that could implicate her. Or maybe, she wanted to advise me to let go of the past and move forward.

I opened her message:

> "Sarito, I just read your notes about Milarepa. I remember you telling us about this disgusting situation when you were in South Africa visiting us. It was disgusting then. It was disgusting when it happened, and it is disgusting now. How trite for him to say he is sorry he ruined your life… that makes me want to puke…. He should be tried for the crimes and put away. I am so sorry that when we were at the ranch, we were no longer so close. And I am so sorry that it all happened whilst I was there, even though I didn't know about it. If I can be of any assistance in any way to you, please do not hesitate to ask."

I felt her support and validation, and then when I read "I'm so sorry it all happened whilst I was there, even though I didn't know about it," my heart sank. I knew that she knew. There had even been other testimonies that indicated that all the Moms knew about the relationships adults were having with us teens. In particular, one of my peers had just commented on my post saying that two of the Moms had asked her and another teen to create a list of all the men who were sleeping with underage girls. Those men were then called to a meeting where they were told to be "discreet." Others mentioned that the topic came up in Moms meetings, and that it was something they didn't want the press to find out about. Learning of the list, which was compiled when I was in Europe, made me wonder if I was sent away because my ties with Milarepa were well known and the Moms didn't want the authorities to find out.

The notion that Vidya didn't know struck me as unfathomable, barring complete dissociation. I felt betrayed again. I had never known Vidya to lie. I was struggling to believe her ignorance. Plus, I thought we were still close at the ranch, just not as close as we were in India. Either she was trying to protect herself from being implicated, or, I suppose, her extreme trauma at the end of the ranch affected her memory. I know that when I saw her in those last months at the ranch, she seemed broken and disoriented. Whatever the truth, I was disappointed.

CHAPTER SIXTY-SIX

RECKONING

THE POSTS from us "then kids" became a catalyst, encouraging many who had joined the movement as adults to air their grievances too. It felt as though people finally felt safe enough to lay it all out there, speaking up about the painful experiences they had carried for years. They detailed their traumatic experiences from Pune and the ranch—from being pressured to get sterilized, to being physically assaulted or raped in therapy groups, to being urged to prostitute themselves to earn money to stay in the commune.

The discussions in the two Facebook groups quickly became polarized and contentious. At one end of the spectrum were those who had become disillusioned with Osho. They relayed stories painting him as a man who used power and exploitation to get whatever he wanted. Some admitted he had undeniable charisma and intellect, but that under the surface he was manipulating his followers to gain power and control. Many agreed he was a narcissist. Some called him a sociopath.

At the other end of the spectrum were those wholly devoted to Osho who accused those speaking out of being on a witch hunt. Some rationalized that there were always dark themes in any society and that we were all making too big a deal of it. They couldn't or wouldn't see how the commune culture and Osho's teachings tilled the soil for abuse—sexual and otherwise. Most insisted that Osho's profound teachings far outweighed the revelations of abuse.

* * *

Then another revelation shook the Rajneesh Facebook groups, and ostensibly the whole community. This time, the bombshell came from one of the commune's elite. Erin was a group leader who lived in Lao Tzu house in the Pune days. She was one of Osho's mediums for energy darshans and someone who received special attention from him even beyond that. After forty-three years of keeping a secret, she revealed that Osho himself had sexually abused her on multiple occasions. She recounted how he would summon her to his room in the dead of night, orchestrating sexual acts under the guise of spiritual energy work. She had unquestioningly followed his directives, rationalizing to herself that it was all part of some profound, albeit uncomfortable, transformation. Now she saw that he had abused his power. Osho had explicitly forbidden her to speak of it, and she never had until now.

The story spread through the Rajneesh community like wildfire. Within a couple of days two other women came forward and told their accounts of abuse at Osho's hand as well. The two Facebook groups were in a kind of virtual battle between the devotees and the disillusioned. I didn't dare speak during the Facebook war. Each new insult or dismissal sent a jolt through my already overcharged nervous system.

Many of the devoted took to posting a barrage of Osho quotes, Osho photos, and testimonies of their blissful experiences as a means of justifying their perspectives and monopolizing the feed. It was blatant that they were trying to dilute the negative experiences by sharing their glowing ones. The dynamic in the groups became outright hostile as the unsavory stories didn't go away.

In mid-November, less than two months after our stories started coming out, someone in the Pune Sannyasins group removed all posts about abuse—not only those from the kids, but also the posts from the women who claimed Osho abused them. The hundreds of comments accompanying the posts were, of course, gone too. The rationale posted was as follows:

"As of late, the original purpose of this group was diverted into various defamation and smearing campaigns. This group was originally intended for sharing our memories, both good and bad. But lately, only the bad is being shared, without any tangible results in sight. I suggest everyone look within."

Those who had enough with what they called the smear campaign left the Rajneeshpuram Residents group where the dark side was still welcome to be discussed. It became the group where people aired their negative experiences, while the Pune Sannysins group was where the devotees shared their positive experiences.

CHAPTER SIXTY-SEVEN

GOING PUBLIC

THE NEXT year was intense. I did my best to maintain normalcy while at work, but every other free moment, from when I awoke and looked at my phone till I went to bed, was consumed with reading new posts and engaging in various discussions behind the scenes.

At times I felt like I was living in a spy novel, especially when a kind of informant using the alias "Zeus" contacted me. He managed to save Milarepa's video before it was taken down. He said he thought I might need it as evidence. I thanked him. Day after day, he sent me incriminating information about other perpetrators and OIF, revealing things nobody had exposed yet. He claimed that some prominent sannyasins were pleading with the girls they had slept with not to expose them. Zeus also said Jayesh, the current president of OIF, was a corrupt businessman with a long criminal history, including drug smuggling, and that he was hiding OIF money in secret Swiss and offshore bank accounts while claiming the foundation was in debt. Whether true or not, it echoed other tidbits I'd heard over the years from various sannyasins.

Osho International Foundation hadn't so much as acknowledged the "kids" stories of abuse and neglect. Several people even wrote to them asking them to take action. Radio silence. I believed that OIF, as the legal entity representing the entire Osho movement, should be held at least partially responsible for the grave oversight concerning the commune kids. When I suggested in a Facebook thread that OIF should pay financial damages to all the kids, I received a message from a man who had been supportive until that point. Now he vehemently asserted that Osho and the commune had nothing to do with the abuse; he said it was the parents and the perpetrators who were responsible. He wrote to me saying, "If Osho's reputation is on the line, Jayesh will interfere."

"What do you mean?" I wrote back.

"Jayesh gets things done and has friends in every secret service agency on the planet; he knows the most powerful people in the highest positions of government—I would not mess with him."

Seriously? It sounded like he was trying to intimidate me. All I could think was, Don't you dare threaten me! But a shiver of fear lodged in my belly. I didn't know Jayesh or what he was capable of. If I exposed my story and called out OIF, would my safety be at risk? Would he send somebody to hurt me or poison me? Would he unite sannyasins to harass me online? Would he destroy my life if I didn't keep my mouth shut? As ludicrous as it seemed for a spiritual institution to do something so sinister, I couldn't ignore the real threat. After all, dark plots had surrounded Osho for a long time.

★ ★ ★

It felt like my only safe haven was with a few peers who also wanted accountability and to speak out publicly. We had each other's backs and supported each other through frequent meltdowns. We spent hours discussing the best way to share our stories and what the potential ramifications might be. It had already been over three years since I decided I wanted to go public. Then my peers and I had spent another year strategizing.

Nothing was happening. While I wanted to do it right, whatever that meant, my patience was wearing thin. Every idea I had, like writing a blog, was stymied by a couple of my peers who insisted I wait. I finally hit my limit when one peer in particular insisted that I don't do anything or talk to journalists without her permission. She had a vision of how it could go, but so far it wasn't panning out. I found myself feeling resentful. While I was willing to work cooperatively with the others, I wasn't willing to give up my autonomy. We wished each other well and parted ways.

★ ★ ★

Meanwhile, Erin had broken her silence when she was interviewed for a podcast. *The Times* of London got wind of her story and interviewed her for a potential feature. They wanted to interview some of the "then kids" too. The journalist had approached a couple of my British peers, all of whom declined interviews. A British writer I had been communicating with said she knew the journalist and asked if I wanted to be put in contact.

I said I did. A couple of days later she got back to me to tell me that *The Times* was still interested. They wanted me to write a pitch. I got straight to work and sent the pitch the next day.

A few days later, my new writer friend got back to me saying *The Times* wanted to move forward. In the meantime, they also had managed to get a few other commune kids to agree to be interviewed too. I was pleased to not have to do it alone.

A couple of days later, I was pacing as I waited for the Zoom meeting I was about to have with *The Times* journalist. My mind was racing, my stomach churning, I was petrified. Now that I was about to tell my story in the public arena, I had no idea how it would be received.

I sat down at my desk, centered myself the best I could, and reminded myself that despite my fear, my need to break my silence was more important. I joined the Zoom meeting. When it was over, the journalist said the story would be a feature in *The Sunday Times* but didn't know when. She would let me know the day before. At that point, she said, she would call Milarepa, Mutribo, and Osho International Foundation for statements. Holy cow!

Then it was a waiting game. After a couple of weeks, the journalist called. "The story will run tomorrow," she said. "I'm calling Milarepa now for a statement." I felt so uncomfortable, I wanted to hide under my desk. I had asked for this, but now that it was coming to fruition, I felt shaky. I tried to focus on work.

An hour later, the journalist called again and, with the utmost calm, said, "Just so you know, I reached Milarepa, and he is threatening legal action if we print the story."

"What?"

"This happens all the time," she said. "I ran it by our lawyers. They say he has no ground for legal action since you have evidence and witnesses, so we're going to print." I was shaking in my boots.

The next morning, Sept 4, 2022, the article ran, titled "Abused in Osho, the middle-class sex cult that stole childhoods." Huh? The title confused me. Osho was a person, not a place, and middle class had nothing to do with it. Nevertheless, the article was accurate and informative.

The journalist even managed to get the first statement about the abuse from OIF. All they said was, "There is no one in Osho International who had any organizational function in any of the entities mentioned, and so they know nothing of these accounts." I wasn't surprised. It just confirmed their dismissal. Milarepa's statement was rather flat too, saying, "There was no grooming or molestation. Apologies were made for youthful mistakes." He had clearly changed his tune since his email and open letter where he said he was glad the abuse was out in the open.

I had finally gone public. I had taken a stand. I had named names. I had used my own voice. I knew that breaking my silence would not go over well with those still devoted to Osho. Almost all of the sannyasins with whom I was still friends had stopped talking to me when I shared my story on Facebook. Now it seemed inevitable that I would be shunned even more. Speaking out meant more loss. My aim was to tell the truth, not to hurt those that I loved. However, I couldn't continue silently hiding in the shadows enduring the hurt and rage to protect other people's feelings. I needed to use my voice to unburden myself. I needed to not be invisible.

★ ★ ★

With *The Times* article published, it seemed like the opportune time to come out of hiding and tell everyone I knew about my sordid past. I braced myself and did the most uncomfortable thing yet—I posted the article on my own Facebook page and unveiled the website I had spent the last several days creating, where I told more of my story. Most of my Facebook friends were not close friends. They were acquaintances and clients who knew little to nothing of my past. I was worried they would now see me in a different light. But so be it.

As soon as I shared my story, responses full of support and empathy flooded in, helping me through my jitters. Everyone was so understanding and kind, not critical or accusing me of being some kind of imbecile or fraud. I was the one who judged myself so harshly, not them. There were a few, though, who were genuinely shocked and worried about my safety.

Armed with mace, I carried on with my usual routine. Nobody came after me. In fact, nothing much happened with the article either. After a few days of buzz, it landed softly with a thud. I wasn't sure why it didn't get the traction even the journalist anticipated. All I could think was maybe the story was so old now that people weren't interested, or maybe the title failed to intrigue readers. It could also have been that the queen died four days after the story ran, capturing everyone's attention.

The response from "the kids" in the WhatsApp group was all but nil. Almost nobody said a word, not even those I still considered friends. It felt like a collective shunning. There was not a lot of reaction in the Rajneesh Facebook groups either. The topic was seemingly receding into dormancy.

CHAPTER SIXTY-EIGHT

LETTING GO

Two years had passed since my peers and I posted our stories on Facebook, yet nothing had changed in terms of accountability. The perpetrators were back to living their lives—Milarepa was even performing at Osho meditation centers and Osho gatherings in Europe and beyond. Word reached me that people believed enough time had passed and he should be forgiven and welcomed back into the fold. Osho International Foundation did nothing either. Likewise, sannyasins who had expressed a desire for healing didn't take the next step to defend us or push OIF for action.

I was disturbed by how desperately the community clung to their vision of utopia, using every tactic in the book to preserve it. I had no idea how thick and impenetrable the fog of devotion would be, nor that they would shield themselves with Osho quotes and teachings, chimeras of spiritual maturity. The dogma was woven into their very beings, it was part of their identities—they weren't going to change. The hypocrisy and dismissal by most of the community were as triggering as the abuse and neglect.

What was it all for? I thought confronting my past was supposed to be healing, but though the topic had died out in the public domain, it was still very much alive inside me. The whole process of bringing my story out of the shadows was disillusioning. I was more enraged than ever that justice and truth weren't overriding principles. For the past two years I had been in the thick of my trauma, triggered right and left, my nervous system about to short circuit. I withdrew from life. I drove my relationship with a man I loved into the ground. I couldn't even remember the last time I felt joy. I was heartbroken and stewing in bitterness and rage.

Week after week, I'd go to therapy, insisting I needed justice—that the Osho community and all the deniers had to face the truth, that everyone needed to wake the fuck up, and everything should be made right. My therapist, Susan, would calmly remind me, "You're consumed with a life from forty years ago; you have a life now, you need to live it," adding, "There most likely won't be justice." Though I knew what she was saying was true, it was almost unbearable to hear. How could I restore my faith in humanity if justice didn't prevail?

As I reflected, I realized I faced a choice: continue waging a futile battle against humanity's ugliness or accept reality and lay down my arms. No one was coming to save me; I had to rescue myself, clichéd as that may sound. I needed to reclaim my spiritual self and embrace the power of goodness and grace, rather than reject it due to my wounds. In fact, my spiritual injuries only deepened my longing for connection. I wanted to trust again—in grace, in love, in goodness —else my bitterness and pain would corrode me like battery acid. Nonetheless, I still hoped that karma would somehow right all the wrongs, but it was out of my hands.

Out of self-respect and self-love, I had to let go. I didn't need to absolve anyone; it was about freeing my heart from the past and standing tall in my own shoes—those of a warrior who no longer has anything to prove. I'm not under any illusions—my trauma will always be with me in some form. But when it grips me, when it thrashes me about, I am committed to meeting it with compassion. Being traumatized is not a mark of weakness; surviving and flourishing alongside it is the true measure of strength and resilience.

Now, I am slowly building the habit of reminding myself that the kindest thing I can do is release the struggle that holds me captive and embrace the things that bring me joy: nature, music, a good cup of tea, art, and all the quiet sources of hope and inspiration. I'm learning to hold the love and the pain together, to live in the bittersweet, and to make peace with both.

YOUR FEEDBACK MATTERS!

Thank you for joining me on this journey through my memoir. If my story resonated with you, I would be deeply grateful if you could share your thoughts by leaving a review. Your feedback not only helps other readers find my book but also supports me in continuing to share my experiences and insights.

How to Leave a Review:

Amazon: Simply visit the book's page on Amazon and click "Write a Customer Review." Your honest feedback is invaluable!

Goodreads: Share your thoughts on Goodreads by finding my book and adding a review.

Social Media: Tag me in your posts about the book—your recommendations and shares mean the world to me!

Every review, no matter how brief, helps spread the word and make a difference. Thank you for your support and for being part of this journey.

With heartfelt gratitude,

Sarito Carroll

ACKNOWLEDGMENTS

To the women who helped raise me:

Mary Jo, thank you for your steadfast support and your big heart.

Vidya, through all the twists and turns, the love between us was real, and your care gave me shelter.

Ira, your kindness and generosity made me feel seen and valued in ways I will always cherish.

Marga, thank you for looking out for me and for teaching me about cooking, botany, and herbs.

I also want to acknowledge the numerous others who took me into their hearts and showed me kindness.

To my mother: Our relationship has been complicated, but I know you've always loved me, and my love for you has never faltered. With time and reflection, I can more readily accept that you did the best you could.

I am deeply grateful to the supportive communities and friends I have had along the way. Your encouragement and steadfast presence helped me find my voice and a sense of belonging when I needed it most.

A special thank you to my therapist, **Susan**: your unwavering patience, dedication, and belief in my ability to heal has been a guiding force on my journey.

Thank you, **Gopa & Ted 2**, for your stunning work on the cover design and layout. **Stuart of Book Architecture**, your developmental editing helped me zero in on what truly mattered. **Susan Pohlman**, your impeccable copyediting and being the first person to read my completed manuscript were invaluable.